Absolute Beginner

Absolute Beginner

Patsy Kensit

SIDGWICK & JACKSON

First published 2013 by Sidgwick & Jackson
an imprint of Pan Macmillan, a division of Macmillan Publishers Limited
Pan Macmillan, 20 New Wharf Road, London N1 9RR
Basingstoke and Oxford
Associated companies throughout the world
www.panmacmillan.com

ISBN 978-0-283-07191-1 HB
ISBN 978-0-283-07193-5 TPB

1 3 5 7 9 8 6 4 2

A CIP catalogue record for this book is available from the British Library.

Typeset by Ellipsis Digital Limited, Glasgow
Printed and bound by CPI Group (UK) Ltd, Croydon, CR0 4YY

Visit **www.panmacmillan.com** to read more about all our books
and to buy them. You will also find features, author interviews and
news of any author events, and you can sign up for e-newsletters
so that you're always first to hear about our new releases.

To James and Lennon
I love you
Mum xxx

Picture Acknowledgements

All photographs from the author's private collection apart from:

Page 6: top © PA Archive/Press Association Images; bottom Rex/Everett Collection. Pages 7 and 8 © Bob Penn. Page 9: top © Rex/Moviestore Collection; bottom © BBC Picture Library. Page 11: top and middle © BBC Picture Library; bottom © REX/ITV. Page 13: © Getty Images. Page 14: top © BBC Picture Library. Page 15: © Redferns. Page 16: top © G.Dalla Pozza/Camera Press; bottom © REX/Moviestore Collection. Page 17: bottom © REX/Moviestore. Page 18: top © REX/Moviestore; bottom © REX. Page 19: top © BBC Picture Library. Page 20: top and middle © Alex Bailey; bottom © REX/Moviestore Collection. Page 22: top © Yuki Mok/PA Archive/Press Association Images; bottom © REX/ITV. Page 23 top and bottom © BBC Picture Library.

Every effort has been made to credit all copyright holders of the photographs in the book, but where omissions have been made the publishers will be glad to rectify them in any future editions.

Contents

Prologue

I picked up my son Lennon from school recently and as he got into the car he gave me a really funny look. 'Mum,' he said, 'you were in that film *Lethal Weapon 2* with the *Mad Max* guy, right?'

'Yes, I was in the movie with Mel Gibson,' I replied.

'Well, it was on TV the other night and some of my friends saw it, and apparently you kiss Mel Gibson.'

'Yes, Lennon,' I said, wondering where the conversation was taking us. 'I play Mel's girlfriend in the movie.'

'Hmmm. But did you *really* do a love scene with him?' he asked, turning his nose up as if it was the most unlikely thing that could ever happen.

'Well, I know it was a long time ago, darling, but back in the days before talkies your mum was actually considered nice looking. Some might *even* say I was a bit of a sex symbol.'

'Ah, don't brag about it!' he shouted, cupping his hands over his ears.

That took the wind out of my sails!

In all honesty, it feels as if that movie happened a hundred years ago to another person. That's also how I feel when someone mentions my name in the same breath as 'Britpop' or 'rock chick'.

I find it hilarious, actually. I'm a working mum with two boys who is on the fast-track to fifty. As I write this, a tube of testosterone cream is winging its way to me in the post to help balance my hormones – and that's not a joke! My perfect evening in these days consists of a pea-sized dab of testosterone cream on my tummy, a glass of rosé and *Coronation Street*. My so-called rock-and-roll years are well and truly behind me. I had a few late nights in the nineties, but I've had many more early calls for filming and long days shooting in my lifetime. And my eldest son, James, was with me the whole time as I travelled the world making movies. I had him so young that we almost grew up together. It wasn't a conventional upbringing, which worries me from time to time, but James said to me recently, 'I don't know what you're talking about, Mum. It was great.'

But this is how glamorous my life is now – James gave me a huge bag of coins the other night and I sat and bagged them all up for him. What's more, I actually enjoyed it.

Because I've been acting since the age of four, I've done a lot of growing up in public and there will be plenty of people who think they know me from what they've read in the papers. But there's a bigger story to tell, a story about a little girl from a council estate in west London who was driven to succeed in an effort to buy her mother's health and to escape a family legacy of secrets, poverty and crime.

And it's been an amazing journey. Never in my wildest dreams could I have imagined Elizabeth Taylor cooking spaghetti for me; being flown across America in the Warner Brothers private jet; having my hair brushed by my hero David Bowie; being asked to shoot with some of the world's top photographers; and working alongside some of the best actors, directors and producers in the business. Oh, and there was also the time a notorious Japanese cannibal decided he liked me . . .

I think, and I hope, this book holds a few surprises.

1

The Blue Bird

I have Elizabeth Taylor to thank for turning me into a hopeless romantic. When I was six years old, I was picked to play her daughter in a movie called *The Blue Bird*, which was based on a fairy tale by Belgian playwright Maurice Maeterlinck. We spent nearly a year shooting the film in Leningrad and Elizabeth would often pop down from her suite in the hotel to visit my mother Margie and me in the room we shared. Even at that age it was impossible not to be captivated by her glamour and sense of fun.

'Catch it, darling!' she'd say, throwing me the huge diamond ring Richard Burton had given her. The Krupp Diamond was breathtakingly beautiful and the size of an egg, and it sparkled like crazy as I turned it over in my little hands.

'Try it on, Patsy,' urged Elizabeth one day.

I glanced up at my mum, who looked completely horrified. My two front teeth had fallen out halfway through shooting, so I had to wear dentures and I was forever losing them. Mum was clearly terrified that this priceless, world-famous gem was about to suffer the same fate.

'Please, Elizabeth, take it back!' said Mum anxiously.

'No, no, let's play catch!' she insisted, throwing her head back and laughing.

It was the beginning of 1975 and Elizabeth was between her two marriages to the great love of her life, Richard Burton. Her companion at the time was a photographer called Henry Weinberg, but he was obviously on his way out! She'd sometimes knock on our door and ask Mum if she could call Richard from our suite. It was Soviet Russia and you had to book calls out of the country twenty-four hours in advance, and everyone was convinced the lines were tapped.

'Look, I need to book a call,' Elizabeth would whisper to Mum. 'Can I come down here and talk to Richard?'

My mum had no idea what it meant at the time, but she was happy to help and would usher me out of the room where our phone was and close the doors behind her so Elizabeth could talk in private.

I imagine it must have been thrilling for my mum to observe the lives of these great movie stars from behind the scenes. And it was a life-changing time for me, too. *The Blue Bird* opened my eyes to a whole new world of possibilities. I was a working-class kid from Hounslow who up until recently had been used to sleeping on a mattress on the floor of our tiny maisonette, which had two rooms and an outside loo. Now I found myself working on a picture for 20th Century Fox alongside Elizabeth Taylor, Ava Gardner, Jane Fonda and legendary Hollywood director George Cukor. The austerity of the Soviet regime was all around us – long, snaking lines of people queuing for bread were a common sight – but I felt like I was living in the lap of luxury in our suite at the Leningrad Hotel, with its faded splendour and grand piano, which I'd sit at for hours playing 'Chopsticks' and driving my mother mad!

I was exposed to so much incredible art, culture and creativeness during that time in Russia and it changed me completely. At weekends Mum would take me around the city's amazing galleries and museums, and on Saturday mornings I took classes with the younger kids at the Bolshoi ballet, who were being groomed to enter the company.

Elizabeth was always coming up with wonderful things to do, too. She'd announce, 'We're all going out this evening! We're going to see *Swan Lake*!' And when we walked into the theatre to take our seats in the Tsar's box, the entire audience would stand up and applaud her. I'll never forget how moved and terrified I felt watching the swan die at the end – my eyes were like saucers!

Going to the ballet was dreamlike and intoxicating, as

were our visits to the Hermitage, a beautiful Russian palace, most of which was closed to the public. It had a room where everything shimmered gold and only the leaders of the country ever got to see it. But we got to see everything, thanks to Elizabeth.

I was just seven when filming wrapped on *The Blue Bird*, but things had already started conflicting in my world. I saw two different paths – one wasn't better than the other, but I often look back now and wonder what would have happened to me if I hadn't got the breaks I did.

My parents, Margaret Rose Doohan and James Henry Kensit, met in the early sixties at a nightclub called the Roaring Twenties on Carnaby Street in the heart of swinging London. Or so the story goes. Much of my dad's life was shrouded in secrecy, so there are facts I still can't quite be sure of today. When I was growing up I had so many questions, but it was impossible to get a straight answer out of my family!

My parents were very different characters. In fact, probably the only thing they had in common was their poor working-class backgrounds. Dad, who was twenty years older than Mum, was born an only child in 1915 in Shoreditch in London's East End, which was an extremely deprived area in those days.

His father was in and out of prison until my dad was

seven for a variety of crimes including robbery, so he never had a strong father figure as a role model. There's a famous saying, 'Give me a child until he's seven and I'll show you the man', and I think that was very true in my dad's case, because he became involved in the criminal world just like his dad before him. He was nineteen when he was first sent to prison for pickpocketing, and he was later charged simply for being an 'incorrigible rogue'. I found out recently he also went AWOL from the army.

Dad became an associate of notorious villains Ronnie and Reggie Kray, who ruled the East End in the 1950s and 1960s. He'd grown up alongside the Kray family in Bethnal Green and went to the same boxing club as Ronnie and Reg, where he watched the brothers fight. In fact, Dad was a champion featherweight boxer when he was a young man. But he was also desperately poor, and in that part of London in those days I guess it wasn't uncommon to become a career criminal in order to improve your circumstances. He was a really bright guy and a genius with numbers, so he became a pretty successful gambler – he would literally bet on two flies crawling up a wall. I believe he was one of the best pick-pockets around, which earned him the nickname 'Jimmy the Dip'.

He was on the fringes of the Kray firm, rather than part of it, and he also worked with the Richardsons, a well-known crime family from south London. The Krays and the Richardsons were arch-enemies, so I have no idea how my dad managed to go between the two gangs. In the sixties he was involved in several long firm frauds with Charlie Richardson. This was a scam that consisted of buying premises and setting up a company, then making big orders, collecting the goods and disappearing without paying. Charlie recruited my dad because he got along with people and was plausible – he was good at selling a firm.

Like Dad, my mum came from nothing, but she didn't have a dishonest bone in her body. She wouldn't so much as jump a red light and I'm exactly the same. Her parents came over from Leitrim in Ireland and settled in Herne Hill in south London. Her father was a sous chef and her mother worked as a nanny in St John's Wood. Mum, who was born in Hampstead in 1935, was their eldest child, then came Uncle John and Auntie Mary. My grandmother also had another little girl called Deirdre, who sadly died of pneumonia when she was a toddler, and I remember Mum telling me that everyone on their street could hear my gran wailing and screaming when she came home from the hospital after Deirdre passed away. Apparently she was the sweetest little thing.

My mum was a great beauty when she was a young woman, with dark hair, very blue eyes and fabulous skin, and she spoke beautifully, too. She had an enduring passion for books and loved to read the classics, which is something I've inherited from her.

Her looks must have won her an army of admirers, and before she met Dad she dated the Aga Khan for a while. Going out with someone from a different culture was probably quite risqué at the time, so she must have had a bit of a rebellious streak in her. I have a photograph of the two of them together and Mum looks like a piece of art – just stunning.

She did a Pitmans shorthand and typing course, and when she started dating my dad she was working in an administrative role in the press office at Christian Dior, which must have suited her down to the ground because she always had great style and loved fashion.

Mum also had this wonderful inner calm and I never saw her fall out with a single person, which I know makes her sound like a saint, but she was a genuinely good person and had a strong Catholic faith.

Not long after she started seeing Dad they split up, but he wouldn't have it and when she left her parents' house to go on dates with other guys, he would jump down from the tree outside her front door! I think he wore her down in the end, but I can see why she fell in love with him. My dad was an incredibly likeable man – charismatic, funny and, despite his size – he was just a couple of inches taller than Mum at 5ft 8in – he had a formidable presence. He was a sharp dresser, too, and wore beautiful suits, crocodile skin shoes and a cashmere Crombie.

He also had an Aston Martin, like the one James Bond drove in the movies, and one day he threw Mum the keys and said, 'You drive it. Go to Margate and take your mum.' Mum told me she was driving the car back to London, showing off with my gran in the passenger seat, when the car spun out of control. Apparently, my gran screamed out in her thick Irish accent, 'Margaret, save us if you can!'

The car flipped over and ended up in a ditch, but miraculously neither of them was injured. They left the car where it lay in a crumpled heap and caught the train home. Mum never told Dad she'd written off his car. Goodness knows what he thought had actually happened to it, but apparently he wasn't too bothered when he discovered it was missing!

There's no doubt that part of the reason Mum was so attracted to Dad was that he could always make her laugh, and I think there was possibly also a certain excitement attached to dating someone so unconventional. Let's face it, he was pretty far removed from the kind of man who went to the office every day in a pinstripe suit and tie.

I have black and white photos of my parents from the sixties looking incredibly glamorous, drinking champagne with my dad's associates at West End night spots like the Embassy Club and the Café de Paris. They could almost be movie stills from *Goodfellas* – Dad in his tux and Ray-Ban sunglasses and Mum looking like a film star in an evening gown and fur wrap with a little diamanté tiara in her hair. I guess because they'd come from such deprived backgrounds, they wanted to enjoy their money while they had it.

The world of organized crime seemed glamorous at the time, and personalities like the Krays were, if not the celebrities of the day, then at least on a par with them. It's a view that's epitomized by David Bailey's iconic photograph of the Kray twins in 1965, which hung alongside his portraits of sixties movie actors, models and pop stars. Of course, the flipside of the glamour was the terror. These villains looked after their own, but clearly hideous things could happen to their rivals. I was very relieved a few years ago to find out that my dad didn't take part in any of the violent beatings that were routinely dished out. I don't know how Mum reconciled my dad's villainy with her own values, but it must have been very stressful for her to be with someone who lived outside the law.

My older brother Jamie was born in 1963 and Dad made Reggie Kray his godfather. We have a photograph of Reggie at Jamie's christening, cradling this tiny vulnerable baby in his huge hands.

The reality of what my dad did for a living hit home hard when he was sent to prison for his involvement with the long firm frauds when Jamie was still very young, and Mum found herself a single parent. She told me later that she really struggled financially during that time and had to stay with a friend.

Jamie kept a letter that my dad sent to Mum from prison at Christmas time, which must have been heartbreaking for her to read:

Hello love, Here is my Xmas letter to you and my son. You can guess how I feel about being away from you both at this time of the year, but I can say to myself over and over again that I love my Marge and Jamie.

I can't explain in words how much Jamie means to me – I keep remembering when he was upstairs in bed before the doctor came, he just looked at me and said, 'Don't leave me, Daddy.'

If only I could do something regarding money for you both. I just can't, I'm at my wits' end. I just know how hard it is for you and also how it will be for you later on. God, please help us just this once. Happy Xmas Darling. I do miss you both so.

I don't know if it was an attempt at intimidation by someone with a beef against Dad, or just bad luck, but Mum told me that at around this time the brakes on her car were cut when it was parked on Box Hill in Surrey and she was with Jamie. I don't know any more than that, just that she didn't drive the car and the two of them were fine.

When Dad got out of prison he had nothing and had to start again from scratch; what he actually did to earn money, none of us will ever really know. It still amazes Jamie and me how little we knew about my dad's life while we were growing up. Mum did everything she could to keep that side of things hidden from us. She must have loved my dad a great deal to turn a blind eye to his villainy, and he loved her, too.

My dad was fifty-three and Mum was almost thirty-three when I was born on 4 March 1968 at the Lying-In Hospital on York Road in Lambeth, which sits between Waterloo Station and Westminster Bridge. They named me Patricia Jude and took me back to their maisonette on the Wellington Road in Hounslow, which was home for the first six years of my life.

My earliest memory is of cowering behind the coal bunker in the backyard when I was about three years old. I was hiding from my parents who were trying to take a photo of me, which was something I was completely terrified of. It's strange when you consider the way my life's panned out – there's a distinct irony in the fact that I've ended up doing a job where I have to be photographed all the time. Maybe I had some kind of childish premonition of things to come – hiding behind the curtains at home to avoid the paparazzi camped outside the front door!

My first home in Hounslow was modest to say the least. We had the ground floor of the maisonette and there were more tenants above. It was very basic – a living room with a sofa, a black and white TV and a little coal fire, a kitchenette, one bedroom, a bathroom just big enough for a plastic tub that we had to fill with the kettle, and an outside toilet. There were no proper beds, just two mattresses on the floor. My parents had one and Jamie and I slept on the other. It seemed entirely normal to me as a child, but looking back it's clear we had nothing.

I never remember feeling deprived, though. There was a little patch of grass out the back and Jamie and I would spend hours outside in the summer, happily painting and making things with Play-Doh. And we had loads of fun jumping from mattress to mattress, until I missed one day, hit the wall and was left with a right old shiner. I was a kid who was always banging my head. In fact, the week after the mattress incident I fell trying to get out of my mum's Mini and whacked my head on the kerb. I'm sure the hospital must have thought I was being battered!

When I was a bit older I remember the blackouts during the miners' strikes in the seventies – Mum used to get the candles out and the four of us would play Monopoly, and usually end up rowing over it, as families do.

Although our house was always clean, Mum was never organized like I am, so the place was always a bit chaotic. As a result I'm borderline OCD when it comes to tidiness. Everything has to be in its place! I was always the kid at ballet with the wrong tights on and my hair falling out of a lopsided bun, but Mum made up for it with an abundance of love, and that's all that mattered.

I was four years old when I got my first acting job. My mother's friend Rhonda Morgan had just started a children's talent agency in Teddington called Magnus Management when she got a call about a casting for a Paramount movie based on F. Scott Fitzgerald's novel *The Great Gatsby*. There were only four kids on her books at the time, but she needed six girls for the audition, so she rang a few of her friends who had children of the right age and my mum agreed to take me along.

The film was a big deal – the British director Jack Clayton was in the hot seat, Francis Ford Coppola had written the screenplay and two of the biggest movie stars of their generation, Robert Redford and Mia Farrow, were playing the lead roles.

I was auditioning to play Mia's daughter, Pammy Buchanan. I was asked to run into the room and say, 'Mummy, Mummy, I've missed you!' in an American accent to a woman who, I discovered years later, was renowned Hollywood casting director Marion Dougherty. I did it three or four times, and every time this little cockney voice would come out – it was before the voice coaching! – but a few days later Rhonda called Mum to tell her I'd got the part. It definitely wasn't on the strength of my acting ability, or my accent, because they ended up dubbing my voice with an American kid's, but I could follow direction and I also had very white-blonde hair, which may have helped me to stand out from the other children auditioning.

All my scenes were shot in Heatherden Hall on the Pinewood Studios lot in Buckinghamshire. A chauffeur-driven car used to pull up outside our house on Wellington Road to take Mum and me to Pinewood, and the driver would get out in his smart uniform and hat and open the door for us. I can still remember the smell of the leather seats and the excitement of being driven to the studios.

Ralph Lauren designed the costumes for the movie and he did my wardrobe fittings. I had little white spats, which I adored, and beautiful chiffon dresses in pretty pastel colours. Just gorgeous!

I don't remember much about my first day on the set, other than the scene where everyone is at lunch and I have to run up to Mia Farrow and say my 'Mummy, I've missed you' line. Luckily at four you don't have any nerves! It just felt like fun, as if I'd been dropped into a beautiful fantasy land, but I still knew I was there to work.

Mia was lovely to me – I couldn't have asked for a more nurturing person to perform with for the very first time – and I remember the day Robert Redford walked on to the set: my mum's eyes were out on stalks. I had no idea who any of these people were, but I knew I was in the presence of something electric.

The filming took about six weeks and I appear briefly in four scenes – blink and you'll miss me, but I'm there!

The movie wasn't released until 1974 and, in the meantime, I signed to Rhonda's agency and worked pretty much constantly after that. I'd had fun on *The Great Gatsby* and Mum realized I'd taken to acting like a duck to water. She wasn't a pushy stage mum, though, or even a 'woo-hoo!' type of person when I landed a role – she was very grounded – but she was always supportive and encouraging. Dad was bursting with pride and more effusive with his praise, but he never got involved with the professional side of my life – he left all of that to Mum.

After *Gatsby* I appeared in my first Birds Eye peas TV ad, which was directed by Adrian Lyne, who went on to make a string of big Hollywood movies, including *Fatal Attraction*. The commercial was about a little girl making a sunflower out of paper at school to give to her mum on Mother's Day, and then dropping it in a puddle on the way home. She has peas for dinner and says, 'Next week we're making paper animals.' That was the line!

I was under contract to Birds Eye from the age of four and a half until I was about twelve and got to work with other really talented guys, such as Tony and Ridley Scott and Alan Parker, who all became big movie directors. Once I started going to school the advert soon earned me the nickname 'Patsy Peapod', which I was less thrilled about.

I also got a small part in a British comedy called *For the Love Of Ada* with Irene Handl and Wilfred Pickles, then I appeared in *Z Cars* and an episode of a BBC series called *The Brothers*. And I was murdered for the first – but not the last – time in my acting career when I was given a tiny part in a 1974 movie called *Gold*, starring Roger Moore and Susannah York. All I can remember about it are the special effects going off to make it look like we'd been blown up at a Christmas party! I came to another sticky end in *Hennessy*, which was a thriller about an Irish plot to blow up the Houses of Parliament. The movie was never released in the UK over concerns it was pro-IRA, so it was only seen in the US. Rod Steiger played my father in the film and he's out to get revenge on the British Government after his family (including me) is accidentally killed during a riot in Belfast.

Rod and I did a rehearsal together, which was fine, but when we did the actual take and I got hit with the squib and fell to the ground, he ran over to me and started wailing and screaming, and he scared me so much I wet my knickers! He was a brilliant method actor, but I had no idea what was going to change from the rehearsal to the take, and all the hysterics were a bit of a shock!

It was at about this time that I started at a little stage school called the Professional Children's School in Teddington, which Rhonda was connected to. Strangely, I have very few memories of my first days there, possibly because I hated school right from the word go and couldn't wait to leave! I think I already knew, even at the age of five, that I just wanted to be an actress. Looking back, it's astonishing that I was so determined to carry on in the business – I never had any doubts.

While school didn't make a big impression on me, when I was five something else happened that was to have a profound and lasting effect on my life. One day my dad took me off to the hospital, where I saw my mum being wheeled out of a ward and being taken down to theatre for surgery. I remember she had a paper shower cap on her head to keep her hair out of the way and my dad was holding me up as he walked alongside the trolley, saying, 'Kiss your mum, Pat. You know she loves you.'

I hadn't realized Mum was ill until that moment. She'd been diagnosed with breast cancer and had been told it was terminal, so she was in hospital to have the tumour removed. She was still a young woman – just thirty-eight.

I'm sure children weren't supposed to be on the ward, but it was typical of Dad to break the rules. I understand why he did it, though. He did it for my mum and for me, in case she didn't come through the surgery, but I think that was the day I lost my innocence. I read a quote from Jack Nicholson many years later about the moment you comprehend your mortality and how it robs you of a certain freedom – it's a view I certainly agree with.

While Mum was having her operation, Dad took me for a Chinese meal and the two of us sat there, eating in silence. I loved my dad, but I couldn't talk to him the way I could talk to Mum. And I guess he was lost in thought, contemplating what it would mean for us if the worst happened to Mum. You know, 'What am I going to do with these kids?' When I was much older he told me about the day Mum called him to break the news that she had cancer. He was playing cards with his friends and he broke down in front of all these tough guys. He was absolutely devastated.

From that day on, whenever we had to visit Mum in hospital, the two of us would go to the local Chinese restaurant and, despite the circumstances, I came to love Chinese food.

When Mum came home she seemed to be OK, but she had to have a course of radiotherapy at the Middlesex Hospital on Mortimer Street and I'd go with her to the sessions. I'd sit up in a booth, looking down on her having the treatment. I was able to talk to her through a microphone and I'd say, 'Hi, Mummy!' and we'd chat.

Looking back, it was like a scene from a science fiction movie – Mum lying there with contraptions all around her and blue ink drawn on her right breast to mark the area they were going to zap. I'm sure a lot of people would think it terrible to allow your child to see that, but Mum and I were so close, and she never made it feel like something negative or scary.

She must have felt so sick after those sessions, but there was a little cake shop opposite the hospital and, when her treatment had finished, she'd take me in there for a treat and then we'd catch the tube home. I never remember her lying in bed sick, despite the fact that she was very ill. She was strong and positive, and carried on cooking, cleaning and caring for Jamie and me. She never burdened us with it. But it didn't change the fact that from then on I worried about her every day of my life. It was a constant, ever-present anxiety.

When I was six the school I'd been attending closed down, so I was sent to another stage school called Corona in Hammersmith, but I ended up only going for a term because I got the role of Elizabeth Taylor's daughter in *The Blue Bird*. The job had come through Rhonda's agency, but to attend Corona you had to be on their books, so my parents asked me what I wanted to do – stay at Corona or leave and go to a school called Newland House in Twickenham. It might seem like a big decision for a six-year-old to make, but I think it was kind of great that they gave me the option. I wasn't very happy at Corona anyway – I didn't like school full stop! So I told them I wanted to stay with Rhonda and go to Newland House when *The Blue Bird* finished. It wasn't a stage school, but it was fee-paying, and my parents used my earnings to send me there.

The Blue Bird was a big deal, not just because of the all-star cast; it was also the first co-production between an American studio and the USSR. I had to go through a long process before getting the role, which involved several meetings and auditions with the director George Cukor, who was then in his seventies, with silver-grey hair and glasses and always well turned out in a cashmere sweater, cravat and blazer. In those days I didn't feel any pressure at all when I auditioned – now I get terrified!

Mum and I had our first meeting with Mr Cukor at the Savoy Hotel, just off the Strand in London – we had afternoon tea together in the foyer downstairs. I'll never forget the waitress bringing our cakes over on an ornate silver stand – one of them was shaped like a swan.

For the next meeting I had to prepare a little scene, and then about three weeks later my mum got a call to say he wanted to screen test me at a studio in Twick-enham. The screen test involved a scene where my brother and I wake up in the middle of the night and start talking to each other, but because we were in bed I did the whole scene with my eyes shut, so Mr Cukor came over to me and said, 'Listen, Patsy, when you're talking you can open your eyes, even though you're half asleep.' So I took the note and we did the scene again.

Afterwards, my mum took me to a restaurant called Pizza Land, which was nothing fancy, but I loved it. Whenever I went up for an audition she always tried to make it a fun day. I was really scared to tell her that I'd been given a note by the director, not because she would have been cross with me, but because I just wanted to please her and protect her from any stress or disappointment. When I did pluck up the courage to say something, she replied, 'Oh, my darling, don't be so silly, it's just a bit of fun.'

Neither of my parents ever put any pressure on me, but I put pressure on myself from a really young age. I don't know if it had something to do with my mum's illness or all the secrecy around my dad's work, but I always felt the need to take responsibility for other people's feelings.

It took so long to hear back from *The Blue Bird* that everyone assumed I hadn't got the role. In the meantime, we'd moved from our cramped maisonette on the Wellington Road to a bigger place in Avondale Gardens, a street where council houses and privately owned properties stood side by side. Ours belonged to the council, although my parents eventually managed to buy it years later.

I was very excited about our new house; it was small and semi-detached, but it felt like a palace after what I'd been used to. I even had my own little bedroom. Everything was brand new and pristine when we moved in, although I remember it getting tired very quickly and nothing being done to improve it. I guess my mum had more important things to worry about than decor and home improvements. Things were constantly breaking and the pipes would often freeze in the winter so we wouldn't have hot water. There always seemed to be a problem, but I loved it and that's where I stayed until I moved out of home and got a place of my own.

My mum was sitting at her dressing table in Avondale Gardens when she got a call from Rhonda, saying I'd got the part in *The Blue Bird*. Almost immediately, I had to go over to the agency in Teddington to do some publicity shots for 20th Century Fox. Terry O'Neill, who ended up photographing me many times over the years, was taking the pictures. He was a world-famous photographer by then and dating Hollywood star Faye Dunaway.

We went to Bushy Park, near Hampton Court Palace, and Terry snapped away for the press shots. There was a lot of media interest in the movie and, for the first time, in me too, and Mum kept all the newspaper clippings. After that, though, she really pulled back on the amount of publicity I was allowed to do, as she wanted to protect me from all the scrutiny so I could enjoy my childhood. I think she was also worried about drawing any attention to my dad and his background.

We flew to Russia on an Aeroflot plane, which looked like it was held together with plasters, but was the only airline allowed in or out of the country at the time. There was a guy sitting near us, one of the film crew, who kept saying, 'Can you see the runway lights yet? Can you see the lights?!' Everyone on board thought it was a miracle the thing had actually managed to get off the ground.

When we arrived in Leningrad – now called St Petersburg – I'd never seen snow like it in my life. Everything was covered in a thick blanket of white. I was so excited about this that when we got off the plane I let go of my mum's hand and dived straight into the nearest snowdrift.

The whole cast and crew were staying at the Leningrad, which became known as the Loonygrad, because we were meant to be there for three months and it ended up being nearly a year – it couldn't have been more different to how we were used to living in the West.

Our suite of rooms was fabulous, if a little frayed around the edges. Todd Lookinland, an American boy who played my older brother in the movie, was staying next door with his mum, Karen, and I developed a huge crush on him. Of course, he wasn't interested in me at all! Ava Gardner was in a room across the corridor and Elizabeth Taylor was above us.

There really were some incredible people involved in the movie. George Cukor was a very famous old-school director, responsible for classics such as *Holiday*, *The Philadelphia Story*, *A Star is Born* and *My Fair Lady*. The cinematographer, Freddie Young, had won Academy

Awards for his work on three David Lean movies, *Lawrence of Arabia*, *Dr Zhivago* and *Ryan's Daughter*.

And Edith Head, another Hollywood legend who'd worked with all the great movie stars, including Katharine Hepburn and Marilyn Monroe, was responsible for the costumes.

In the cast, alongside Elizabeth and Ava, were Jane Fonda, Cicely Tyson, Will Geer (aka Grandpa Walton) and two British actors Robert Morley and George Cole, who went on to play Arthur Daley in the TV series *Minder*.

On the first day of rehearsals with Mr Cukor, Elizabeth walked in, and the first thing I noticed were her eyes – they really were the most incredible violet blue colour. She was in her early forties at the time and still very beautiful, with an amazing figure and the tiniest waist. George Cukor called me over so he could introduce us. 'This is Miss Taylor, Patsy,' he said. He always insisted on being called 'Mr Cukor', never George, and he was so revered in the business that even Elizabeth referred to him as Mr Cukor.

'Oh, hello, Miss Taylor, so nice to meet you,' I said politely.

'Oh my God, call me Elizabeth!' she said straight away.

At the time, she was probably the most photographed woman in the world, with the exception of Jackie Onassis, but I knew none of this at six. All I knew was that I'd worked with older actors before who weren't very patient, but Elizabeth was warm, generous and supportive from day one.

When rehearsals got underway George Cukor said to me, 'Don't walk in tempo with Todd.' Now I was six years old, so I had no idea what 'tempo' meant. Realizing this, Elizabeth took me aside and said gently, 'What he means is, try not to walk in time with Todd, as if you're doing a dance routine. So if Todd's right foot is forward, walk so your left foot is forward.'

She explained it in a way I could understand, and she carried on guiding me like that throughout the entire movie.

On the first day of shooting Elizabeth arrived at work with her dogs and entourage in tow – her assistant Raymond, a dresser called Joyce, and hairdresser to the stars Sydney Guilaroff, who'd been the chief stylist at MGM since 1934. He came over to Russia to set her look and then headed back to the States.

She had a red Valentino cashmere cardigan over her shoulders and looked fabulous, and everyone in her entourage also had a subtle touch of red somewhere on their outfits. Every day after that, whatever colour Elizabeth was wearing, her entourage would wear something in the same shade. I watched a documentary recently on Halston – the seventies fashion designer who was a favourite of the jet set, including Elizabeth – and he did that, too. The models and muses who travelled with him

– the Halstonettes – all wore colour-coordinated outfits. It didn't seem at all contrived with Elizabeth, though – it's just how it was.

These days a lot of movie stars have a big entourage as a barricade against media intrusion, but although Elizabeth was probably the first celebrity to start that exploding world of magazine gossip, I never saw her lose her temper. She was always gracious and polite. There are lots of stories about her being demanding and high maintenance, but I never saw it. On *The Blue Bird* she always turned up on time, knew her lines and was lovely to everyone.

As two huge stars working on the same picture, you might expect there to be rivalry between Elizabeth and Ava, but there was none at all. In fact, one day Ava was upset about something, so Mr Cukor called a halt to the filming. Some actresses might have rolled their eyes and made a fuss about it being unprofessional or used it as an opportunity to score brownie points, but Elizabeth couldn't have been nicer and took Ava off to her dressing room. A couple of hours later they were back on set.

The studios were piping hot when we were shooting the interior scenes and Elizabeth would comb my hair and blow on the back of my neck to cool me down. I have a great photograph of her doing that. She needn't have bothered with Todd and me, but she did. She had this knack of making everyone feel good.

Back at the Loonygrad, I think there was a kind of siege mentality among the cast and crew. We'd all been thrown into a very different culture, and the experience brought everyone together. We were all assigned interpreters, but as soon as we got too friendly with any of them, they'd disappear and be replaced with someone else. And outside the hotel there were always gangs of kids wanting our jeans – we called them the Levi's gangs – so Elizabeth had some sent out from America to give to them.

Decent food was in short supply – apart from caviar, which was everywhere! I only wish I'd liked the stuff back then. We all got hotplates delivered to our rooms, but some nights my mum or Todd's mum would cook something or Elizabeth would make spaghetti and invite us up. She also got Fortnum & Mason hampers flown in once a month with lots of goodies in them. She would always be saying, 'Come up, Patsy! Come up and play with the dogs.' My mother never wanted to impose, but Elizabeth really liked my mum. I think she admired her style – Mum used to wear headscarves, which were quite bohemian, and soon Elizabeth started to wear them, too. I have a great photo that stills photographer Bob Penn took of Mum and me, where she's wearing one of her signature headscarves and she looks fantastic. Like Elizabeth, Ava Gardner – who had the most marvellous husky voice – was very generous and lots of fun. I'll never forget her doing a headstand while drinking a glass of champagne. She was very into yoga at the time!

Our stay there could have been really isolating and depressing, given the austerity all around us, but everyone made the most of the situation, so it wasn't like that at all. In many ways we were lucky they chose Leningrad to shoot the movie, as opposed to any other Russian city – as it had been the Imperial capital of the country, the architecture was stunning and it was steeped in history and culture, so there was lots to see.

As well as the ballet and the museum visits, Elizabeth took us to the American Embassy every week, where they screened movies for us. Once I remember the movie starting and Mum saying suddenly, 'We have to go, Pat,' so we collected our things and left in a hurry.

'Why did we have to leave, Mummy?' I asked as we walked back to the Leningrad together.

'That was the film I went to see the day my little sister Deirdre died,' she explained. She just couldn't sit through it.

Elizabeth would also arrange trips to Riga, where there was a long sandy beach, and I loved that. It was the seventies, so of course we'd all smother ourselves in Ambre Solaire and bake in the sun!

Being at work was fun for me, too. It was a dream job for a kid – the costumes and sets were wonderful and our roles were magical. Todd and I played two peasant children who go in search of the Blue Bird of Happiness and are given a hat with a magic diamond for their journey, which brings objects to life. At the end of the story, they discover the blue bird has been in their backyard all along. In some of the scenes I had to have loads of birds perched on me, which I loved. They were just ordinary pigeons dyed blue, but because my dad had taken me to Trafalgar Square to feed the birds, I wasn't frightened at all!

I still had to keep up with my schoolwork, though, and I had a lovely tutor called Betty Wickland, which was so much better than being in school.

At one point we had a break in filming because it appeared as if the movie wasn't going to be finished, so we all went home for a few weeks. I was looking forward to going back to London as I was a bit homesick by that point and missed my dad and my brother. Jamie came out to Russia for some of the time we were there, but he had to attend school back in London.

My relationship with Jamie was pretty regular brother/ sister stuff – I loved him to bits and always looked up to him, and I'm pretty sure he thought of me as his annoying little sister! Jamie was a beautiful-looking boy with thick dark hair, and he was good at sport and art. He had the opportunity to try acting, but he was never interested.

I think my relationship with Mum was possibly different to his experience because she spent so much time with me, chaperoning me on jobs, and we were very close. That must have been hard for Jamie, especially as his other role model in life was my dad. Probably as a result of that, he became closer to my gran and my Auntie Mary than I did. I know Mum missed him desperately when he wasn't with us in Russia, though, so it was good to be going home.

We flew back to London via Finland, and when we landed in Helsinki, everyone on the plane was whooping with joy and Elizabeth shouted, 'Let's get hamburgers!' We couldn't get that kind of food in Russia and we were all craving it.

When we got off the plane, dozens of paparazzi were swarming around, all clamouring to get a shot of Elizabeth. My mum and I hung back, but Elizabeth turned round and said, 'Come on, Patsy,' and took my hand. I'd overcome my fear of cameras by that point, but I wasn't used to that level of attention. It was just incredible the way she dealt with the press – as the shutters clicked and the flashbulbs went off, she lifted her chin and strutted through the airport with such confidence. She was so comfortable in her own skin.

We stayed the night in Helsinki and had an amazing dinner. In our hotel there was a jewellery shop in the lobby, where Elizabeth bought gifts for everyone. She gave me a beautiful gold heart pendant. 'Now at your age you can wear it here,' she said, draping it around my neck so it hung in the centre of my chest. 'And when you're my age you can wear it as a choker.'

Mum and I went back to London and didn't hear anything for three or four weeks, then we got a call to say the film was continuing, which we were delighted about. As we were getting ready to return to Russia, Elizabeth phoned Mum and asked us to fly back with her.

'Listen, I'm in London. Come to the Dorchester and have lunch. I can pick you up or send a car,' she said.

But my mum didn't want her, or anyone else, to see where we lived, so she politely declined. I guess she felt embarrassed by our circumstances. Our house in Avondale Gardens might have been an improvement on the maisonette on Wellington Road, but it was still very modest.

'Well, I'm flying tomorrow,' said Elizabeth. 'So why don't you just meet me at the airport and come with us?'

Mum checked with one of the production staff to make sure it was OK. 'Yes, of course it is,' she said. 'Elizabeth wants you to travel with her.'

So the next day we got to Heathrow and were driven straight on to the tarmac to the plane. It was a Swissair Boeing 747 with an upstairs and it was chartered just for us – there was no one else on the plane. It was incredible! I'd probably been on holiday twice in my life at that point – on a Freddie Laker flight. I was living two lives really, but although I could see that one was impossibly glamorous, I never thought any less of where I was from – Hounslow was home and I loved it.

It didn't take long to get back into our routine in Russia, but then one day Mum took me with her to a doctor's appointment. She'd obviously started to feel ill again. I'll never forget walking out of the consultant's office, glancing up at the door, which had a glass panel, and seeing the doctor turn to a nurse and shake his head solemnly. It was obviously bad news. I never told my mum what I'd seen because I didn't want to worry her.

Not long afterwards she had to go back to the hospital for another check-up, but this time I couldn't accompany her as we were filming an important scene that day. I had to dance on a table and have cake smeared all over my face, which upset me and I became very tearful. I didn't like it at all. But George Cukor wasn't sympathetic – in fact he was horrible about it. He just pushed on with the scene and kept saying, 'More cake, more cake.' He was a genius director, but the last child actor he'd worked with was Freddie Bartholomew for *David Copperfield* in 1935! Elizabeth wasn't there that day, either, so I just had to do what I was told.

When my mum returned and found out what had happened, she took Mr Cukor to one side and had a very frank conversation with him, and he apologized. I loved that about my mum. If she'd been a proper stage mum, she probably wouldn't have been very sympathetic either and would have just expected me to get on with it, but she was very protective. Of course the shot was needed, but the way he dealt with it was unnecessary. He scared the life out of me, to be honest!

Overall, though, I had a lot of fun making the movie. Most people think show business is incredibly glamorous, but most of the time it really isn't. *The Blue Bird* – and *The Great Gatsby* – were truly glamorous, though, and were probably among the last movies made that felt like the old Hollywood studio system. When we started shooting *The Blue Bird* in 1974 there was a new wave of movie-making coming through, driven by directors like Martin Scorsese, Brian De Palma, Steven Spielberg and George Lucas, so looking back I feel very fortunate to have been involved with it. Given my background, I still think it's miraculous what's happened in my life.

The year I spent in Russia was a very formative time for me and I learned a lot. Working with Elizabeth had a huge impact on me. She was professional, but playful, too, and very maternal. Without wanting to sound overdramatic, she became almost like another mother figure, which may also have had something to do with the fact that I had this underlying anxiety about Mum getting ill and that I'd wake up one day and she'd be gone.

I saw a change in Mum after Russia – not in a way

that's unpleasant or selfish, but I think it would be impossible not to have been affected by the experience. I could tell that things were never quite the same between my parents afterwards. Looking back, I think Mum saw opportunities for me, and how my life could change for the better.

Not only did I love performing, I wanted to work. I wanted to make money so I could buy my mum her health. It was a childish dream, but it became my quest.

2

Secrets and Lies

I prepared myself to say my final goodbyes to Mum at least six times before the age of eleven. After we returned from Russia, her bouts of illness became quite regular. I got used to her going into hospital for treatment and, miraculously, she always managed to bounce back.

She went for a check-up at the Middlesex after *The Blue Bird* and that's when her consultant Dr Spittle, who was a wonderful woman, told her the cancer had spread to her other breast. Mum never talked about it at home, though – we were only told what we needed to know. She obviously wanted to protect Jamie and me from her illness as much as possible and she did a good job of it. I'm glad she had us, because we were her reason to carry on and keep fighting.

In those days, people didn't discuss their health so much. I remember her saying to me once, 'There's no such thing as depression, Pat,' which is a very English thing to say. Other people might have dealt with cancer differently, but she was determined to get on with life and she never let it get in the way of things or allowed anyone to see her looking ill. I've never witnessed anyone else display that kind of positivity in the face of such bleak odds.

It was tough waking up every day knowing Mum was sick, though. Even as a little girl, when things were going well and I felt happy, I'd suddenly think, But my mum's got cancer and she's going to die. I'd be doing the super-market shop with her and I'd go off to another aisle to find something and I'd literally stop in my tracks and think, There's going to be a time when I do this and I'll walk back round to the aisle and Mum won't be there. I'd often tell my family I'd had a 'bad thought'. I never said what it was about, but it must have been my way of expressing the trauma I felt over Mum's illness.

My work was probably a welcome distraction for her and something positive to focus on. After *The Blue Bird*, which wasn't released until 1976, I worked pretty solidly in the UK, mostly in the school holidays, although some-times I'd have to take a week or two out of school. I appeared in *Alfie Darling*, a sequel to the 1966 movie *Alfie*, with Alan Price in Michael Caine's role, then there was *Churchill's People*, a BBC historical drama, and then a Yorkshire TV mini-series called *Dickens of London*.

While I enjoyed being in front of the camera, I couldn't say the same for school, which I continued to loathe. I started at Newland House in Twickenham after coming back from Russia and it felt like the most academic school on the planet. I remember gazing out of the classroom window and seeing a flock of birds, and wishing I could fly away, too.

It wasn't that I was yearning for the glamour of Russia or Elizabeth's Fortnum & Mason care package, I just wasn't suited to that type of school. I loved to read and was interested in history and geography, but maths was a complete mystery to me – I couldn't count for toffee and I still can't. It was a hard adjustment to make after having one-to-one tutoring for a year. I remember crying a lot in the mornings and telling Mum I didn't want to go to school. It must have been very hard for her to send me off.

I was teased a bit, too, and called 'Patsy Peapod', which was awful because when you're that young you just want to blend in with everyone else. The kids used to copy the moment from the advert where I put my finger in my cheek and make a popping sound. So I never spoke about work at school as I didn't want the other kids to know what I was doing. As Newland House wasn't a theatre school, Mum signed me up for ballet, tap and singing lessons on Saturday mornings at the Italia Conti stage school, which was much more fun.

Although I probably wasn't the most popular kid at school I got along well with most people and always had a little group of good friends around me. In all honesty, though, Mum was my best friend, which I know might sound a little odd, but we really were soulmates, if you can say that about a parent. I could tell her absolutely anything and we were interested in lots of the same things. We both loved going to the movies, so sometimes we'd go to a matinee on a Saturday and occasionally she'd take me into the West End to see a show. I remember seeing Liza Minnelli perform at the Palladium and being totally and utterly knocked out by her – she is a powerhouse of energy.

One thing I wasn't allowed to do, though, was accept playdates and invitations for sleepovers from my school friends, because we couldn't reciprocate. The girls I mixed with at school were quite well-to-do and Mum was very conscious of our more modest circumstances. But it wasn't only that – because of what my dad did for a living, the police could have shown up at any moment and turned the place over, which they did on occasion. Whenever it happened, Mum would say to Jamie and me, 'Right, kids, go outside and play,' and we'd run into the backyard or take our bikes out onto the street. If I'd been her, I'd have been a complete mess in that situation, panicking about what they might find or if they'd take Dad away, but Mum was always totally calm.

When I was a kid, the police turning up at the door never bothered me, but not being able to have friends over had a long-lasting impact, so much so that I still panic now in one-on-one situations with people I don't know. I just never had the chance as a child to learn how to behave in certain social situations, which sounds crazy because I can walk onto a film set or go on stage in front of hundreds of people and feel confident. But as I got older I always worried about what I was going to talk to someone about or whether they would like me. It's probably why I relied on Mum so much and why today I have a close group of friends I've known for twenty or thirty years.

Growing up, there were lots of uncertainties. One feeling that's been familiar to me my whole life up until fairly recently is anxiety, which was a result of worrying about my mum's health and the fact that my dad could get arrested at any minute. There were times in Avondale Gardens when we had no money at all – if my dad had done well one week, or the horses had won, we'd eat like kings and go to a restaurant every night, but the next week there might be no food in the fridge. On lean weeks, Mum would make corned beef and cabbage or we'd have a slice of ham and a couple of potatoes. Sometimes we'd just have bread and butter with water, which I loved. Mum used to say, 'You could live on a prison diet, Pat!' But I remember thinking as a kid that when I grew up and had children, there would always be a full fridge and a drawer with snacks in it, which is something I did do.

Unfortunately, it also helped me to put on a lot of weight at one point (more of which later!).

It wasn't deprivation – well, not on the scale of what my dad must have experienced as a kid. On Christmas Day or if we were having a proper Sunday lunch, which we couldn't afford to have every week, Dad would call from the kitchen, 'Pat! Jamie! Come and look at the bird.'

'But why, Dad?' we'd whine as we traipsed into the kitchen. We couldn't understand why he wanted us to look at a raw chicken or turkey sitting in a roasting tray waiting to go into the oven. But if you've starved at any point in your life, which he had as a boy, it's an achievement to put that on the table. He appreciated food because he'd gone without for so many years.

Dad was an amazing cook and loved nice food. On weekends when he had some cash in his pocket, we'd get up at 5 a.m. on a Sunday and go over to Petticoat Lane to have bagels and smoked salmon for breakfast, then we'd pop by Tubby Isaacs and pick up seafood for dinner. On other weekends, it was corned beef hash all the way. I loved going out with Dad for a slap-up dinner of double pie and mash with green liquor – it was my favourite meal. I used to eat jellied eels as a kid, too, and one time I got an eel bone stuck in my throat, which meant a trip to casualty – again!

My dad particularly liked kosher food, which is why I always assumed he was Jewish, but apparently he wasn't.

Maybe it was because a lot of the guys he grew up with around Bethnal Green were Jewish. There was a kosher butcher in Richmond where we'd go to buy chicken, and we'd have latkes and chicken noodle soup for lunch at a kosher restaurant called Bloom's in the East End.

Jamie and I only ever got glimpses of Dad's criminal activity. His associates used to come over to Avondale Gardens and go into the sitting room, where Dad would draw the curtains. Jamie and I would have to leave, but we could hear them doing the count up from outside the door. I think they were involved in credit-card and traveller-cheque fraud, connected to Heathrow Airport, but I can't be sure of exactly what was going on – he could have been selling goats for all I know!

Sometimes I'd accompany Dad to meetings with his associates at hotels in the West End, which I loved because all the posh hotels had swimming pools. I'd go for a swim while he chatted to his mates – God knows what was going on, but I had fun.

I definitely saw some odd things. Dad used to go fishing. Allegedly. I'd come home from school sometimes and there would be a whole salmon or a small shark in the bath. I still don't know what to make of that today, but I do know that he was banned from Harrods for life for stealing from the store. Luckily, the ban didn't extend to the rest of the family, as I love Harrods.

Other things weren't so funny. We went on holiday

to Spain one year and got home to find we'd been burgled. Dad had stupidly given the house keys to someone he knew to keep an eye on the place and it got ransacked. Of course we couldn't go to the police and report it like anyone else would have done, and that must have been tough on my mum. It wasn't as if we had a lot to steal.

Mum did a brilliant job of hiding most of my dad's activities from Jamie and me, but we got used to covering things up and keeping secrets from a really young age. We were told to say that Dad was an antiques dealer, which we knew he wasn't, but that's what we'd tell our friends.

No one ever found out what my dad actually did, which seems incredible, so we weren't ostracized. Back then things were more puritanical and I might not have worked again if people in the industry had found out. It's amazing that Mum managed to keep that side of things private, although I'm not sure if she'd have managed to do the same in the times we live in now.

It meant that the four of us very much relied on each other. We didn't have a big extended family for support – my dad had no living relatives, and although my mum's siblings, Auntie Mary and Uncle John, were around, we didn't see each other all that often, though we were a bit closer to my gran – my mum's mother, Bridget.

Very occasionally, Mum and Dad would go out on a Saturday night, so Jamie and I would stay with my gran and my grandfather, who we called Papa. We'd pick up

Gran from the department store in Peckham where she worked and go back to her house in Dulwich, which I loved because it was very neat and orderly. We'd have fish and chips for tea and drink Tizer. Gran would listen to *The Goon Show* on the radio and then Auntie Mary would read aloud from Agatha Christie books and change all the names. Jamie and I had to sleep in the same bed, but we'd draw an invisible line down the middle! Then on Sunday I was allowed an hour on the piano, playing 'Chopsticks'. It was rare for us to have sleepovers but we enjoyed them when we did.

The constant worry over what my dad was up to and the stress of keeping it secret must have been incredibly hard for Mum to live with. When I was older I thought she should have moved on from Dad but, even as a kid, I remember thinking that I wouldn't put up with anything like that. I decided pretty early that I wouldn't stick around in a relationship if things weren't right.

Mum had her faith to fall back on, but she must have found it difficult to reconcile that with living on money that had been earned illegally. Her faith was something that gave her comfort and routine, though. Jamie and I went to mass with her every Sunday at St Michael's & St Martin's Church, which is off the Wellington Road in Hounslow. We'd usually be late, but we'd be there! I'd go and do the Stations of the Cross with her over Easter, too, and we always observed Lent, giving up chocolate and sweeties. We said our prayers at night, which is something I still do today, and Jamie and I both made our First Holy Communion and Confirmation.

Despite all the underlying tensions at home, I remember my parents laughing a lot together, too; there was always laughter in our house. And when Dad had a bit of money, he'd spoil Mum rotten. She loved nice clothes, so he'd give her a roll of fifty-pound notes and she'd buy cashmere sweaters and designer pieces from Zandra Rhodes, Yves Saint Laurent and Dior. I used to love watching Mum getting ready to go out, sitting at her dressing table at Avondale Gardens, applying a little base and then making up her eyes. She was so beautiful she looked like an angel to me.

My parents didn't socialize a lot – they went out for dinner now and then, and sometimes we'd be invited to parties at Charlie Mitchell and his wife Pat's house. They were a great couple – Charlie was a very charismatic guy with a wonderful sense of humour and Pat, who I called Auntie Pat, was one of the most beautiful girls in London, with dark hair and blue eyes just like my mum. Dad had known Charlie since the late fifties. They became friends after having a run-in watching a boxing match at the Albert Hall. Dad worked for the Richardsons, who were Charlie's enemies, so it was perhaps inevitable they would get into an argument. It was brave of my dad, though, because Charlie was much bigger than him! Just as they were about to come to blows, the promoter Jack Solomon walked past and said, 'If you two want to carry on I'll put you on the bill.' It broke the ice; Dad and Charlie started laughing, and from that moment on they were firm friends.

A party round at Charlie's was a lot of fun – a proper East End knees-up – and we'd all be expected to get up and sing something, which was OK up until the age of eight or nine, but after that I used to cringe and think, Please don't ask me! But inevitably Charlie or someone else would shout, 'Come on, Pat! Give us a song!'

It was like something straight out of *The Sopranos*, with all these crooks around, but they were very smart and funny and incredibly entertaining. They all had nicknames – Fat Roy and Manly Mick to name but two of the guys who would come to our house. Mick was an Australian and only dated air hostesses. In those days, air travel was still super-glamorous and he was seeing a Pan Am stewardess called Ingrid, who was Swedish and gorgeous. She used to give me her Pan Am hat to wear – oh, how I loved that hat!

I knew all these characters quite well because they'd come over to Avondale Gardens to do the count up, then afterwards they'd sit in deckchairs in our backyard, chatting and soaking up the sun – everyone was a sun worshipper in those days! I remember them all being very proud of my acting work. They've all passed away now, but I'm still friendly with some of their children – Charlie's son Sean and a guy called Adam, whose dad was a money-lender. My dad used to take me to see them box and I had a big crush on them both! What's nice is that we've been there for each other over the years. I guess we understand each other because we grew up in the same world.

By talking about my dad and his friends in this way, I'm not condoning what they got up to or trying to glamorize it – I've been burgled three times, so I know how awful it is to be on the receiving end of criminal behaviour. But it's just how things were. And whatever wrongs they did to escape the poverty of their backgrounds, they were always very loyal to each other.

My dad was a colourful character, too. I remember him going off to the dog track in his sheepskin coat and pork pie hat and sometimes he'd let me go with him. When I was older, Auntie Pat said to me once, 'You know, Jimmy had more money than anybody; he just gambled it all away.'

By the time I was nine, my parents could see I was still obviously hating school with a passion and miserable there, so they took me out of Newland House. Instead I started going to a local Catholic state school called St Edmund's, which I loved. It was a great school and I was so much happier as there was less emphasis on being an academic prodigy. I remember doing a lot of painting, which suited me just fine because I was good at art.

One break time I sat in the toilet because I was getting teased for being the new kid and I didn't want to go out into the playground, but I overcame that pretty quickly and never did it again, which I suppose shows an inner strength. I won't be bullied and I can stand up for myself if I have to, which are traits I must have inherited from my dad.

I worked a lot while I was at St Edmund's. I got a regular job on an ATV Friday night drama called *The Foundation*, which ran from 1977 to 1978. I played the daughter of a businesswoman who takes over her husband's company when he dies.

I also landed a role in a French movie called *Lady Oscar*, which was a period piece set during the French Revolution. It meant Mum and me relocating to Paris for eight or nine weeks during the summer holidays as the film was being shot in and around the city. Every day, the entire production would grind to a halt for lunch, which was always the most incredible feast, and the table would groan under the weight of delicious food and carafes of wine. God knows how the afternoon's filming ever got completed, but somehow it did! I was too young to enjoy that side of things, but I had a great time and picked up loads of French words while I was there.

My biggest movie project after *The Blue Bird* was an

Anglo-American Second World War movie called *Hanover Street*, which is about a married British nurse (Lesley-Anne Down) who has an affair with a USAAF pilot, played by Harrison Ford. Christopher Plummer played Lesley's husband and I was their daughter. I was very excited about working with Christopher because he'd been Captain Von Trapp in *The Sound of Music*, which was one of my favourite films, and he didn't disappoint as he was lovely to me and it was a fun movie to work on.

Lesley, who is best known for her role in the TV series *Upstairs, Downstairs*, was fab, too. Like me, she had attended the Professional Children's School in Teddington, so we had something in common straight away.

One day she said to me, 'Patsy, I'd really love to know the lyrics from "God Save the Queen" by the Sex Pistols.'

At the time, my brother had just become a punk and had all their records, so I knew the lyrics off by heart.

'I can teach you,' I piped up, feeling extremely pleased with myself, and the two of us sat together on set singing 'God Save the Queen'!

The movie was filmed at the EMI studios in Elstree and on different locations around the city. One day we were shooting in Belgravia and the movie's stars had their Winnebago trailers on site. I was chatting to Lesley when I suddenly found myself desperate for the loo.

'Use the toilet in my Winnebago,' she said, ushering me inside.

After I'd been, Harrison Ford, who'd just flown in from the States, knocked on Lesley's door to invite her to lunch, and apparently there was a very nasty smell coming from the toilet! Lesley thought it was the funniest thing ever. Luckily, I think he realized it was me, and not his leading lady, who was responsible for the odour. Well, I was just a kid.

The picture was released in 1979, and the following year I was nominated for Best Juvenile Actress in a Motion Picture by the Young Artist Awards, which I was thrilled about.

I was also in a kids' movie called *Quincy's Quest* and played schoolgirl Tessa Justin in a six-part ITV drama based on Antonia Fraser's novel *Quiet as a Nun*, which was part of the channel's Armchair Thriller series. The story involves the faceless ghost of a murderous black nun, who stalks a girls' convent school. In one scene I walk into a room to find the faceless nun sitting in a chair. I was ten years old at the time, and even though my mum was there, as well as the entire film crew, it scared me half to death and I had nightmares for months afterwards – along with countless other kids I'm sure, because it was screened before the traditional 9 p.m. watershed. The last scene, where the heroine climbs into the attic and the black nun moves towards her, made it into Channel 4's Top 100 Scary Moments list.

While I was at St Edmund's I also started working a

lot with the BBC and appeared in several drama series between 1978 and '79 – *Prince Regent*, which was about the life and times of George IV, *Penmarric*, which spanned generations of the same family from Victorian England to World War II, and *The Legend of King Arthur*, where I had to dye my hair red for the part of Morgan le Faye. They promised me it would wash out, but I ended up being strawberry blonde for about a year!

Around the same time, I left Rhonda to sign with a big talent agency called William Morris, which also had offices in the US. I'd been getting a name for myself in the industry as a kid who could deliver, but I wasn't that well known to the public at this point – Mum had done a great job of keeping me out of the press and she still insisted on that when I moved to William Morris.

Something else came into my life when I was ten – a pony named Fella. I'd been desperate for a horse and had nagged my dad about it for ages. Then one Sunday morning, he knocked on my bedroom door and said, 'Pat, I've got a surprise for you! Get your coat and let's go.'

We drove to some stables near Heathrow Airport and waiting for me there was Fella! God knows where Dad got him from – he could have stolen him for all I know. The place was no la-di-da pony club either – it looked like a junk yard and Fella hadn't been schooled, so he kicked me a lot. Within a week of having him I couldn't cope. Owning my own pony certainly wasn't what I'd expected it to be – it was like having a child, with all the mucking out every day.

I was bullied terribly at the stables, but it was my own fault. There was one girl who was the leader of the pack, and one day somebody was bad-mouthing her and I joined in. Then the girl who'd been bitching told her what I'd said! After that I lived in fear of getting beaten up, although I never was.

I felt too indebted to my parents to tell them how unhappy I was, because I'd wanted a pony so badly. I ended up keeping Fella for seven years, without ever letting on to my parents because I didn't want to upset them. I did love Fella and he served me well, but I also couldn't wait to get rid of him!

Towards the end of the seventies, things started to change for my dad. There was a man who used to come round to Avondale Gardens who was very high up at Scotland Yard. I'm not going to name him because although he's dead now I don't think his family knew what he got up to. My dad and his associates were paying off the police. This policeman, who was a lovely guy, would be driven over in an expensive car with a big aerial on the roof and my dad would give him a whole smoked salmon! This kind of thing had been going on for years. Then one day we were in the front room watching *World in Action*, which was a documentary investigating bent coppers at

Scotland Yard who'd been taking backhanders from crooks. I remember my dad turning round to Mum and saying, 'Well, it's all going to change now.' I never saw the policeman again after that and it was the start of my father's journey back to jail.

Not long afterwards we had to flee the country. Dad had been hiding out at a hotel near Heathrow before boarding a flight to Paris. Mum and I left the house in a hurry one day and met Jamie at a coach station, as he'd been staying with our nan and Auntie Mary. The three of us took a coach to Heathrow and then caught a plane to Paris to meet up with Dad. From there, the four of us flew to St Martin in the Caribbean, where we boarded a cruise ship for three or four weeks – long enough, I guess, for whatever was going on in London to calm down.

When I look back on it, having to flee our home like that could have been pretty traumatizing for a child, but it didn't scar me. To be honest, I found it all very exciting. Mum never made anything seem awful – she always managed to put a spin on things and turn it into an adventure.

My dad's associates had arranged the whole thing and Dad was masquerading as a top travel writer for some publication, so we were at the captain's table every night on the cruise, when in reality we may as well have been stowaways!

The weather was beautiful and the Caribbean seemed so exotic – to me it was the holiday of a lifetime, and I couldn't understand why Mum looked so sad the entire time we were away. Now, of course, I know it was because Dad was on the run.

When we came home things went back to normal for a short time, but then Dad was arrested for the airport fraud and had to stand trial.

My mum didn't go to his hearings because every time she'd been in the past he'd gone down, so Dad was convinced she was bad luck. We were at home in Avondale Gardens when she got the call from my dad's lawyer to say he'd been found guilty and was going to jail. She was sitting in our tiny back room on one of the horrible plastic chairs that my dad had swapped for her really nice leather ones when we were in Russia. (I don't think she ever forgave him for that!) Usually, Mum was so composed, but suddenly she seemed very vulnerable; she looked as if she'd shrunk into the chair.

It was the first and last time I ever saw her cry. She wasn't sobbing, there were just a few tears tumbling from her beautiful big blue eyes – what was she going to do? Again, she found herself on her own with no money and two kids to provide for.

Mum never expected anything of me, but I felt a huge responsibility to look after her. All I wanted was for her to be OK. I'd just written a book called *The Naughty*

Pyjamas, which had won an award at school, and it was about pyjamas that flew away and scared people. It was just a silly little kids' book, but I knelt down at her feet and said, 'Don't worry, Mum, I'm going to send off my book to get published and I'm going to look after you.'

'Darling, that's a wonderful idea,' she said, wiping her tears away and pulling me in for a hug.

'It's such a great story. Let's send it off, but everything's going to be fine. Don't you worry.'

Mum was as resourceful as ever and managed to get a job at a computer firm in Wembley on the strength of her Pitmans shorthand and typing skills. We had to tell people that Dad had gone to work in South Africa to explain his absence. I remember Mum swearing Jamie and me to secrecy and I never told a single person that my dad had gone to jail, which for a kid of eleven is pretty incredible. To this day, I'm very good at keeping secrets.

It's a sobering thought, but I honestly believe that if Mum had died after being diagnosed with breast cancer when I was five years old, Jamie and I would probably have ended up in care. My grandmother was getting older and leaving the house less and less, and my Auntie Mary was a single woman, so I doubt either of them was in a position to take on the responsibility of two children. I dread to think what could have happened to us.

3

Hounslow to Hollywood

After Dad went to prison, I had to get used to looking after myself because Mum's time was taken up with work and she was also in and out of hospital. Every afternoon I'd come home from school, stick my uniform in the washing machine and start getting dinner ready, peeling the potatoes and chopping vegetables. I remember thinking, My kids will never come home to an empty house. I didn't resent Mum at all – she was doing what she had to in order to keep a roof over our heads – but I desperately missed our old life.

One week she took a couple of days off work and it felt wonderful – just like it had before Dad went away. She picked me up from school in the car and took me home to a lovely warm house, and she'd made my favourite thing in the world for dinner: lasagne. I can honestly say they were two of the happiest days of my childhood.

Dad going to jail was devastating, but my mum made

the decision not to take Jamie and me to visit him. As far as I know she went to see him on her own, but I don't think she wanted to expose us to that environment and, in retrospect, I'm glad.

At first I sent a letter to Dad every week and, because I loved writing stories, I suggested that we wrote a Sherlock Holmes book together while he was away. The idea was that I'd write a chapter and send it to him, then he'd write the next one and send it back to me. But he wrote to me and said, *Darling, I think we're going to have to wait until I come home to finish the book because I'm not allowed to do it.* I don't know whether that was true or whether he just couldn't be bothered, but I still kept in touch with him by letter, especially during his first year in jail. At the same time I had to adjust to him not being around and get on with life. What else could I do?

That same year I started secondary school. Mum got me into a private girls' convent school in Twickenham called St Catherine's, which was paid for out of my earnings. You often hear about kids in showbiz who end up financing everyone else's lives, but my parents never touched a penny of my money – it was always ploughed into my education. I was very conscious that Mum had less money after Dad went to prison. My school shoes had holes in them, but I didn't want to worry my mum with it, so I lined the insides with plastic bags and put tissue on top.

Although the fees at St Catherine's were extortionate, it was a good decision to send me there – I'm sure if I had gone to Heathlands, which was the local comp, my life would have been a total misery. As it was, I had to walk past that school on my way home from St Catherine's, and I got chased and had bricks thrown at me because I was in this ridiculous 1950s-style uniform, complete with blazer and hat. We weren't allowed to take off our hats, even on the bus home. If we did we got reported and were sent to see the headmistress, Sister Christina, who'd inevitably dish out a detention. I've no idea how the nuns found out we'd taken off our hats – they must have had spies!

But if I was jumped by one of the kids from Heathlands or caught by a flying brick, I'd always turn round and give as good as I got. I'm a scrapper like my dad. That kind of thing was horrible, though, and I went out of my way not to put myself in situations where I might get picked on. I never sat upstairs on the bus, for example, in case I got teased by the other girls.

I liked St Catherine's as much as I was going to like any school. People say your school days are the best years of your life, but in my opinion that's only if you have a normal, carefree childhood, which I didn't. I worried about my mum constantly while Dad was in 'South Africa'. There was just too much going on in my life to allow myself to let go and enjoy school. However, I responded well to the routine and discipline at St Catherine's – I'm the kind of person who loves order and structure, and I work best in that environment. I made some good friends there, too, including Selena Bubb, who was my best friend all through school and who, all these years later, is in a relationship with my brother Jamie, which is fab.

St Catherine's was also responsible for me seeing my first dead body when I was still only eleven! One of the nuns died, so the girls were taken through the underground tunnel, which was called Pope's Grotto, to get to the other side of the river where all the nuns slept. It was pretty spooky actually – dark and cold with lots of little caves off to the sides. We all had to go into this dead nun's room and pray for her soul. I'm not sure now whether it was compulsory or whether we had a choice, but I remember one of my friends saying, 'I really need to see this because I want to be a doctor.'

She wasn't a nun I knew, but when I saw her body, all I remember thinking was how much I wanted to push her false teeth back in because they were coming out of her mouth. Imagine if your kids came home from school now and told you they'd been taken to visit a dead nun. You'd be livid!

During my first year at St Catherine's I appeared in a BBC period drama series called *Hannah*, and in my second year I got the role of the young Estella in an adaptation of Dickens's *Great Expectations*, which was another BBC production. It was a fantastic part and I happened to be reading the book at school at the time, so it was wonderful to get the opportunity to take it apart and get right inside the story, as you do when you're working on a drama. I loved working for the BBC, too, as it was a very nurturing and inclusive system.

My next job took me to Los Angeles for the first time. Although I'd worked for big Hollywood studios, I'd never actually been to LA until I was flown out there when I was thirteen to screen test for the part of Pollyanna Harrington in a Disney pilot, *The Adventures of Pollyanna*. It was hoped the pilot would get picked up by one of the networks to develop into a TV series.

Mum and I were put up in a ramshackle Howard Johnson inn (that's how far down the ladder I was). The walls were paper-thin and the first night we were there the people in the next room were having an Olympic sex session and we could hear everything! Welcome to LA.

I think the studio saw me as a young Hayley Mills, who'd played Pollyanna in the 1960 Disney film, so I got the part and, as a gift, Disneyland was closed to the public for a day so I could have the run of the park along with some other young actors working on pilots and VIPs. It was amazing.

Mum accompanied me when I went back to shoot the pilot – her bosses at the computer company were very generous and understanding when it came to giving her time off to chaperone me on jobs. But our first adventure in Hollywood wasn't what we'd hoped it would be. It was tough, actually. We were living in furnished apartments near the studio in Burbank, which is miles away from anywhere. When I went back to LA years later I realized the place to stay is West Hollywood, but it was our first visit and Mum just assumed it would be practical to stay near the studio.

One Thursday night something very sinister happened. We were in our little apartment, asleep in our two single beds, when Mum awoke with a start to see a man standing at the end of her bed holding something in his hand. He walked very calmly over to the side of her bed, stopped for a few seconds and then turned, jumped over my bed and ran out of the apartment. Mum was frozen with fear, so she didn't scream or call out for help, and I slept through the entire thing. He was probably in the bedroom for a matter of seconds, but it was terrifying for Mum and that weekend the studio moved us to the Sheraton hotel. As usual, she didn't want to worry me, so at the time she didn't tell me the real reason we were moving. I was meant to be having a sleepover with a friend from the cast that weekend, whose parents owned a big house in Malibu, but Mum wouldn't let me go and I was so disappointed.

'But why, Mum?' I whined, as kids do.

'I just don't want you to go,' she replied brusquely.

'We need to move from these apartments because they're too noisy.' And that was the end of the matter.

My mum also started to get really sick again at this time. She'd had a cough she couldn't shake and she kept getting abscesses in her mouth, which looked really painful, and she'd wrap herself up in lots of clothes, even though it was very warm in LA. I remember looking over at her one day when she was sitting in the sun at the Disney studios; she'd fallen asleep in the chair and I just knew she was ill again.

When we got home to London, Mum went into hospital for tests and began more treatment. She'd go in and have her lungs drained, then she'd come home and get back on her feet. The cancer had obviously started to spread, but she didn't want to discuss it. I think she believed that talking about the disease gave it power. She just wanted to make the most of her life, and who's to say that kind of positivity didn't help keep her going? She'd been told she had terminal cancer nearly a decade earlier and had defied all the doctors' prognoses. In those days cancer screening and treatment wasn't anywhere near as sophisticated as it is now, so it's even more incredible that Mum was able to keep coming back from it.

I'd had to miss a bit of school because of the filming in LA, and when I went back to St Catherine's there was a maths teacher who seemed to have taken a dislike to me. I felt as if she was picking on me in lessons, bellowing,

'Patsy Kensit!' across the classroom, using my full name for emphasis. I put up with it for about two weeks and then I stood up in class one day and said, 'Do you know what? That's it! I don't want to be taught by you any more,' and I packed my bag and got up to leave.

'You can't do that!' she shouted after me. 'Go straight to Sister Christina's office!'

'Fine,' I replied as I was halfway out the door. 'I'm on my way.'

When I was sat in front of the headmistress she said, 'So, what's with all the dramatics, Patsy?'

'Call my mum now,' I said confidently. 'Expel me if you want to, but I feel like this woman has been picking on me since I got back from America. I'd be happy to go.'

Of course they didn't kick me out, and after my outburst the teacher involved left me alone. I wouldn't have complained if I'd been the type of kid who walked around school boasting about my work or being disruptive in class, but I really wasn't. I was discreet about the acting part of my life because I didn't want that kind of attention at school. I felt embarrassed by it. I'm actually pretty shy and not naturally confrontational, but perhaps because my mother was sick, I felt I'd been pushed too far and decided I wasn't going to put up with this woman's nastiness.

*

Pollyanna wasn't picked up by any of the networks during pilot season, so it ended up being screened as a one-off TV movie. In retrospect, it was probably a good thing for my career because I don't know whether I would have been considered for Hollywood projects later on if I'd become a child star in the States. It's a very different system there, and once you've been pigeonholed in that way it's very hard to break away from it.

Back in England, I returned to working for the BBC in a drama called *Frost in May*, which was an adaptation of an Antonia White novel about a young girl's experiences at a Catholic convent school. It meant I got the chance to appear alongside Daniel Day-Lewis, who was lovely, and I remember thinking how gorgeous he was! It was wonderful to get the opportunity to see him work. And it was a good part for me because I could draw on my experiences of Catholicism and my own school, St Catherine's. I understood the character, Nanda Gray, and I was able to really immerse myself in the role.

There's a scene at the end where I get accused of having lesbian feelings towards other girls at the school, and I have to go to the headmistress's office and break down in tears. It's not easy to cry on cue and I was a bit worried about it.

On the day we were shooting that scene my mum made me late for work, which was really unlike her and I couldn't understand it. We were always punctual and I felt really stressed and upset when I arrived on set. But I nailed the scene and afterwards one of the producers explained to me gently that they'd asked Mum to make us late, so I'd feel unsettled and be more likely to deliver those difficult emotions. It wasn't cruel and I'm not sure I could have done it if I hadn't been helped in that way – in any case it was worth it as it got incredible reviews. As I've got older I've realized you need to use certain triggers from your life to help draw the emotion out of you. I never had to try hard – the sadness I felt over Mum's illness and the fear of her dying were always just below the surface.

I saw Daniel again about six years later when we were both doing a photo shoot for *Blitz*, which was a very hip fashion and pop culture magazine. They wanted me to wear a tiny denim jacket with just a skimpy bra underneath and I remember Daniel saying, 'What *are* you wearing, Patsy?'

'Oh, just this bra thing,' I replied nonchalantly.

'Be careful, Patsy. You're too good,' he replied. I guess he was trying to warn me about the publicity side of things overshadowing my work. And he was right.

Even though I was getting regular acting work, I decided I wanted to find myself a Saturday job in a hair salon. I'd had a long run of BBC costume dramas, which I felt made me look sort of drab, and I had fantasies about getting discovered, like Twiggy was when a celebrity hairdresser roped her into a makeover and cut her hair short.

One day Mum and I were shopping on the King's Road in Chelsea when I had a brainwave. 'Mum, I just have to do something. I'll meet you back here in five minutes and we can go for a burger,' I said, turning round and heading back down the road.

We'd just walked past Daniel Hersheson's hair salon, which was called Neville Daniel at that point, so I went back and spoke to the girl on reception.

'I just wanted to enquire if you need a Saturday girl to sweep up and make tea and coffee?' I said enthusiastically. 'If I give you my number will you consider me? I'm fourteen.'

The manager said, 'Actually, yeah, we do need someone, you can start this week.'

I ran back up the King's Road to find Mum. 'I've got my first Saturday job!' I squealed.

'What?!'

'They've hired me at Neville Daniel!' I announced, feeling very pleased with myself and grinning from ear to ear. Mum was so proud of me for taking the initiative. She'd drummed into me that life can be wonderful but you have to work for it, so I was always looking for opportunities – that drive was there from a young age.

I swept the floor at Neville Daniel's for about six months, but I never got 'discovered'! When my friend

Beatrice got a job at a branch of Warehouse in Knightsbridge, I followed her and ended up working there on Saturdays for about two years.

When it came to boys, I guess I was a late bloomer. My parents were quite strict in that respect, and I wasn't boy crazy like a lot of the girls at St Catherine's who didn't have brothers. I was used to Jamie's friends being around, so boys weren't such a mystery to me.

Teddington Boys was one of the nearest schools to St Catherine's and at home time the boys would cycle past our school on their racers and check us out. There was a boy from Teddington called Darren Stone, who was my first big crush. I actually liked him because he looked like Nick Heyward, the lead singer of Haircut 100. I think every girl in my year was in love with Darren, but he was going out with someone in my class, so he was out of bounds. Then as luck would have it, he finished with her.

Now that I was fourteen, I was becoming more independent and Mum allowed me a little more freedom socially, so I was able to accept invitations for sleepovers. One night I was staying at my friend Nicola's house and we were outside in her garden, swinging on one of those very eighties garden chairs that had a sun canopy over the top, when Darren and his mate Graham turned up.

When it came time for the boys to go home, Darren said to me, 'Walk me to my bike, Patsy.' When we were alone we had a kiss and I chipped my front tooth in the moment. I couldn't believe it had finally happened because I'd liked him for such a long time!

We ended up going out for about six weeks. All we did was hold hands and do lots of snogging. He used to meet me at the school gates and cycle slowly next to me as I walked to the bus stop. And on Saturday afternoons we'd meet up and go to the movies – Darren on his racer and me on my bike.

I finished with him, though, when he showed up at my house one day wearing a Slush Puppies T-shirt. That's how shallow I was. I'd been on at him for ages to get a yellow mac like the one Nick Heyward wore at the time – he had a kind of fisherman's look going on which was oddly sexy – but Darren wouldn't dress up like Nick for me, so that was that!

Funnily enough, Darren's dad was an in-house paparazzo at Heathrow, and years later when I was being photographed all the time, I'd be coming through the airport and there would be Mr Stone with his camera, clicking away. He was very sweet and we'd always have a quick chat about what Darren was up to.

My dad was released from prison when I was fourteen. Although I accepted that he was a flawed man, I still loved him very much. Whatever wrongs he'd done and bad decisions he'd made in his life, he'd served his time and paid his debt to society. And I can honestly say, hand on heart, that neither his villainy nor his stint in prison scarred me in the way my mum's illness did – that was absolutely soul-destroying.

When he came home to Avondale Gardens, it was obvious that he'd changed. He just wasn't the same man. I don't know how to explain it, other than to say that the light behind his eyes had gone out. He never talked about his time inside, but being in jail for nearly four years had clearly taken its toll.

The week he got out, he said to me one day, 'Right, come on, Pat, I'm taking you to the cinema. We can have some food afterwards.' He was trying to recreate the wonderful afternoons we'd spent together in the seventies when he'd take me to J Sheekey in the West End to have lobster, which I loved, and then we'd head over to Soho to one of the little movie theatres that showed cartoons (they'd probably started showing dirty movies by this point!).

So off we went to the local Odeon in Osterley, which looked like it was practically falling down, then we had a bad fish and chip supper afterwards. Of course, it was impossible to recreate the times we'd had – things were different: he'd changed and I'd grown up.

When we got home that day my parents had an almighty row and I heard my dad say to Mum, 'You know what, Margie? I don't know what you want. You haven't been near me in years anyway.' I stopped listening. I'd heard enough.

It was almost as though Dad had been institutionalized and he found it very hard to adjust to living back at home. My parents didn't share a bedroom. When Dad came out of jail, he took my room and I shared with Mum. He used to keep really odd hours – he'd go to bed early and wake up at 4 a.m. because he'd been used to getting up at the crack of dawn to slop out.

Obviously, we'd been struggling financially while Dad was away, even though Mum worked, but he was in his late sixties by the time he got out, so he was at an age when most people start to slow down. He couldn't throw himself back into the kind of work that had put him away, but what else could he do? In the end he set up a money-lending and gold-buying business with Charlie Mitchell in a room above a shop on Dawes Road in Fulham, but who knows what was really going on. He could have been up to anything, to be honest.

There were long periods when work was pretty quiet, so his friends used to visit him there and they'd all sit around playing cards for money. My dad was a great card player and taught me how to play. The two of us used to play pontoon together for hours.

One day, Dad was coming into the place on Dawes Road with the milk and papers when two robbers barged in. One of the intruders was armed with a gun. But Dad, even though he was getting on for seventy, scared the life out of these guys and chased them off the premises and down the street. Maybe Dad got lucky, but he was a tough guy and absolutely fearless.

The softness in his heart was still there, though, and Sean Mitchell tells a lovely story that proves it. One day a young South African backpacker came to the place on Dawes Road with some stones she wanted my dad and Charlie to appraise. It was a Friday afternoon and Sean was back from boarding school for the weekend so had turned up to meet his dad. The girl put her rucksack on the table and got out the stones, which were quite sizeable emeralds. Sean said my dad was very matter of fact about it and told her, 'I'll write you a receipt and we'll grade and appraise the stones over the weekend. If you're happy with the price we'll give you the money; if not, you can take the stones and be on your way.' The girl agreed and left, saying she'd return on Monday.

Charlie decided to have a bit of fun with my dad so he winked at Sean, then stepped forward, clapped his hands and said, 'Right then, Jim, we've got those stones now.'

Apparently, my dad looked horrified and said in his lovely quiet voice, 'Ah, you can't do that, Charlie.'

Charlie burst out laughing. 'Oh, really, Jim? Right you are then.'

The girl came back on Monday and got her money – a few thousand pounds. For all their faults, men like Dad and Charlie weren't violent and they had a wonderful sense of humour. Sean Mitchell once said that there was a light in me that came from having two loving parents. I think the same is true of him.

A lot of villains decamped to Marbella in the early eighties and bought these amazing mobile homes on the beachfront while they were having their villas built. The same year Dad got out of jail, he took me there on this incredible holiday with Charlie Mitchell and another one of their friends, and Dad and I stayed together in a little caravan.

I'd never eaten so well in my life. I was a skinny little thing and all they wanted to do was feed me up, so I was eating these huge meals every day – proper English fry-ups, fillet steak with sautéed tomatoes and gratin potatoes, kosher chicken, big pasta dishes, barbecued seafood, smoked salmon and caviar. These guys could cook! I didn't have to lift a finger. I'm pretty sure I came back from that holiday at least a stone heavier.

I had a fantastic time. The men were all so larger than life and entertaining, and I loved just sitting quietly in the corner, listening to their stories while they sliced garlic and chopped veg, as the steaks sizzled on the stove in the background.

Dad and I laughed so much in Marbella, but I guess

it must have been hard for him, too, as Charlie and the other guys out there were clearly doing very well for themselves, while we'd fallen on hard times again because of Dad's stint in jail. The two of us were walking along the beach one day when out of the blue he said to me, 'You know, Pat, I could go back to villainy to get all the things we had at times, but I don't think I could do it.'

He'd reconciled himself to the fact that those days were gone. The criminal world had changed, too. It had probably started to become about drugs at that point and my dad was old school – jewellery theft and traveller's-cheque fraud. It was a different world.

I was glad that he'd confided in me and I was happy we'd been able to spend that time together, laughing, sunbathing and playing cards in our stuffy little caravan. The holiday gave me some great memories that I would cherish in the years to come.

Back in Avondale Gardens, though, Dad wasn't finding it any easier to adapt to life as a free man, and I probably didn't help matters by acting the classic moody teenager (I slammed a lot of doors!).

Now that I was older, I was finding it harder to understand why my mum would settle for the kind of life my dad gave her. At least in the past he'd always been a doer, but he'd lost that spark and, although he'd joined Gamblers Anonymous in prison, he was back down the betting shop pretty much every day once he got out.

It seemed as if he'd become an old man overnight. Of course he was much older than Mum, but the difference in their ages suddenly became much more apparent. Despite her ill health, Mum was kind and funny and still beautiful, and it upset me that throughout her life she could have had anybody she wanted. But she always did the honourable thing when it came to my dad. When we were in Russia shooting *The Blue Bird*, one of the bosses of 20th Century Fox was madly in love with my mum, but she would never have been unfaithful. It just wasn't her style. I couldn't help thinking that her life could have been so different, though, and it strengthened my resolve that I wouldn't stay in a relationship if it wasn't working. Of course I was too young at the time to understand that relationships are complicated and life isn't as straightforward as it seems at fourteen.

Sadly, I'd started to lose respect for my dad, which I felt bad about later because he was seriously ill at the time, although I didn't know it then. Thinking back, he hadn't been well before he'd gone to prison, but it was the 'South Africa effect' all over again, and Jamie and I were kept in the dark.

The life my dad had led was catching up with him in all sorts of ways. His last stint in prison broke him, and it broke my heart to see it.

4

West End Girl

Growing up I was really into music – Bowie was my hero and my bedroom pin-up – so when I was fourteen I started going to see bands with my brother Jamie. One Friday night I begged my mum to be allowed to see a Scottish band called The Bluebells, who were playing at one of the colleges in town. They'd supported Haircut 100 on their tour and a couple of my friends from school were going, so Mum agreed to let me go as long as Jamie went, too. We were standing near the front and afterwards we ended up getting invited backstage (aka the janitor's office!) because we were with Jamie and he knew everyone. He'd started his own band by then and was a real scenester. He was such a handsome guy – a cross between Elvis and John Travolta, with very dark hair and piercing blue eyes, which he'd inherited from Mum. He was really popular, so he got into all the cool clubs and was invited to lots of parties.

We were all hanging out backstage – me, Jamie, my

best mate Selena and another girl called Beatrice Beatle (she'd renamed herself as a tribute to her favourite band!) – when in walked Nick Heyward with his brother and a few friends. As soon as I clocked him my legs just went from underneath me and I fell on the floor in a heap. I immediately sprung to my feet and tried to look composed. It was almost like the royal line-up as he walked past everyone. It was 1982, Haircut 100 were riding high in the charts and lots of girls were a little bit in love with Nick – I was one of them! He was about twenty-one at the time, but he looked more like a fifteen-year-old. He was very boyish.

As they got to us, Nick looked at me and said, 'Birds Eye Peas?' and I just nodded, lost for words.

'I love that commercial!' he continued. 'Can you do that popping thing?'

It was the first and only time I was delighted to put my finger in my cheek and make it go pop! At the end of the night he asked for my number, then someone obviously told him how old I was, so that was the end of that.

But although I was too young to be his real girlfriend, I did end up being asked to play his girlfriend in a video for his song 'Nobody's Fool', which was good enough for me.

At the time I was working on a TV show called *Luna* for ITV, which was conceived and directed by Micky

Dolenz from Sixties pop group the Monkees. It was a bit like *Metal Mickey* – a sort of futuristic sitcom for kids – and just as bad!

I had to wear these little pastel mini-dresses or a leotard, and I had waist-length hair at the time, which was held back with a matching Alice band. I got a lot of requests from older guys to sign pictures of me in those outfits, which I wouldn't do because even at that age I realized it was inappropriate.

One day I received a phone call on the payphone outside the rehearsal rooms at Elstree where *Luna* was filmed and it was Jamie saying that Nick Heyward had called the house to speak to me and wanted me to ring him back. Intrigued and feeling incredibly excited, I dialled the number straight away.

'Oh, hi, Patsy,' he answered. 'I was just wondering if you wanted to be in my next video?'

'Um, yes!' I almost offered to clean his windows as well! For a fourteen-year-old girl it was just about the best job in the world.

I had to ask Micky for the day off to shoot the video and luckily he managed to rejig the schedule to accommodate me. We shot on location in the West Sussex countryside and I loved every minute of it, riding a white horse around the pretty village location and pretending to be Nick's girlfriend.

*

On the work front, *Luna* might have been a turkey, but around the same time I won the role of Lady Margaret Plantagenet in the film *The Tragedy of Richard III*, which was a co-production between the BBC and the Royal Shakespeare Company. Then the following year, when I was fifteen, I landed the lead role in a BBC drama series called *Diana*, based on the R. F. Delderfield novel about the daughter of a rich landowner and her relationship with a poor country lad. The story spans the decades from the 1920s through to post-war Britain, and Jenny Seagrove played the older Diana.

The character I had to play was quite sexually precocious and I wasn't at all like that, so it worried me a bit. There was one scene where I had to wear a flimsy slip dress and I also felt embarrassed about the kissing side of things. Of course it was the BBC and, looking back, it was pretty tame, but I was just a young girl and it felt intimidating, particularly showing that sexual energy in front of my mum, who would be on set. But I really wanted the role because it was such a fantastic part.

I'd already been in to see the director three times, so I went in again with Mum and he said to me, 'Look, I'm not going to keep going round in circles, Patsy, I'm going to ask you one question: Do you like her? Do you like the character?'

'Yes,' I replied without hesitation.

'Well, then, you have to play her.'

It made me realize that in order to play a role well, despite how terribly a character might behave, you have to like them. So that was another lesson.

It turned out to be a wonderful drama to work on. As always at the BBC, it was a truly collaborative process, and there was always lots of discussion on set about how to get things right. It was a real coming together of creative thinking and positive energy, which is why it was so good and received such glowing reviews from the critics.

This was the point where I started to become known outside the industry, and the media were keen to find out more about me. However, thankfully my mum still kept me well away from the press.

In May 1983, while I was still working on *Diana*, I was invited to a lunch for up-and-coming young things at Palookaville restaurant in Covent Garden. It was a Capital Radio event and I went along in one of my mum's little black Dior dresses, accessorized with a pair of Ray-Bans! I was still only fifteen, but I must have looked at least seventeen in my outfit. When I walked in Gary Kemp, the songwriter and guitarist from Spandau Ballet, was there with the band's manager Steve Dagger. Spandau were the band of the moment and they'd recently had a massive hit with their single 'True', which was at number one for weeks. I didn't know Gary or Steve at the time, but Steve, who ended up managing me for years, told me later that I made an impression on him that day because I was dressed so differently from the other girls at the lunch. Apparently, I looked like I belonged in the sixties rather than the eighties, with my mini-dress, blonde hair and big sunglasses.

I wasn't introduced to Steve that day and he wasn't aware of my film and TV work, but apparently he made a mental note of my name because he could see something in me – a bit of 'star quality' to coin an old-fashioned phrase. Steve is a huge admirer of the Rolling Stones manager Andrew Loog Oldham, who'd discovered Marianne Faithfull at a party, and I think he always kept his eye out for someone who fitted in with that idea!

I chatted to Gary, though, who was sitting next to me at lunch, and we exchanged numbers and ended up going out on a couple of innocent dates. We went to the pictures to see one of the *Friday the 13th* movies in 3D with Beatrice Beatle and her boyfriend Gary Crowley, who was a DJ on Capital Radio at the time. And on another occasion we had dinner at an Italian restaurant, but that was it. He dropped me back home in Hounslow after our first date and he looked pretty taken aback when he saw our little council house in Avondale Gardens. He was a working-class lad himself, but I guess he knew me from these classic BBC dramas and assumed I had a privileged middle-class background.

As I got out of the car Gary said, 'What are you working on at the moment?'

'I'm filming this thing called *Diana*,' I replied.

'Oh, who do you play in it?'

'Diana.'

'Well, that's a good part then, innit?!' He laughed.

Once again, I was too young to be dating Gary, so nothing ever happened between us, but we became good mates after that. I think I was just desperate to be in love. I wanted to have a grown-up relationship because I'd been hanging out with people who were quite a lot older than I was.

I'd already started going to nightclubs in the West End with Jamie. I'm sure I badgered him so much he let me tag along just for a quiet life! In London in the early eighties punk was over and there was an exciting club scene, fuelled by the new wave of electronic dance music and the New Romantic bands, who were influenced by the likes of Bowie, Roxy Music and Kraftwerk. It was a really happening scene; similar, I imagine, to how London was in the sixties.

It was almost as if the city had burst into life again after the seventies and there were suddenly all these incredibly glamorous and creative kids who were at the centre of club culture – musicians, fashion students, artists, writers, photographers – many of whom went on to be very successful. Everyone seemed to be aspiring to do something and be someone; it was fabulous.

The Blitz club was the first place where all of these people partied, after Steve Strange and the DJ Rusty Egan started running a Tuesday night there called Club For Heroes. Boy George and Marilyn were cloakroom attendants, Spandau Ballet were the house band, and other regulars included Midge Ure, Billy Idol, Sade, fashion designer John Galliano, jewellery designer Dinny Hall, milliner Stephen Jones, the dancer Michael Clark and Steve Dagger (aka the Blitz Kids). It was a hotbed of creativity.

When I ventured on to the club scene with Jamie, things had moved on a little and we went to the Le Beat Route and Taboo (where the performance artist Leigh Bowery ran a night), but mostly to the Wag club on Wardour Street, Soho. Saturday nights there were incredible – all these very hip people in amazing outfits with a backdrop of great music. Bands were regularly getting signed from playing gigs there.

I'd put on Mum's black Dior dress and Jamie would drive us into the West End, sometimes with Selena and a couple of my other friends. Either Ollie O'Donnell or Chris Sullivan, two of the owners, would be on the door, picking out regulars and fashionable kids, and turning away others. Door Nazis! One night when Selena and I had invited along another girl from school, Ollie wouldn't let her in, despite my pleas. 'Nope, she has to go home and change,' he said. Brutal! It was that whole Studio 54 mentality – you had to look the part to be allowed in.

Chris Sullivan was a musician as well as a promoter, and he was in a band called Blue Rondo à la Turk, who'd had the huge dance-floor hit 'Klactoveesedstein' a couple of years earlier. They were an amazing band, but they never broke through commercially. We'd often turn up and Chris and Ollie would be in costume. I remember one time Chris was dressed as a kind of SAS soldier.

'Er, why are you dressed like that, Chris?' I ventured.

'Because when the Wag closes tonight I'm going out the window!' he said in his thick Welsh accent. He was a real character.

When we got inside the club and bought our drinks (Coca-Cola for Selena and me), it was a feast for the eyes. The hippest people in London were lining the walls and filling the dance floor. The second time we went there I was walking up the stairs when I saw Martin Kemp and his girlfriend Shirlie Holliman kissing by the coat check – they were just the most beautiful couple I'd ever laid eyes on.

I also saw Sade perform before she got a record deal and she was incredible, as well as exquisitely lovely. She was always very nice to younger girls like myself and Selena, as was Paula Yates, which we appreciated because a lot of the older girls on the music scene at that time could be horrors.

The guys from Spandau Ballet would be there, along with George Michael and Andrew Ridgeley from Wham!, Boy George, Madness and the journalist Robert Elms, who was dating Sade and wrote for *The Face* magazine.

Selena and I never talked about the Wag at school – it was as if we had this secret life. We were too young to really be a part of that world, but we loved watching from the wings and people seemed to like having us around.

For me, it was a chance to experience a little glamour, to dress up and be part of something wonderful. I was working at the BBC a lot, which was great, but it wasn't like being on set with Elizabeth Taylor. And of course I was still at school, which I'd never grown to love.

Some nights when Jamie wanted to have a drink we'd catch the night bus home from Soho, which was most definitely not glamorous. It was full of drunken clubbers and the air was thick with cigarette smoke. I remember thinking to myself, Life's going to change. I'm going to make sure I don't have to use public transport when I'm older. Funnily enough, these days I love the tube and wouldn't be without my Oyster card, which was given to me by my assistant JD, who I think of as the Jewish mamma I never had! But trundling back to Hounslow from central London on the night bus at 3 a.m. is enough to put anyone off public transport for life.

After seeing all those bands bringing the house down at the Wag, I then decided I wanted to be a pop star.

Clearly my fear of having my picture taken had gone. I was just about to see a whole new world – I was so lucky.

My dad, Henry James Kensit, with his mum.
This was probably taken around 1920.

My beautiful mum, Margaret Rose Doohan, is in the middle of
this photo, with her sister Mary on the left, brother John on the right,
and their parents behind.

Mum and Dad in Trader Vic's. Years after they passed away I asked their friend Pat Mitchell why Dad was wearing dark glasses. 'Well, Pat,' she said, 'he was in disguise.' I fell on the floor laughing.

This picture fascinates me. Reg Kray holding my brother Jamie, this tiny baby, in his powerful hands and looking at him with what appears to be tenderness. Reg was Jamie's godfather. Auntie Mary is next to him, and Mum and Dad are on the left.

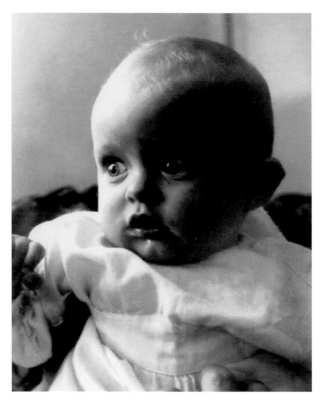

Here I'm about six months old, in summer 1968.

With Mum and Jamie. I'm looking very serious.

This is my earliest memory – cowering by the coal bunker in our back yard because I was terrified of having my photo taken.

My parents were a bit more successful with this shot, but I'm still not happy.

Were they casting
for Tweetie Pie?
Mum was clearly
not on point with
this outfit.

Messing around
with Jamie.

Looking at this it's hard to believe I got so many modelling jobs! Here, aged four, I'm wearing a stylish outfit from the Absorba autumn range.

My first acting role, also aged four, was in *The Great Gatsby*. Mia Farrow was an angel and very maternal. The women were like cats on heat around the gorgeous Robert Redford.

With Elizabeth Taylor on the set of *The Blue Bird* when I was six.
This picture is so authentic, not staged or created as a still.
I think it is a beautiful, very private moment.

The room Mum and I shared at the 'Loonygrad'. Also with us are Todd Lookinland (I had such a crush on him!) and his mother Karen. When I realized Todd was only interested in his acting and his skateboard, I had to have one too.

I love this photo of my mum, taken by stills photographer Bob Penn. The beautiful Margaret Rose Doohan – not Kensit, as she was living in sin with my dad. I think my rebellious streak came from her.

There weren't many girls in bands at the time – there was Clare Grogan from Altered Images, who I wanted to be like, and I was also obsessed with Bow Wow Wow and their singer Annabella Lwin, who was a thirteen-year-old punk when she was discovered doing a Saturday job at her local dry cleaners.

I started hanging around Jamie and his band Spice when they rehearsed, and they'd let me sing backing vocals sometimes. I was desperate to join the band properly, which Jamie was against, but after a lot of badgering I eventually wore him down and they took me in. The band was renamed Eighth Wonder and I ended up becoming the lead singer. Looking back, I feel so bad that I did that to Jamie because it was his thing and I muscled my way into it.

We started writing songs and rehearsing at our drummer Jake's parents' house in Battersea. Somehow, a guy called Bill White heard about us and told his immediate boss, Graham Ball, that he thought we were worth taking a look at. Both men worked for Steve Dagger. So Graham came down to see one of our rehearsals in Jake's bedroom and told Steve that although we were embryonic as a band, we were actually OK and we had a female singer, which was fairly unusual. Steve remembered me from the lunch at Palookaville and, on the basis of that first meeting, he instructed Bill to keep an eye on us.

On a few occasions I went into town after school to

see Bill at Steve's office in Great Portland Street, wearing my St Catherine's uniform and hat. I think Steve was pretty shocked when he saw my head peeping round the corner to say hello, because the last time he'd seen me I was in my mum's Dior dress looking a lot more sophisticated and a good few years older. Steve told me later that he thought it took balls to come up and introduce myself at the office, and he liked the fact that I showed such confidence. In the end Bill set about trying to book us some gigs and they began acting as our agents.

I'd only ever had one birthday party, when I was five, and I was terrified even then that no one would show up or that they'd have a bad time, and I had exactly the same anxiety when Steve organized my sixteenth birthday party in March 1984 at a place in Soho called the Banana Club.

To be honest, I look back at it and cringe. Jamie and Selena were there as well as some other friends but all these huge Eighties pop stars came along too, including George Michael and the guys from Spandau Ballet. Gary Crowley was the DJ. My party outfit was all Azzedine Alaïa: a black dress, ankle boots and a little leather jacket. Alaïa was one of the hottest designers of the decade and became known as 'the king of cling' for his bodycon frocks. I'd bought the dress from the Alaïa store on Sloane Street on a shopping trip with Mum. We would often hop on the Piccadilly Line on a Saturday and go shopping in

Knightsbridge, where I'd spend some of my earnings. I bought quite a few fabulous dresses that I still wear today.

Someone told me that Paula Yates defended me at a dinner party once when some girls were bitching about my outfits and saying, 'Who does she think she is in Chanel?' and 'How did she get those clothes?' But Paula stood up for me and told them she'd known me since I was fourteen and that I'd always bought my own clothes and jewellery, which was the truth.

I thought the Spandau girlfriends disliked me and seemed very territorial, with the exception of Martin's girlfriend, Shirlie, who was always lovely. But I had to see them quite a bit because at this point Steve Dagger had come on board as Eighth Wonder's manager. I remember going to a Wham! gig at Wembley with Steve and the Spandau crowd and there was a party at Stringfellows afterwards. I was standing next to the Spandau girls when Nick Heyward came over to say hello to me, and I was pushed in the back and nearly went flying!

On another occasion a few of us were travelling in a car somewhere late at night and I was sitting next to one of the band members and his girlfriend. I ended up falling asleep and my head accidentally dropped onto his shoulder, and I got a really hard dig in the ribs from his girlfriend! I would have understood if I hadn't been a girl's girl, but the truth is, a woman's approval has always meant much more to me than a man's. I was young, though, and probably annoying. Maybe I wouldn't have liked me!

The problem was, I was still a kid and the people I was socializing with were all in their twenties. I wanted to be accepted and I was desperate for romance in my life, but the minute someone found out how young I was, they weren't interested. They just thought of me as a child. It meant I ended up feeling quite lonely and lost among those people. I guess I should have been running around in my trainers with other sixteen- and seventeen-year-olds.

My party was a success, though, and everyone had a good time. The only downer was that Nick Heyward, who I still held a torch for, came with his girlfriend, so at the end of the night I went home feeling awful. We did end up having a little kiss at another party when I was seventeen but I was still too young for him. Sadly, for me, it was a case of unrequited teenage love.

Back in the real world I was in my last year of school and had just sat my O levels. I had a little scooter with L-plates on the back, which I'd ride to school and back, but if I could get out of going, I would. I still hated school and I'd finished my exams, so I didn't see the point in going any more. I was only ever interested in English literature – the rest I didn't care about. I didn't want to go to university and I never worried about making a living because I was already working. I can honestly say that I have never used anything I learned at school other than how to pray. My spiritual side was nourished at St Catherine's, but that was about it. Eventually I started refusing to get up for school some mornings, which I feel terrible about now.

'Come on, Patsy, you're going to be late!' Mum would shout from the kitchen.

'I'm not going to school,' I'd shout back from the bedroom.

'You've got to go to school.'

'Well, I'm NOT going!'

'Right,' she'd say, exasperated, picking up the phone to speak to Miss Edwards, who was Sister Christina's secretary. 'Patsy's going to be in a bit late this morning, but she *will* be in.'

This little charade went on for a while, but I always ended up going to school, albeit reluctantly. I did OK in my exams, too, but only because I have a good memory.

In retrospect, I probably would have been a lot happier if I'd gone to a drama school, but I was working and learning on the job, which is, I think, the best way.

My first gig with Eighth Wonder was in a wine bar in Wimbledon in November 1984. Steve Dagger was there, as well as some A&R guys from record companies who'd heard about it. I was convinced we were going to blow them away. I'd seen all these artists like Sade, Animal Nightlife and Blue Rondo à la Turk, who'd been such a hit with London's hippest clubbers, and naively I assumed we'd get the same reaction. I didn't think about the fact that they'd all been writing and playing music for years. We were bloody awful! We had the nerve to do a cover of the Isley Brothers classic, 'Summer Breeze', and I remember someone saying to me afterwards, 'That was a bit ambitious, wasn't it? You know, trying to tackle that.'

So it didn't go very well, but afterwards we started doing lots more gigs around pubs, clubs and college venues to hone our skills.

Around about the same time I heard about a film role in a new Brit flick adapted from the Colin MacInnes novel *Absolute Beginners*, which is about life, love and racial tension in London at the end of the fifties. The movie was incredibly hyped before it even began shooting. It was a musical and David Bowie was going to be in it, along with Ray Davies from the Kinks. Julien Temple, who'd made the Sex Pistols documentary *The Great Rock 'n' Roll Swindle* and who had shot Bowie's videos, was directing it. And the producer was Stephen Woolley, who'd just made a film called *The Company of Wolves*, which I'd tested for, but didn't get. I have massive respect for Steve – I was a fan then and still am.

One Sunday I was watching a music show on TV called *20th Century Box* and Julien was a guest on it. He held up this picture of Brigitte Bardot and said, 'If anyone out there looks like this, write in because we've got to find Crepe Suzette,' which was the lead female role in *Absolute Beginners*.

I wasn't arrogant enough to think I actually looked like Brigitte Bardot, but I had blonde hair and I was obsessed with her, so after that I became determined to get the part.

My acting agents William Morris spoke to the movie's casting director, Susie Figgis, but she wasn't keen on seeing me. Her impression of me was of this girl who wore dowdy costumes in period dramas, and Crepe Suzette was quite a provocative, sexually aware character. I guess she just didn't see me in the part. But I was in a band now (trying to be Debbie Harry!), and *The Face* had taken photos of us, which I sent to Julien, along with letters, asking to be considered for the role. He still wouldn't see me.

As it turned out, Steve Dagger had known Stephen Woolley for years – they'd been in the same class at school – so he invited him down to one of our gigs in Kensington. It was actually one of our good shows and loads of regulars from the Wag came down, including Sade and Robert Elms. I think Stephen saw a different side to me when he watched me perform with the band.

'Julien should definitely meet Patsy,' he told Steve after the gig.

'She's tried to get a meeting, but he won't see her,' replied Steve.

'Well, when's the next gig?'

'In two weeks.'

'OK, I'm coming down and I'm going to bring Julien.'

True to his word, Stephen brought Julien to our next gig, at the YMCA in Tottenham Court Road. My stage outfit for the night was a silver dress by the American designer Stephen Sprouse. I loved his Sixties-inspired designs because I was also obsessed with Sixties icons Edie Sedgwick and Marianne Faithfull (such a cliché, I know!). He also made a lot of Debbie Harry's clothes, and he went on to design the Louis Vuitton graffiti logo luggage.

So I went on stage in this silver dress, which turned virtually transparent under the stage lights, and almost immediately I heard someone in the audience shout, 'Fucking hell, her dress is completely see-through!'

Oh God, I thought. Of all the nights for that to happen!

Afterwards, Stephen and Julien came backstage to talk to me. When I say backstage, it was a cupboard with a sunbed in it, and Julien and I sat on the sunbed, crouching under the canopy.

'Look, I think you should test for the film,' he said.

'But I've been trying to get you to see me for ages.'

'Yeah, but after what I've seen tonight, I can imagine you in the part now.'

So I screen-tested and got the role. In a celebratory mood, Selena and I went off on holiday to the Canary

Islands, where we stuffed our faces and baked in the sun. I came back as pink as a lobster and about six or seven pounds heavier.

I was called into Shepperton almost straight away to test with the guys who were auditioning for the part of Colin, the male lead, because they still hadn't found their man. One of the guys who tested was Suggs from Madness, who I love. I wish he'd got the part, but they ended up casting an unknown actor called Eddie O'Connell opposite me instead.

A few days later one of the production assistants called to say Julien wanted me to meet him at Nitrate Films in Soho, but I wasn't told what the meeting was about. When I turned up, Julien said, 'We're going to walk to a screening room in Wardour Street. I want to show you something.'

Once we were there and settled in our seats, the lights went down and up popped the screen tests I'd just done with the guys. 'Look at that,' said Julien, pointing at the screen. 'You've got to lose weight. You've got to sort it out, Patsy.'

Then he played the screen test I'd done before I went on holiday. 'This is what you looked like before. You need to sort your hair out, too.'

I could see that I didn't look quite the same as when I tested for the role – the sun had bleached my hair a whiter blonde and I did look bigger – but I didn't know how to respond to Julien. I was too shocked and upset.

He had a right to point out those things, and maybe he believed he was doing me a favour by being honest. Maybe he thought I needed to toughen up a bit – the business can be cruel after all – but I'd never experienced that side of things and I was too young to detach myself from it. In the past Mum had always protected me, chaperoning me on set, but once I was sixteen having a chaperone wasn't a requirement.

In the end, they hired a trainer to work out with me and the weight fell off in a week; my sunburn calmed down and I put a toner through my hair. It was all sorted out really quickly, but I felt Julien could have handled it better.

Before we started shooting, Julien did lots of interviews in which he said, 'We've cast Eddie and Patsy because they are absolute beginners, they are new to this.'

But I wasn't new to acting. At sixteen I was already a veteran, although I wasn't at all prepared for what was about to unfold. I was about to get the biggest wake-up call of my career.

5

Crepe Suzette

When it was announced that I was going to play Crepe Suzette, the interest in Eighth Wonder from record companies sky-rocketed. There had already been a degree of expectancy, as our manager Steve Dagger also looked after Spandau, so most people in the music industry assumed we must be the next big thing. But Steve had been trying to keep things low-key, so that we could get used to performing, putting us on at dodgy off-the-beaten-track pubs. The bush telegraph had been buzzing for a while, though, and the more he tried to fob off the record companies, the more interest it generated. Somehow the A&R guys used to get wind of where we were playing and they'd turn up at the gig and pester Steve about us signing with them. When word got out about *Absolute Beginners*, the interest shifted up several gears. Suddenly every major and independent label wanted to sign us, including EMI, Warner Bros, CBS, Virgin and Geffen, and a frenzied bidding war followed.

Steve managed to negotiate a deal with the movie's bosses so that Eighth Wonder provided a song for the soundtrack, alongside incredible artists such as Bowie, Ray Davies, Sade and the Style Council. Not intimidating at all, then! We were given a brief for the song so, along with guitar player Geoff Beauchamp and keyboard player Alex Godson, I wrote 'Having It All'. With the movie due to go into production in July 1985, we recorded the track that spring with top producers Clive Langer and Alan Winstanley, who'd produced lots of Madness hits. Then, on 25 April, Eighth Wonder signed an impressive deal with CBS – it was a time when bands were being offered crazy advances on record deals. It was exciting but it felt a bit daunting, too, because there was a lot of expectation that we'd be successful.

The interest around the band was nothing compared to the buzz the movie was generating, though; the media was obsessed with it. The British film industry was in the doldrums at the time, and it felt as if everyone was looking to *Absolute Beginners*, which was a big-budget movie, to revive its fortunes.

There was a huge level of expectancy before the movie had even been made, not least because of the people who were involved with it – wonderful musicians as well as respected actors, including James Fox and Steven Berkoff.

To add fuel to the fire, the whole world was looking at London at the time. It was the year of Band Aid and

Live Aid, so the city was the centre of the music universe, as well as a vibrant hub of popular culture, and *Absolute Beginners* was being made in that context.

Naturally, the press started to focus its lens on me as the star of this much-hyped movie-of-the-moment. Steve started getting inundated with requests from magazines for interviews and photo shoots, but when it came to the media I was incredibly naive, clueless even. As I've already said, Mum had never allowed me to do interviews because she didn't want my dad's villainy to be exposed. But while staying out of the papers had kept my background under wraps and helped me to make the transition from child actor to adult performer, it also meant that when I *was* thrust into the media spotlight, I didn't know how to handle it. I ended up saying a lot of stupid things that have dogged me to this day, including the 'I want to be more famous than anything or anyone' quote I gave to a music journalist. I'd actually said it in a jokey context, but that's not how it came across, and it didn't win me a lot of fans, particularly in the music press, which was incredibly snobbish at the time.

But I was just a seventeen-year-old kid who wanted to be Debbie Harry! I didn't really have an identity of my own – I was channelling all these female artists who I was a fan of, and I got caught up in the hype and excitement around the band and the movie.

In the weeks running up to shooting *Absolute Begin-*

ners, it started to become clear what sort of movie it was going to be – and it wasn't what most people were expecting. Julien arranged screenings of musicals including *West Side Story* and *Guys and Dolls* for the cast prior to filming because his intention was to make a traditional musical. But no one outside of the production got that – the media assumed it was going to be a cool rock-and-roll movie about youth culture with music in it, almost like a prequel to *Quadrophenia*. So right from the start there was a misconception about the style of the film.

The novel is a cult classic, set in Notting Hill and focusing on teenage life in a fast-changing society on the cusp of the Sixties – a world of jazz music, sharp clothes, hip hang-outs, sex and simmering racial tensions. In the book, my character, Suzette, has a definite edge to her and she's sexually confident. The narrator of the book – played by Eddie O'Connell – is in love with Suzette, and she drives him nuts because she's always running off to sleep with West Indian guys. The film script was far less gritty than the novel, so I needed time to understand the character and direction on how to play the role, but I didn't get any, and as a result I felt out of my depth. Julien seemed preoccupied with the look of the film instead of engaging with the actors. It was a shock for me because I'd been used to working on sets where there was a lot of pastoral care, but it was evident that I was on my own with this one. I guess Julien wasn't used to dealing with actors because his background was pop promos. Whatever his reasons, I felt he didn't get to grips with me as an actress, or as a person, right from the word go.

Unfortunately, there was no chemistry between Eddie and me either, which didn't help matters, though there was nothing either of us could do about it. I'm sure Stephen Woolley and Julien thought I hated Eddie, but I didn't. We simply didn't gel on screen or off, which must have been a huge disappointment.

Most of the movie was shot at Shepperton, but one of my major scenes was filmed at the Café de Paris night-club in the West End. We'd had endless dance rehearsals prior to shooting it because it involved a complicated song-and-dance routine on a catwalk, where I get thrown around by dancers and my dress gets ripped, so I'm wearing just a tiny scrap of fabric.

Typically, on the day of shooting my period showed up, so I had to ask to go to the bathroom and there was lots of eye-rolling from behind the camera. One of the costume girls came over to ask me what was going on and I burst into tears. When I explained to her that I was worried there was going be carnage on the dance floor she was completely unsympathetic and just shrugged her shoulders and wandered off.

'What was all that about?' Julien asked when I returned to the set and, feeling uncomfortable and embarrassed, I had to explain. Still there was no sympathy, and I felt as if he thought I was being difficult.

To make things worse, negative stories also started to mysteriously leak out from the set. One newspaper was constantly running little stories about me being unprofessional on set, none of which were true. I'm not trying to sound grand, but having worked on film sets since the age of four, I realized the importance of turning up on time and knowing my lines, and I understood the technical side of filmmaking, too.

In spite of all this, I always bounced back and got on with the job. One thing I'm not is a person who throws in the towel easily, so I worked hard and did everything that was asked of me. In retrospect, I probably brought some of that stuff on myself by saying silly things to the press, but you live and learn.

It wasn't all backstabbing and bitchiness, though, there were some lovely people and some great performances. James Fox, who played my husband Henley, is always fabulous. I remember the first day on set we just looked at each other and laughed because it was total chaos. Bruce Payne and Steven Berkoff were both fantastic, and of course my bedroom pin-up David Bowie was also in the movie. I was beyond excited about that and expected him to instantly fall in love with me the moment he laid eyes on me (as you do when you're seventeen). As a result, the day we met was a big disappointment because he just said,

'Hi,' and walked away! Then one day I was sitting in the make-up chair and he walked over to me, picked up a hairbrush and started brushing my hair. He didn't utter a single word, just put down the brush after he'd finished and left the room. Wow! All I could do was swoon.

There's a brilliant scene in the film where David dances on top of a globe, and on the day it was being shot, the soundstage at Shepperton was packed because everyone wanted to watch him perform, and he was amazing. We were all in awe of him.

In between shooting *Absolute Beginners*, the band had started recording material for release and I was being invited to do more interviews and photo shoots. Over the August bank holiday I was asked to do a shoot with iconic photographer Annie Leibovitz for the cover of *Tatler* magazine. Annie wanted me to wear as little as possible for the shots – in fact, she wanted me to hold this painted disc up in front of me, so I appeared to be naked behind it. When Steve Dagger showed up, the colour drained from his face when he found out what I was being asked to do. He told me afterwards that all he could think was, Oh, God, she's seventeen and we're responsible for her. What the hell is her mother going to say? Margie is *not* going to be happy!

So for the whole afternoon Steve was locked in a battle of wills with Annie over how naked I was going to be.

'Does it have to be *that* small?' I kept hearing him ask.

I guess it could have been quite an intimidating situation for me because it was the first time I'd been asked to do something like that, but I was pretty fearless at that age and I was prepared to give it a go because Annie was such a respected photographer. I ended up in a leather jacket and beret, and the photographs were wonderful.

In October 1985, towards the end of filming on *Absolute Beginners*, Eighth Wonder released their first single, 'Stay With Me'. The record company felt that because people had been hearing about the band for months, they ought to put something out ahead of the movie's release. But with the benefit of hindsight, they should probably have waited for the movie and capitalized on the publicity, because the single was a big flop in the UK.

We did a lot of gigs and college tours that autumn, travelling all over the country to promote the single, and we appeared on several TV shows, too. But when the single came out the music press turned on us, and I remember being spat at during some of those gigs. At one university a girl hurled abuse at me throughout the show, so I jumped down off the stage and decked her. It's not ladylike and I'm not proud of it, but she wouldn't stop and I just snapped. A couple of days later a little story appeared in the papers, but these days you'd probably have a lawsuit on your hands!

There seemed to be a misconception among the music press that I was this spoilt middle-class girl who was playing at being a pop star, and if it didn't work out I could run back to Daddy. Also, the music scene had started to change and we were at the tail end of the eighties pop movement. The moment had gone. Hip-hop artists like the Beastie Boys and Run DMC were emerging and stadium rock bands such as Simple Minds and U2 were huge. Red Wedge artists including Billy Bragg and the Style Council (who wanted to help oust the Tory Government) were also popular, and there I was, going around town saying stupid stuff like I wanted to be more famous than anyone. Of course, ten years later the Spice Girls were just as blatant about wanting fame and success, but back in the mid-eighties, saying that kind of thing was a big no-no.

But while the single bombed in the UK that wasn't the case elsewhere in Europe. In November we went to Italy for three days on a promotional tour, taking in Milan and Verona, and by the time we'd stepped off the plane back in England, the single was at number one in the Italian charts.

Although filming on *Absolute Beginners* rumbled on until the end of the year, I started work on a BBC adaptation of George Eliot's novel *Silas Marner: The Weaver of Raveloe* alongside Ben Kingsley, playing his daughter Eppie. It should have been shot before *Absolute Beginners*, but ended up being postponed because of a writers' strike. At one point I wasn't sure I wanted to do it because there was so much going on with the band, but my acting agents William Morris told me in no uncertain terms that I was doing it, and thank God they did! It was a great piece of work and it also stuck two fingers up to all those people who'd been giving me a kicking in the press, because when it was screened in December it received fantastic reviews and went on to win a BAFTA. I was so bloody pleased! After getting panned for the band and enduring a challenging time on *Absolute Beginners*, *Silas Marner* came at just the right moment and restored my confidence.

Working for the BBC again felt like coming home. The director Giles Foster, like all of the directors I'd worked with at the BBC, was brilliant at creating a nurturing environment where everyone worked together to get the best out of the script. Sadly, working in movies has become a far more solitary experience, as I discovered for the first time on *Absolute Beginners*. These days directors are mostly interested in their shots and their edits, so actors either have to turn up and trust they're going to nail the performance or they have to work on the script with someone prior to shooting.

On 3 April 1986 there was a royal premiere for *Absolute Beginners* in Leicester Square, with Princess Anne in attendance and a party in a marquee in the square afterwards. There was no doubt that a very big deal was being made of this movie. When I turned up on the red carpet with my mum Margie, the paparazzi went nuts. Up until that point I'd appeared in the style press and women's magazines, but this was the first time the national press had latched on to me and pictures of me from that night, wearing a pale pink mini-dress, appeared in the tabloids for about a week afterwards. There were stories discussing everything from my VPL to speculation over who I might be dating! The press also realized I'd had a career as a child actress and, inevitably, journalists started delving into my background to see what else they could discover.

Thankfully, there was nothing awful written about me – in fact the coverage was incredibly positive and I was being talked about as Britain's brightest new star – though the same couldn't be said for the movie, which received a critical mauling. The reviews were awful, regardless of the fact that the movie went straight to number one in the box office and stayed there for weeks. At that time musicals were considered old-fashioned and naff, and the critics couldn't quite believe that the guy who'd given them *The Great Rock 'n' Roll Swindle* had trashed a book they all loved.

For some reason, I became the focus of a lot of this negative reaction, which was a big shock to me because I'd never experienced that level of scrutiny before, and everything I'd been involved with up until that point had been successful. I guess I was an easy person to blame because I'd given lots of stupid interviews. After the movie came out Julien accused me of having 'thick ankles' in an article – as if that was the reason the film had been a critical flop! I really thought he believed I'd ruined his movie. I couldn't understand why all these grown men were putting the responsibility for the success of a feature film on the shoulders of a seventeen-year-old girl.

In reality, the picture had been hyped so much, it couldn't possibly have lived up to people's expectations. But I learned from the experience, and I'm sure other people involved with the production did too.

Interestingly, other countries perceived the film very differently – American critics got it, and it was a huge success elsewhere in Europe. Over the years it's become a cult movie and is now considered a classic. It was referred to in the opening sequence of Robert Altman's *The Player*, where a studio exec says, 'What about *Absolute Beginners*? That was an extraordinary shot,' paying homage to Julien's opening sequence. And when I worked on a movie with Martin Scorsese a few years later, he said, '*Absolute Beginners* is one of my top ten films ever. I mean, that opening shot, it's like Coppola's *One From the Heart*.'

I ran into Julien in 2003, when we were both on a panel for the Festival du Film de Paris, alongside other English actors and directors, including Rupert Everett, Mike Figgis and Danny Boyle. We were there to present a film we'd been involved with – in my case *Absolute*

Beginners. Julian and I had a lovely chat and I was reminded of what a good guy he is, and obviously he went on to be very successful. I always had the upmost respect for Julien as a director whilst we were filming, and wanted to please him. I'm sure everyone's heart was in the right place making the movie; we all wanted it to be a hit and we all learned something from it.

6

Fame and Family Heartache

In the spring of 1986 things with the band started to take off. We'd had a number one record in Italy with 'Stay With Me', and now the Japanese arm of the record company wanted to put out the single with an album. We hadn't finished recording it yet, but we had some B-sides, so we put together a mini album and got some press shots taken to accompany it. When the single hit the record shops it sold 200,000 copies almost immediately and went straight to number one.

Steve Dagger organized a promotional trip to Tokyo in May on the back of it. We happened to fly out on Virgin Atlantic's first flight to Japan, so Richard Branson was on board and I did a little disco dance with him in the aisle! We didn't play any shows, but we did lots of press interviews, as well as TV and radio. I was staggered by the number of fans who'd congregate outside the hotel, and we also started getting sack-loads of fan mail delivered to our rooms. In among the letters was one addressed to me from a man called Issei Sagawa, saying he was a huge fan and that I reminded him of his girlfriend. That would have been quite sweet – if he hadn't murdered her. It turned out that Sagawa was a notorious Japanese cannibal, who'd killed his Dutch girlfriend (the one I bore a resemblance to) in Paris in 1981 and partially eaten her. It was a really big case at the time, so much so that the Rolling Stones wrote a song about him called 'Too Much Blood', which appears on the 1983 album *Undercover*.

Sagawa was declared insane by the French court and sent to a mental institution but after three years he was transferred to a similar hospital in Japan. Controversially, he was released just over a year later into his parents' custody. So I was getting letters from a cannibal who was essentially a free man and could have been camped outside the hotel with all the other Eighth Wonder fans!

I would love to have been a fly on Steve Dagger's wall back in London when our tour manager John Martin called him and said, 'Look, we've got a problem here. Patsy's getting fan mail from a cannibal.'

Once Steve realized that John wasn't pulling his leg he had another Annie Leibovitz moment – times ten. 'Jesus, what the hell is her mother going to say?!' he replied, head in hands. 'Call the police, John. You've got to get them involved. This guy is a nutter of the first order!' He just couldn't believe it.

I was actually pretty cool about the whole thing, probably because it was such a busy week that the enormity of it didn't quite hit home. The police stepped in and the band was moved to another floor in the hotel, and they put a bodyguard outside my room twenty-four hours a day. I also had a personal bodyguard who accompanied me wherever I went, and this guy took his job extremely seriously. His face was completely expressionless – I never managed to get a reaction out of him. One day we visited Tokyo's version of Disney World and I tried to persuade him to get on the Space Mountain ride, but he was having none of it! Happily there was no more drama. Nevertheless, Steve was counting the minutes until I stepped off the plane at Heathrow.

We had to get the album finished, so at the end of May we went to LA to record with Mike Chapman, a producer who'd had lots of success with Blondie. Steve had sent Mike some of our material, as well as magazine covers and interviews, to see if he'd be interested in working with us, and he was.

This was my first time in Hollywood as an adult, and what became apparent immediately was the different attitude towards *Absolute Beginners* over there – my US agents at William Morris were really excited about me being in LA. The movie opened there on 2 June, and that morning I had a meeting with director John Hughes, who made some of the biggest movies of the eighties – *The Breakfast Club*, *Weird Science*, *Pretty in Pink* and *Ferris Bueller's Day Off*. Then in the afternoon I met with director Rob

Reiner, who went on to make *When Harry Met Sally* and *Misery*. The next day Steve and I were due to catch a flight to New York, where we had more meetings. Just before we left for the airport, Steve got a call to say that John Hughes wanted to cast me in his next movie, *Some Kind of Wonderful*. We were both thrilled to bits, and when we got on the plane we ordered champagne to celebrate.

However, by the time we landed in New York, the deal was already off! Steve got a phone call to say the studio didn't want an English actress in the movie – apparently they just didn't want to risk the incredibly successful Hughes franchise by chucking an English person into the mix. Hughes wanted to rewrite the script to make me an exchange student, but the studio wouldn't buy it, so unfortunately that picture went away.

In July I went to a film gala in Rome to promote *Absolute Beginners* and also did a shoot with iconic photographer Bob Carlos Clarke. Then in August we went back to LA to record with Mike Chapman and meet with Dave Stewart from the Eurythmics, who wanted to write a song for the band. I love Dave and was a big Eurythmics fan. Steve and I had dinner with Dave at a restaurant in the Valley, then the next day he invited us to play tennis at his house. When we showed up, this lovely dog bounded over and was jumping all over us.

'This is a nice, dog, Dave,' said Steve, patting it on the head. 'Did you bring him over from England?'

'No, it's a rented dog,' replied Dave, without missing a beat.

When Steve and I left that day we couldn't stop laughing. A rented dog? You couldn't make it up!

Back in the relative sanity of Europe, *Absolute Beginners* opened in Rome on 11 September and it was an incredibly glamorous premiere. I was a proper pop star in Italy, thanks to our number-one record, so I was swamped with journalists and photographers on the red carpet. Later that month, we decamped to the San Sebastián Film Festival in Spain, where *Absolute Beginners* got a wonderful reception. On the day of the main event it was a beautiful balmy late-summer evening and we were in the green room surrounded by all these incredibly glamorous people, including Ursula Andress, who looked so stunning I couldn't take my eyes off her. Just as we were about to be ushered into this magical open-air amphitheatre, the mood was broken for me when Julien Temple walked in. Sadly, at the time there was still tension between us.

Back in Italy a couple of months later I accidentally pushed my celebrity status to another level. I was there with Eighth Wonder to perform at the Sanremo Music Festival, which is a huge event out there with a TV audience of millions. Unfortunately, during our second performance I had a spectacular wardrobe malfunction when my Stephen Sprouse dress fell down to reveal one of my breasts. Some people thought it was premeditated, but it absolutely wasn't. I was mortified!

There were lots of other British bands out there, including the Pet Shop Boys, who'd obviously become hugely successful since their first single 'West End Girls' had launched them onto the scene a few years earlier. One night I left the hotel with the rest of the band to go to the venue, and Neil Tennant and Chris Lowe from the Pet Shop Boys were standing outside. This big shiny limo drew up at the kerb to pick us up and, as we walked towards it, all these fans who'd been waiting outside the hotel started chanting madly, 'Patsy! Patsy!'

Neil and Chris just looked at each other, totally bemused by all the attention Eighth Wonder were getting. I hadn't met either of them before, but I shouted over, 'Are you going to the venue?'

'Yes,' they replied.

'Well, come with me. Hop in!' I said, waving them into the car, so they jumped into our limo amid much hilarity. They found the whole thing hysterically funny. After all, I was literally being spat at back in England and felt lucky if the record company gave me my train fare home from a gig!

After the festival we went on to Milan to do TV shows and press interviews, then I flew on to Paris where I had a meeting about a movie with the French actor Christopher Lambert, who was a huge star at the time thanks to starring roles in *Greystoke: The Legend of Tarzan* and *Highlander*. Unfortunately, the film didn't get made in the end.

Towards the end of February the band went back to Italy for more TV appearances and to attend the Festival of the Mask in Venice, as our music had been chosen as the theme tune. We were about as hot as we could possibly be in Italy!

I flew back to London to model in a Vivienne Westwood show at Olympia, which was a real honour because I love her clothes, then it was over to Germany to shoot the cover of *Miss Vogue*. My schedule was jam-packed and I seemed to be flying off to a different country every two or three days. It was mostly to promote the band, but although we were very popular all over Europe by this point – Spain, Germany and France, as well as Italy – we still hadn't had a hit record in the UK. When filming had wound up on *Absolute Beginners* I'd been convinced I wanted to be in the band, but a year on I was already starting to have doubts. Also, I knew deep down that I didn't have the ability to become a good singer. You realize very quickly if you're going to be able to improve or not.

I turned down a lot of acting work during this time, including a really fab part in a costume drama, which is something I regretted later. Strangely enough, the bad press surrounding *Absolute Beginners* in the UK didn't have a negative impact on my career as an actress – in fact, it made Hollywood sit up and take notice – but I think being in the band did and, with hindsight, I wish I'd just concentrated on acting, as trying to sing and act gave out mixed messages about the direction I wanted to go in.

What the band did do, though, was give me an international profile, which enabled me to go on to make films in Italy, Spain, France and Germany in the years to come, so I benefited from it in that way.

While things were busy and exciting on the work front, the situation back home in Avondale Gardens, where I was still living with Mum and Dad, was far from rosy. My mum's illness continued to be a dark presence in all our lives. As usual, she never made an issue of it, to the point where I only found out by accident that her cancer had spread.

One day after she'd been to the hospital, she'd stopped for petrol and had driven off without paying, so the police turned up on our doorstep and I overheard her talking to them from upstairs.

'I'm so sorry,' she said to the officers. 'I was on my way home from a hospital appointment and I was told my cancer has come back. I just wasn't thinking straight and completely forgot.'

It turned out, her doctor had told her she might have only weeks to live, so naturally her mind was elsewhere. At first I was really angry with her, which I'm sure was the last thing she needed, but I wanted to know what was going on so I could help her. Even though Jamie and I were older now, she still wanted to protect us, and she knew I was a terrible worrier – I worried about her all the time.

A year or so earlier, prior to starting work on *Absolute Beginners*, I paid to have all her teeth fixed because she'd been suffering terribly with mouth ulcers. I didn't know if they were a side-effect of her treatment or because her immune system was depressed, but I hated seeing her in pain and I was terrified she might have oral cancer. I would have done anything to help her. Anything.

After she was told the cancer had spread, she went into hospital for surgery. I believe she had a mastectomy and that they took skin from her back to patch up the scar, but she refused to discuss it, so I never knew the full details. I know she didn't want a reconstruction, though, because to her that was just vanity.

She must have been in hospital for a couple of weeks, and one day I was so desperate to see her that I got in my car – even though I hadn't passed my driving test yet – and drove to the hospital with the L-plates on it. When I got home to Hounslow after the visit, the phone rang almost immediately and it was Mum, who went absolutely mental because I'd driven the car without a licence. She'd looked out of the window when I'd left and saw me driving off. There was no fooling her! I took it as a good sign that she was getting better, though, and I promised not to do it again. Once again, the doctor's grim prognosis proved to be wrong and Mum battled on with treatment.

But while Mum, thankfully, had been given yet another reprieve and it was such a relief to see her getting a little stronger every day, my dad was in really bad shape. When he came out of prison it emerged that he had leukaemia, which Jamie and I were kept in the dark about for a long time. We could see he'd changed after being inside, and at first we assumed it was just down to the effects of being institutionalized, but it turned out he was also ill. He'd actually been diagnosed before he'd gone to jail and had received treatment, which meant he was in remission when he was serving time, but after he was released he started to suffer again.

One of the first signs that something was amiss was when he stopped driving as he'd always been a man who loved cars. One day I was driving home along the Wellington Road in Hounslow when I saw this frail figure in the distance walking on the pavement. As I got nearer I thought, Oh my God, it's my dad. I didn't recognize him. I pulled over, wound down the window and said, 'Dad, jump in.'

'No, Pat, it's only down the road,' he replied, dismissing the idea with a wave of his hand.

'Don't be silly, Dad, get in!' I insisted.

He was still sleeping in my tiny box room in Avondale Gardens while I bunked in with Mum, and one day, when he'd gone out to meet Charlie Mitchell at the place in Dawes Road, I went into the bedroom to collect a few of my things. I noticed the bed sheets were soaking wet and there was a really strong chemical smell, which was probably his medication, so I'd stripped the bed and put fresh sheets on it. Whenever I was at Avondale Gardens, I tried to keep on top of the housework, and I'd do the food shop and cook an evening meal. Mum was still working for the computer firm, even though she wasn't well herself, so I did as much as I could to help out. I think my compulsion for tidiness and order was a way of dealing with the uncertainty and chaos at home. And focusing on practical things helped me push away the reality that I was going to lose my dad.

Soon after that, Dad was admitted to King's College Hospital near Dulwich in south London where he stayed for two or three months. When he came home, things returned to some kind of normality, but he gradually deteriorated as the illness took hold.

He was admitted to King's again towards the end of the summer of 1987 and I remember going to visit him one day with Mum and Jamie. Dad was a huge Tottenham Hotspur fan – he used to get so nervous watching the match on TV that he'd have to leave the room, and sometimes he'd come up to my bedroom and ask me to say a prayer for the team. 'Pray to Saint Jude for us, Pat,' he'd say. Before he'd gone into hospital there had been a record in the charts by Spurs players Glenn Hoddle and Chris Waddle called 'Diamond Lights'.

'Glenn Hoddle was here earlier,' said Dad when we were sitting at his bedside.

'Oh, was he, Daddy?' I said gently, realizing he must have been hallucinating because of his medication.

'Oh yes, he was dancing around the bed. We had a great time!'

'We'll get you that record, Dad,' said Jamie.

That was the last time I saw my dad alive. He died at the beginning of September, and sadly none of us were with him when it happened. He was seventy-two. A nurse called to give us the news and Jamie and I went to the hospital with Mum to see him.

I think it was a defence mechanism, but I almost felt a bit removed from the situation. One moment will be etched in my memory for ever though – my mum going over to Dad's bed, holding his face gently in her hands and repeating his name over and over again, 'Oh, Jim, Jim, Jim.' She was distraught and it was heartbreaking to witness. For some reason, I hadn't expected to see her grieve like that, and it was like watching someone I didn't know. I'd never really understood their relationship, and for the past few years they'd had separate bedrooms and pretty much lived separate lives – Mum put all her energy into Jamie and me, and of course held down a job, too. I suppose it was a glimpse of something I hadn't seen for years: how much she really loved my dad.

I was working a lot during Dad's last stay in hospital, and I carried on working after his death. I'd been in Turin shooting an Italian movie called *Don Bosco*, about the life of the nineteenth-century Italian priest, opposite American actor Ben Gazzara. I decided to go back to Italy after Dad died for a couple of days filming, then I returned to London for his funeral on 11 September.

Steve explained to the movie's bosses that my father had passed away, and I'm sure they wouldn't have made me return to the set so soon, but I wanted to carry on. I remember saying to Steve, 'My dad would have wanted me to keep working,' and he would have.

The acting world was the antithesis of my dad's world and he'd never got involved in that side of my life. My mum was better equipped to deal with it – she'd read all the classic novels that the BBC adapted into dramas and which I appeared in. My dad wasn't a reader, even though he was sharp and a genius with numbers, but I never doubted that he was proud of me. When he came out of prison I was playing *Cinderella* in panto at Richmond Theatre, and on a sleepy weekday matinee I'd often go on stage to see my dad sitting in the audience. I remember thinking, How can you sit through this bloody pantomime over and over again? But it was his way of showing me how proud he was and we never discussed it.

We had a very small funeral for Dad, attended only by immediate family, then the following day I flew to Milan to record a duet with Italian pop star Eros Ramazzotti, then it was on to Turin, then Rome to complete filming on *Don Bosco*.

I can't really explain why I just carried on working – maybe it was my way of coping. I'd also been around sickness and the possibility of losing a parent my entire life, so I didn't experience that shock element. I suppose I was hardened to that reality of life, which lots of kids, thankfully, are sheltered from. But afterwards I felt terribly guilty that I hadn't gone to see my dad enough when he was in hospital. Grief has to come out somehow at some point. I remember going to a CBS conference in Brighton not long after Dad passed away and I felt very low. I'd realized I didn't want to be in the band any more, but it was a similar situation to my pony Fella. I felt a duty to Jamie to keep the band going, even though I wasn't enjoying it. Suddenly the sadness was overwhelming. I sat in the ladies' loos and cried my eyes out, and when I came out I told my manager, Steve, that I needed to go home. It was just a horrible, horrible time.

After Dad had been dead a few months the police called round to Avondale Gardens, asking to speak to him because they'd heard he'd attended a premiere with me and wanted to question him about a street burglary. I'm convinced it was just an excuse to have a nosey round our house, because at that point my face was all over the papers. I found it so offensive and I could feel rage boiling inside me.

'What are you talking about?' I snapped. 'My father is dead!'

7

I'm Not Scared

One evening in autumn 1987 I was walking down Old Compton Street in Soho on my way to the Wag with some friends when I spotted a hairdresser friend of mine called James Lebon, whose brother Mark had recently directed a pop promo for Eighth Wonder. I'd known James since I was fourteen, but he was with another guy I didn't recognize – an incredibly handsome guy with dark hair, who had a baseball cap pulled down over his eyes with 'BAD' written on the front.

'Patsy, this is Dan,' said James, introducing us.

'Hi!' I beamed, trying hard not to swoon.

It turned out he was Dan Donovan, the keyboard player with Big Audio Dynamite – a very cool band at the time. Dan was a really good classical pianist, and had been working with Big Audio Dynamite when Mick Jones (former guitarist and singer with the Clash) asked him to join the band officially. He was also a very talented photographer (his dad was the legendary photographer

Terence Donovan) and he'd been David Bailey's assistant, as well as working with Irving Penn in New York.

A few days later I was getting my hair cut at Vidal Sassoon in Knightsbridge when I got chatting to a model I knew called Rachel, who was sitting in the chair next to mine, and she told me she was dating Mick Jones.

'Oh my God, do you know Dan Donovan?' I asked. 'He's so gorgeous.'

I'd heard through the grapevine that Dan was going out with a really sexy model called Charlotte Weston.

'No, he's single now,' said Rachel. 'Why don't you come to the Café de Paris tonight because the band are going to be there?'

So I went along and Dan was there with Mick and the rest of the band. These guys were all really cool musicians while I was considered deeply uncool when it came to my band! Nevertheless they were all lovely to me and I soon got chatting to Dan, and literally fifteen minutes later we were in my black Fiat Panda heading back to his tiny flat in Fulham, which he shared with a photographer friend. We went upstairs and had a kiss and a cuddle and then I drove home to Hounslow.

Dan called the next day and we went to the movies on the Fulham Road, and from then on we were pretty much inseparable. As well as being handsome, Dan was a lovely guy – funny, kind and gentle, and very hip. The first time I stayed the night at his place he took me for breakfast on the King's Road in Chelsea the next morning and he took the BAD badge off his Harrington jacket and pinned it on my coat. I can't express how much that meant to me at the time – I was nineteen and crazy in love.

I started going to Big Audio Dynamite gigs and hanging around with all these iconic musicians. I met Joe Strummer and I remember him saying to me, 'Patsy, I'm really happy to talk to you about acting and anything else, but we're never going to talk about music.' Brilliant! I would have been happy to talk to Joe about the weather to be honest – I was a huge Clash fan and he was one of my musical heroes.

Dan invited me on a trip to Paris where Big Audio Dynamite were playing a gig, and while we were there he said, 'Why don't we move in together?' I was ecstatically happy and didn't have to think twice before saying yes.

I was struggling with living at home at the time and I felt ready to move out. Although I was back in my own room after Dad had passed away, I didn't have much space and things always seemed really chaotic. After the stress of the past few months, I felt I needed to make a fresh start.

When we arrived back at Heathrow I suggested paying my mum a visit in Hounslow because it was near the airport. I wanted to introduce her to Dan and I was excited about telling her that we were moving in together. But when we turned up at Avondale Gardens Mum was mortified. 'How can you bring Dan here, Patsy?' she said once we were alone for a few minutes.

'For God's sake, Mum,' I began, exasperated. But it was pointless trying to explain that Dan wouldn't give a monkey's what our house was like.

Around about the time I started dating Dan, I bumped into Neil Tennant at the Wag. I don't know how I had the nerve, but I cheekily asked him, 'Will you write a song for me?' And instead of laughing me out of the club he said, 'Actually, I think that's a really, really interesting idea.'

So in November I went into studios in London with the Pet Shop Boys to record the song they'd written for me, which was called 'I'm Not Scared'. They didn't want the band to be involved in the song, so Eighth Wonder didn't play a note on the track, but I fought for the record to be released under our name, and I'm glad I did.

I adored working with Neil and Chris – they're both lovely guys and lots of fun. Their nickname for me was Cheesy Wotsit! I was in the mic booth one day and they were tinkering around at the sound desk and being driven mad by this noise – 'cha, cha, cha, cha' – because they couldn't work out where it was coming from.

'Patsy, what the hell's that noise?' asked Neil.

'Oh, I'm just filing my nails. Sorry!'

I had a laugh, but I took it seriously, too – it was an

amazing opportunity and the track was great. For the B-side I rapped the song in French, which also worked really well. We were all thrilled with 'I'm Not Scared' when we heard the final mix. It was poppy, but it had an interesting edge to it that made it a bit weird, too.

We also finished mixing our album, *Fearless*, which was due for release in July of the following year. Neil and Chris actually wanted to do an entire album with me, and suggested including a cover of the U2 song 'Where The Streets Have No Name', which would be released as a single. It would have been interesting, but I felt too much loyalty to my brother to undermine what we were doing with the band. The Pet Shop Boys went on to have a hit with their version of the U2 track a few years later.

The beginning of 1988 was busy with work projects – in January we shot the video for 'I'm Not Scared' in Paris and London, and the following month I met director Michael Winner to talk about a part in a film adaptation of an Alan Ayckbourn play called *A Chorus of Disapproval*, which follows the exploits of a young widower who joins an amateur operatic society and has several liaisons with female cast members.

In March I went to the Sanremo festival again with Eighth Wonder and we got our first UK hit single with 'I'm Not Scared' and appeared on *Top of the Pops*.

*

On a personal note, Dan and I moved into our own place when I bought a tiny flat in Notting Hill. It had walls like paper and a prostitute lived above us while a drum-and-bass engineer lived below. He used to wait until Dan left the flat for the day, then his music would start up; it drove me bonkers. I remember calling Dan at Mick's house nearby, where the band rehearsed. 'It's bloody started again!' I'd shout down the phone, so Dan could hear me above the racket coming from below.

Sometimes Dan would come back with a couple of guys from the band – usually Don Letts or Leo Williams – who were gorgeous but could look quite imposing! They'd knock on our neighbour's door and say, 'Turn it down, mate.'

In the evenings we'd often go out locally for a bite to eat or to the pub and the woman from upstairs would be standing on the street corner. It was very colourful! 'Hi,' we'd shout and she'd shout 'hello' back. She was very friendly – and very successful it would seem.

Mum was happy for me to move in with Dan but, looking back, it must have been hard for her after I left. She understood that I needed to spread my wings but she was always coming over, to the point where I think she drove Dan mad sometimes. Once when I was away filming he phoned me and said, 'Patsy, I can't believe your mum came round first thing this morning with some "nice ham" to make me a sandwich!'

Mum just wanted to keep an eye on us both and make sure we were OK. She adored Dan and he was very fond of her, too.

I'd accepted the part in *A Chorus of Disapproval*, so in April I decamped to Scarborough for a month, where the film was being shot. It had a stellar cast, including Anthony Hopkins, Jeremy Irons, Richard Briers, Prunella Scales, Sylvia Syms, Jenny Seagrove and Alexandra Pigg. Alexandra had starred in the movie *Letter to Brezhnev* a few years earlier and we became good mates. I ended up having the most fun I'd ever had making a movie.

It was an ensemble piece so no one was singled out for star treatment and the cast and crew were all staying at the same hotel. I remember sitting watching daytime telly with Anthony – who was adorable – and we were both glued to an American soap called *Knots Landing*. 'I want to be in that show. It looks great,' he said, with a completely deadpan expression on his face. He was very funny, and so was Richard Briers. In fact, everyone on the cast was fabulous company.

We'd sometimes stay up at night telling stories, which was fascinating, and there were plenty of high jinks – someone would usually end up falling asleep in the broom cupboard!

Michael Winner was a wonderful director, but you had to stand up to him. If you didn't, you were mincemeat.

One day on set he really laid into me about something and I turned round and gave him just as good back – we were fast friends from then on.

During that month I also married Dan, which I think was a surprise to most people because we hadn't been dating for long, but we really were nuts about each other. He was the first guy I'd truly been in love with and I had no doubts we'd be together for ever. I can't remember if it was my idea or his, but I took my passport up to Scarborough with me and Dan drove up from London and we got married in a register office. I had just turned twenty and Dan was twenty-five.

I remember Michael saying to me before the wedding, 'You're absolutely mad, Patsy.'

'Well, I'm doing it!' I replied.

'Congratulations, then,' he said.

For the ceremony I wore a little silk dress with blue flowers on it by Lolita Lempicka and Dan was dressed down in his usual BAD garb and biker boots. Afterwards we went back to the hotel and everyone celebrated with us.

When Dan and I were walking up the stairs to our room at the end of the night, we both saw a ghost. Everyone who reads this is probably going to think I'm crazy, but a woman suddenly appeared in front of us halfway along the hallway and then disappeared into thin air.

We both stopped dead in our tracks.

'Did you just see that, Dan?' I whispered.

'Yeah,' he said. And that was the beginning of our marriage!

We went back to my room and lay on the bed listening to 'Alphabet Street' by Prince over and over again. We had a really lovely time, but two days later Dan had to head back to London to work with the band and I had to stay up in Yorkshire.

When filming finished, Eighth Wonder embarked on a promotional tour of Europe, after which I travelled on to Monte Carlo to do a shoot with the iconic photographer Helmut Newton for the German magazine *Max*. It was a challenging session, but not without moments of humour. Helmut had a reputation for taking beautiful pictures that were quite provocative and erotic, so I guess, in retrospect, we should have known what we were letting ourselves in for.

Helmut's 'people' picked up Steve and me from the airport and took us out to this extraordinary house with stunning views over the ocean. And once we were there, the shoot turned out to be another battle of wills centred around how naked I was going to be. We started shooting outside, but it began to rain and Helmut's trousers got wet, so he casually took them off. Hang on, I thought, I know I agreed to strip off but I didn't realize this was a party . . . Thankfully he stopped there, and spent the rest of the shoot in a pair of polka dot boxer shorts looking exactly like Benny Hill.

He was a canny old thing, who was used to getting his own way, and in the end my attire was reduced to strategically positioned fox furs. Helmut wanted the fox's head to rest on my private parts, so I said, 'Look, Helmut, I'm not comfortable with that, so can we just move the fur over a bit?'

It became a bizarre sort of battle with me moving the fox fur a few inches and then Helmut moving it back. It was exhausting. In the end he was stamping his foot and shouting, 'I vant to see the pussy! I vant to see the pussy!' in his thick German accent. He never got to see the pussy! I was very comfortable with my body at the time, but I drew the line at having a dead fox's head between my legs.

Steve said to me a number of times, 'Look, you don't have to do this if you don't want to, Patsy,' but I could handle myself and I was determined to carry on and to do battle to get a shot that everyone was happy with. In the end, the photos were beautiful and I kept my dignity!

That summer I seemed to be constantly travelling to different European cities with the band, and in June we released our next single, 'Cross My Heart', which was also a hit in the UK. On the down side, though, our busy schedules meant that Dan and I were spending a lot of time apart and we missed each other.

My past also caught up with me in the summer of 1988 when I received a letter from East End villain Reggie Kray, who was incarcerated in Gartree Prison, Leicestershire. After *Absolute Beginners* I'd become very well known and Reggie had obviously seen me on TV and in the papers. His letter read:

Hello Patsy,

This letter will come as a surprise, but I have wanted to get in touch with you and your family for some time, but had to wait till I got your address.

First of all, please accept my sincere condolences on the sad passing away of your dad, who I always admired and liked his personality, and he was one of the best dressers and money getters around.

Please say hello to your mother for me, she is in my thoughts and prayers. Say hello to Jamie and tell him as his godfather I am around should he or yourself ever need me, even though I am in here.

I am really glad for you that you have made the grade in life – your family must be very proud of you. I watched you on TV and you are a smashing singer and a great mover. Please send a large signed photograph of yourself if possible and try to reply – God bless, your friend Reg Kray xxx

It was like getting a letter from Al Capone, I suppose. It felt like he was reaching out to me in some way and I was intrigued. I guess it also felt like a link to my dad.

I wrote a polite letter back to Reggie and he continued to send me letters.

It was around the time *The Krays* movie with Martin and Gary Kemp was first being talked about and Reggie was keen for me to play his wife Frances Kray, who committed suicide:

> *Gartree Prison,*
> *Leicestershire,*
> *August 1988*

Hello Patsy,

Thanks for your cards and beautiful notes. I was really happy to hear that your mother is well. Please give her my love, and to Jamie.

Keep it confidential between you and your family at this stage, but I want to try to influence the decision in favour of you to play the part of Frances. I should know better than anyone who is best suited to play her, Pat, and you are ideal for the part. I have a photo of Frances wearing a black chiffon dress just like yours and she looks like you in the photo.

I will keep you posted on my request to get the part for you.

Keep smiling. My best wishes to your husband and wish you both happiness, God bless.

Your friend, Reg Kray x

My mum had known Frances in the sixties and said she was lovely, but that she seemed sad, too. They were first introduced at a nightclub and Frances was wearing a beautiful necklace that she was playing with absent-mindedly.

'That's gorgeous,' said Mum, complimenting her on her jewellery.

'Oh, Reggie got me this,' she replied dismissively. 'I'm not sure I like it.' She was clearly unhappy even then.

I did end up being offered the part in *The Krays* movie, but it felt too close to home for me at that point. My mum was still alive and she struggled with the idea of people knowing her business or finding out what Dad did.

In the end, though, we couldn't keep a lid on it for much longer and stories started to appear in the tabloids about my dad and his association with the Krays. I guess it was bound to happen at some point.

What was interesting, though, was that for the first time, people saw me for who I really was – a girl from a very poor background. Prior to those stories emerging, everyone just assumed I led a privileged life.

After my reintroduction to Reggie Kray, I went off to Turin in September with my mum for an audience with the Pope at the premiere of *Don Bosco*. Yep, I had a hard time getting my head around the juxtaposition of those two events, too!

The premiere took place in a huge hall and there were thousands of people there, as well as stallholders outside the venue selling official merchandise, including T-shirts and scarves with the Pope's face on them.

I was used to being around pop stars and attending red carpet events, but I had never seen anything like this. Pope John Paul II arrived with an impressive entourage of clerics and nuns, and the atmosphere felt electric.

Getting the opportunity to meet him and receive a blessing made my mum's year. She told me afterwards that it was like being 'kissed by God'.

It felt wonderful to have been able to do that for her. I always tried to take Mum with me when I was working abroad or going to a lovely event, so she could share the smart hotel suites and private jets. But nothing could compare to meeting the Pope – that was really special. I have a photograph of me being blessed by him and I look as if I'm in a trance because I'm so awestruck.

Later on that month our next single, 'Baby Baby', was released; it was a flop in the UK, but our album was doing really well in the rest of Europe. Then, at the end of October, Jamie and I went to New York with Steve Dagger to promote the album and our single 'Cross My Heart', which was being released in the US.

While we were there, our boss, Jerry Greenberg, threw a party in a recording studio to launch the album.

The head of CBS, Tommy Mottola, was also at the party and was talking to Jerry and Steve when a pretty girl with very long corkscrew hair kept trying to join the conversation and give one of them her demo cassette. Everyone was in high spirits, so they were all joking around with her and passing the cassette between themselves. Tommy ended up with the cassette in his pocket, and in his limo on the way home he asked the driver to put it on – as soon as he heard it, he told the driver to turn the car round and go back to the party. The girl was Mariah Carey and the demo was 'Vision of Love'. By the time he got back to the recording studio, the party was over and she'd gone. The next day, he tracked her down and signed her – and went on to marry her. And it all started at my party!

After that we flew to Los Angeles for more promotion, and it turned out to be an amazing trip. William Morris sent me to meet Jack Nicholson, who was going to direct *The Two Jakes*, which was a sequel to *Chinatown*. I went to his house on Mulholland Drive in Bel Air, which had real Picassos on the walls, and spent an hour chatting to him. I didn't get the part, but it was an incredible experience and he was a really interesting guy.

Something else was just around the corner, though. Before going out to the States, I'd met Tim Burton at the Halcyon Hotel in Notting Hill about a small part in the new Batman movie, playing Jack Nicholson's girlfriend – a part Jerry Hall ended up getting. The casting director was Marion Dougherty, who'd cast me in *The Great Gatsby* all those years before, and had worked on lots of amazing movies, including *Midnight Cowboy*, *Shampoo* and *Chinatown*.

'Do you remember me, Patsy?' she said before reminding me about *The Great Gatsby*. Of course, I didn't remember her at all, because I was only four at the time.

She walked me out of the meeting and said, 'Listen, I don't think you're right for this one, but there's something else you are right for, so just sit tight.'

It's incredible the amount of times you hear that in the business and it turns out to be a load of rubbish, so I didn't think much of it. But while I was over in LA, Steve got a call from William Morris to say that Marion had been trying to track me down and wanted me to get across to Warner Brothers for a meeting that morning. So he put me in a car and I headed out to the studios in Burbank with no idea what they wanted to see me about.

When I arrived Marion was there to meet me. 'I'm so glad to see you, Patsy. It's so fantastic you happened to be in town because I thought we were going to have to fly you out here. I want you to meet some people.'

She took me into a room where I was greeted by Mel Gibson, the director Richard Donner and producer Joel Silver. I'd watched Mel in *The Bounty* that Christmas and I remember thinking, Why have I never acted opposite anyone as beautiful as that? At the time, Mel was the hottest star in Hollywood, and here I was being introduced to him, though I still had no idea why.

We sat down and had a chat about the movie they were working on – a sequel to *Lethal Weapon*, which had been a huge blockbuster – then they asked me to read a scene with Mel. When we'd finished Marion said, 'Dick and Joel, can you come outside with me for a minute because Patsy's leaving town in a couple of days,' so the three of them left the room, leaving me sitting there with Mel.

I didn't have a clue what to say, so I piped up, 'Um, so . . . so, you're Catholic, right? Cos I am, too.'

'Oh, OK,' he replied. 'Practising?'

'Yeah.'

'God, that's unusual these days,' he said, then there was an awkward silence, which luckily was broken by the others returning to the room.

'How do you feel about nudity?' asked Joel.

'Well, if it's called for . . . in what context are you talking about?'

'There's a love scene,' he said, at which point I'm looking across at Mel thinking, There's nothing I'd like to do more!

'Not a problem,' I replied confidently.

'Also, you're going to die in the film and you're going to be naked, chained in a tank, as if you're at the bottom of the sea.'

'Er, I think I'd have a problem with that,' I said.

'Oh really, why?' enquired Joel.

'Well, because I don't think nudity's necessary in that context,' I said. 'If it's for a love scene nudity is fine, but that seems gratuitous,' I explained.

'This could lose you the role,' he replied, raising his eyebrows.

'Well, you asked my opinion and that's what I think.'

'OK, go to costume and get your sizes done. You start in two weeks.'

I couldn't believe it – that wasn't what I was expecting to hear at all. You never get parts like that – never! It was like something out of an MGM musical.

When the guys had left the room I whispered to Marion, 'Oh my God, I can't believe I got it!'

'I told you, didn't I?'

We didn't have mobile phones in those days, so I asked Marion if I could use the office phone, then I called Steve to give him the good news.

'Patsy, don't get too excited,' he cautioned.

'No, Steve, you don't understand. I'm going for costume fittings now! I start in two weeks' time.'

While I was still on the phone to him, William Morris were on the other line, telling him the contract was being faxed over.

When I got back to the hotel, there was great rejoicing, then that night we went to a record company party to celebrate the album being released. I was desperate to call my mum to tell her I'd got the part, so Steve found an office phone and I rang her, even though it was the middle of the night in London.

'Mum, Mum!' I squealed when she picked up the phone, barely able to contain my excitement. 'I've just got a part in a film with Mel Gibson. I can't believe it!'

'Oh my darling, I'm so happy for you,' she said.

It turned out to be a life-changing break.

8

A Hollywood Blockbuster

Dan and I finally managed to book a honeymoon to Barbados over Christmas, and the plan was for me to fly straight to Los Angeles afterwards to start work on *Lethal Weapon 2*.

Michael Winner, who I'd remained friendly with after *A Chorus of Disapproval*, went to Barbados every winter and stayed at a very smart resort called Sandy Lane, but when he found out where we were going to stay he laughed and said, 'You won't last a night there, Patsy!'

How bad could it be? I thought, assuming he was exaggerating because he was used to the high life. But when Dan and I turned up at our hotel, the only way to describe it would be a scruffy B&B (and that's being kind), so it definitely wasn't the romantic honeymoon hotel of our dreams. We called home, and after explaining our plight to Dan's dad Terence, he helped us out financially and we were able to book ourselves into a gorgeous hotel called Glitter Bay.

Michael was also in Barbados over the Christmas holidays, and on New Year's Eve he threw a fabulous party and invited Dan and me along. We had an incredible night – all these amazing characters were there, including Michael Caine and John Cleese, who I was sat next to at dinner.

The entire holiday was wonderful, but all too soon I had to fly to LA and Dan had to head home to London. I had a knot in my stomach on the morning I had to leave because I didn't want to be separated from him.

I flew to Miami first and then picked up a connection to LA, but I didn't realize I had to clear my bags through customs because I was coming from outside the US, so I lost my suitcase in transit. When I arrived in Los Angeles I had to go straight to Warner Brothers for a costume fitting, wearing nothing but the flimsiest beach dress – and it was a lot colder in California than it had been in Barbados. Joel gave me a really funny look when he saw me. 'Don't ask!' I said, realizing I must look like a poor little waif and stray. I'd arranged for Mum to ship out some warmer clothes, but they hadn't arrived yet, so all I had was the outfit I was wearing.

Interestingly, Dick and Joel decided to shoot some of my biggest scenes first, and I'm convinced now that it was because they figured that if they didn't like what they saw they could get rid of me and try someone else. It happens all the time in Hollywood. It meant I was thrown in at the deep end, but thankfully it went well as there was great chemistry between Mel and me right from our first day on set together.

In the movie, Mel and Danny Glover reprise their roles as LAPD detectives, who take on a gang of South African drug dealers hiding behind diplomatic immunity. I play Mel's love interest, Rika van den Haas, who's a secretary at the South African Consulate. The previous film had been very macho, so this was the first time there had been a love story, too, which gave the franchise a different angle.

Originally, I was going to be English, but they changed their minds at the last minute to make me South African, so a few days before filming I had to work with a dialect coach to get the accent right. For years afterwards people used to ask me to say 'diplomatic immunity' in a South African accent! It's pretty normal to do rewrites on these big Hollywood pictures, even during filming, so you have to expect changes to the script. Sometimes rewrites can even change the whole course of a movie. At one point things were going so well with Mel and me that Dick and Joel didn't want to kill me off, so they shot two endings. But they had to kill me in the end, otherwise they couldn't justify the killing spree Mel goes on after he finds my murdered body in a watery grave at the bottom of the harbour.

I was pretty fearless in those days, so I agreed to do the drowning scene myself instead of getting a body double. I had to get my diving certificate first, so I was taught how to do buddy breathing in Dick Donner's pool at his beautiful house in the Hollywood Hills. He had a revolving front door like you'd see at a posh hotel!

For the drowning shot I had to be submerged in a 40ft-deep immersion tank on the lot at Burbank. I was taken down to the bottom of the tank with divers, and when the moment came for the big reveal of my corpse floating in the sea, they took the mask away and I held my breath and played dead with my eyes open. It was quite daunting, but there were divers hovering out of shot with oxygen so I knew I was safe. The shot wouldn't have had the same impact if we'd used a double, though, so I'm glad I did it.

During my time in LA I stayed in a suite at the Mondrian in West Hollywood, which was lovely, but in LA you have to drive everywhere and I couldn't hire a car because I wasn't yet twenty-one. It meant I was quite lonely, to be honest, as I didn't really have anyone to hang out with. Everyone in the cast and crew was lovely, but it was a pretty macho set. On every other movie I'd worked on there were plenty of women around – a continuity girl, hair and make-up artists, wardrobe assistants – but on this project it seemed to be all men. I've no idea why – maybe the execs thought there would be women fainting all over the set at the sight of Mel!

In fact, pretty much the only woman I saw was

Sigourney Weaver, who came on to the set one day to say hi to Mel as they'd worked together on a movie called *The Year of Living Dangerously*. She sat on Mel's lap and she was gorgeous – just fabulous.

It was also the only job I've had where every Friday we finished at 3 p.m. on the dot, so everyone could go home and have a lovely long weekend. I would have been quite happy to stay at work because all I did was go back to my hotel, eat dinner and go to bed. I remember Mel saying to me after a couple of weeks, 'What did you do this weekend, Patsy?'

'Well, I walked down Sunset Plaza and then the police stopped me,' I said.

'Why did you walk?' he asked, puzzled.

'Because I can't hire a car.'

'What do you mean you can't hire a car?'

'I'm not twenty-one yet.'

'How old are you, then?'

'I'm twenty. I'll be twenty-one in March.'

I don't think he could believe it – they all assumed I was in my mid-twenties. Almost immediately, Warner Brothers sorted it out so I could hire a car and I didn't have to be a prisoner at the hotel any more.

I flew back to England as much as I could, though, because I was homesick. If I had a three-day break I'd get on a plane to see Dan as missing him was the hardest bit about filming. The studio bosses were fine about me going back to the UK and cut some deal where they wouldn't have to pay me for certain things while I wasn't in the US. To be honest, at that point in my life I would have paid them to be in the movie! But when I told Dan's dad Terence about the money side of things he said, 'You're bloody mad, Patsy! What are you doing?'

'I miss Dan,' I said.

'Patsy, go back to LA, do the job and take the money! Don't be silly!'

So I ended up flying my mum out to the US for the rest of my stay and she brought a little taste of home with her in the shape of Wall's sausages. God only knows how she managed to smuggle them past US customs. I was literally desperate for English sausages, even though the catering on the movie was out of this world – lobster for lunch, fillet steak for dinner and so on. But all I wanted was a Wall's sausage, which the caterers kindly cooked for me.

'Go on, try one,' I urged. 'They're lovely.'

'Oh, no thanks, honey, we've had breakfast burritos,' said the caterers politely, while looking on in horror as I chowed down on these pink things that looked like condoms filled with God knows what!

At the end of January Steve Dagger came out to see how things were going, then in February Dan came out for an all-too-brief visit. The day he arrived we were doing pickups – on big movies they can afford to edit as they're going along, so if they need more shots they get you back on set. On the day Dan came on set we were doing pickups of a scene where there are lots of close-ups of Mel and me snogging. In the end I had to banish him because I just felt too awkward.

'Go and have lunch in the commissary,' I urged, pushing Dan gently in the right direction. 'I'll meet you afterwards and we'll go to Disneyland.'

Mel was just a dream, though, very charming and a total gentleman, as was the director, Dick Donner. There was one particular scene that we had to shoot on the beach at night and they wanted to capture it with a crescent moon in the sky, so we literally spent a month of nights camped at the beach because it was always cloudy, sitting there for hours hoping the moon would appear.

I didn't have a big posh trailer, I had what they call a honey wagon, which is pretty much the size of a toilet, and I used to sit in there gazing at a picture of Dan! Then one night Mel knocked on the door and said, 'Patsy, come and join us in my trailer.' The hair and make-up guys that worked on all Mel's films were in there playing Scrabble with him. I joined in and it ended up becoming a regular thing to relieve the boredom, eventually turning into dirty word Scrabble! It was very silly, but we had a laugh.

What struck me most was how different it was to my experience on *Absolute Beginners*, even though this was a huge American movie. We watched playbacks of our performances on set, and although Dick Donner was interested in making it cinematic, he was also totally invested in our individual performances. I remember him looking at one scene where Mel and I were saying goodnight to each other and he said, 'I just believe it. I believe every word you're saying to each other.' It was wonderful to get feedback and encouragement, and he also allowed Mel to improvise a lot.

I loved the fact that Mel seemed so grounded, even though he was the biggest star in the world at the time. He'd rock up to work in his own car instead of being driven and we'd just talk about regular stuff. The two of us definitely bonded over our Catholic faith and it was nice to have some common ground.

It was supposed to be a six-week shoot, but it ended up dragging on for about three months. During the last week of work, Mel and I shot our love scene, which caused a lot of excitement on set because it was a first for the franchise. They built the interior of Mel's character's caravan in the studio to shoot the scene. I had to be butt naked for it, although Mel wore a modesty pouch! But he and Dick Donner were both true gents and it was a closed set, so I felt as comfortable as possible in a very unusual situation.

Interestingly, though, although it was a closed set, during the week we shot the love scene every studio boss and executive visited to watch the action on monitors outside. I remember Mel saying, 'That's so fucking typical. So typical.'

'Can't you say something?' I ventured.

'No,' he said.

It made me like him even more as it clearly bothered him and he wasn't happy about it because those scenes are never easy to shoot. But even the biggest star in Hollywood didn't feel in a position to object. It's just the way it was.

In the end the scene worked really well and, I must be honest, it was a very pleasant week at work! Mel was easy to 'fall in love with' for the scene because he was just so charming. And he was a great kisser.

When filming wrapped on *Lethal Weapon 2* my agents William Morris were keen for me to stay on in LA and I was finally starting to feel at ease in the city after being so homesick. It had rained for an eternity during filming, which it can do in Los Angeles from November until the end of February, but when the movie was winding down the sun started shining and the skies were blue. I began to think that I might be able to live out there, but I had a husband and a life back in London. I returned to the UK in March and was cast in a BBC film adaptation of the George Bernard Shaw comedy *Arms and the Man* alongside Helena Bonham Carter. It got a good critical reception when it was screened at BAFTA on 3 April and broadcast on TV later that month, and it was the ideal project for me to take on after *Lethal Weapon 2* because it was so different to working on a Hollywood movie.

Later that spring, I returned to LA to do promotion for *Lethal Weapon* and I took Mum with me. We travelled on the Warners' jet, first to Vancouver where Mel was filming *Bird on a Wire* with Goldie Hawn, and then we flew on to New York. We had penthouse suites in every hotel, all our extras were picked up by the studio and we developed a taste for caviar and Cristal champagne. The promotion on those big movies is relentless, though, so I didn't feel guilty about eating like a king! It was an incredible experience.

Back in the UK I started rehearsing new material with Eighth Wonder, with a view to making another record, but to be honest my heart wasn't in it. We were about to embark on a tour of Japan, which meant that Dan and I would be spending yet more time apart from each other. Although I went a bit reluctantly, the tour was very successful and we played some really big venues – I think I finally found my feet in terms of performing on stage, but it turned out to be the last time I'd do it.

In the summer I was cast in the movie *Chicago Joe and the Showgirl* by a production company called Working Title, which was just starting to become a force in British cinema. Bernard Rose was directing, who I already knew because I'd become friendly with his wife Alexandra Pigg on *A Chorus of Disapproval*. It was shot in London and also starred Kiefer Sutherland (I played his girlfriend) and Emily Lloyd, who'd enjoyed huge success with her movie *Wish You Were Here* a couple of years earlier.

At the time, *Lethal Weapon 2* had just been released in the States and I remember Kiefer saying to me in make-up, 'Wow, congratulations, Patsy, you've gota number-one movie on your hands!'

Kiefer was totally lovely to work with and is one of the funniest men alive. I just adored him and we had the best laugh. We both loved the Rob Reiner movie *Spinal Tap*, about a fictional English heavy metal band, and used to quote lines from it to each other and get terrible fits of the giggles, which I think started to annoy the crew in the end. In fact, I probably fell a little bit in love with Kiefer! The whole thing was a really positive experience.

That summer, *Lethal Weapon* opened around the world and then in the UK in September, and was an enormous commercial success. When it came to doing the publicity, Warner Brothers were surprised and delighted that Italy and France were desperate for me to be there in person to promote the film because Eighth Wonder were such a big deal in those countries. Actors are often cast in movies simply because they have a foreign profile and can make money in different territories, so it was a real bonus for the studio.

There's no doubt that *Lethal Weapon 2* was a big moment in my career in terms of showcasing me as an actor and raising my profile worldwide, and it marked the beginning of a very exciting time in my life.

9

A Boat, a Break-up and an Indie Hit

'Never do a boat movie,' Mel Gibson had warned me when we were chatting on the set of *Lethal Weapon* one day. 'Anyone who's ever done one never will again.'

He went on to explain that continuity is a night-mare on those films because the wind changes every five seconds and everything moves, so it can end up taking for ever.

'Yeah, that sounds like a big headache,' I agreed, making a mental note to turn down all offers of boat movies.

So what did I do for my next film project? Yep, a boat movie!

I was offered a part in a German film called *Kill Cruise* opposite Jürgen Prochnow, who'd starred in the critically acclaimed war epic *Das Boot* about men serving on board a U-boat. Elizabeth Hurley, who'd just appeared in Dennis

Potter's acclaimed BBC drama series *Christabel*, was also cast in the film.

It was a big-budget project, and I figured that Jürgen's last movie about a boat had done really well, so why not? It was being directed by Peter Keglevic, an Austrian director, and was being shot entirely in Malta. Jürgen plays the skipper of a boat who agrees to take two English girls – Elizabeth and me – to the Caribbean.

Before I headed out to Malta at the end of August, Elizabeth called me and asked if I'd like to go over to her flat in London and do a read-through of the script. I didn't know Elizabeth, but I'd met Hugh Grant (who was then her boyfriend) on a few occasions over the years because he was also signed to William Morris at the time.

As soon as we started reading the script, it became apparent to us that it was unlikely to be winning many awards. At one point we were laughing so hard we had tears streaming down our cheeks. We played two friends called Su and Lou from Manchester, and we had the worst accents you'll ever hear. There was no nudity in the movie – we just had to wear a lot of dodgy bikinis. There's one particular scene where I've slept with a sailor the night before and wake up to discover I have beard rash, and my line is, 'Shave, pig.' The signs weren't good for this being an Oscar-winning project.

Things didn't improve when we got to Malta. Elizabeth and I had been booked into what I can only describe as a prefab hotel, which was full of teenage kids getting absolutely lashed every night because it was their first holiday away from their parents. It was really noisy in the evenings, and then you'd get up the next day to find empty beer bottles and vomit by the pool. I'd like to emphasize here that I have a camping spirit, but *Kill Cruise* was a long shoot – three months – and there was no way we could stay in that hotel and be fresh for work every day.

When William Morris negotiated my contract, it was agreed that the hotel would be of a certain standard. If they'd said OK to a rubbish hotel, then fair enough, but they hadn't. So after I made a call to my agents back in London, the film company agreed to move me, and Elizabeth, to another hotel. After that I think the pair of us were tarred with the diva brush by the rest of the cast and crew, who were all German.

For the first couple of weeks we did pretty much nothing because we were told that Jürgen had 'the pox'. It was so dramatic – it was almost as if he had some sort of medieval plague because he'd been sent to an island off Malta to be in 'isolation'. In fact, all he had was bog-standard chicken pox.

The hotel we'd been moved to was called the Grand Phoenicia. It was right in the centre of the capital, Valletta, and it was considered the best on the island. It had clearly been a very swanky place in its heyday, but it had a touch of the Grey Gardens about it when we stayed there –

elderly eccentric characters inhabiting the lounges and bar areas and there were silk ceilings that looked like they hadn't been dusted since the 1920s. However, it was quiet and had nice linen sheets, and we were very grateful to be there.

Dan, Hugh and Steve all came out during the first week at our new hotel. Dan and Hugh came to collect Elizabeth and me from work on the Friday afternoon, and as we were leaving we shouted, 'Bye, have a nice weekend!' to the rest of the cast and crew, and not one person said goodbye back to us.

'Jesus bloody Christ!' remarked Hugh. 'You'd think you would have started to make friends with people after two weeks.'

We already knew it wasn't going to be a great movie, but from then on we laughed every single day. And by moving to our new hotel in town we got to meet some extraordinary people and had a lot of fun.

Malta was actually quite a dull place – it might have been swinging in the Sixties, but by 1989 it definitely wasn't. However, the locals made a tremendous fuss of us – they were thrilled the movie was being made in Malta and they were all incredibly friendly and welcoming. *Midnight Express* and Robert Altman's *Popeye* were the last movies to be shot there, and the boat we were filming on was docked at Anchor Bay just below the cartoonish, derelict village that was built as a film set for *Popeye*.

At the hotel we were mingling with the island's jet set, one of whom was a fairly elderly guy called Maurice Mizzi, who was head of Coca-Cola in Malta. He was a very sweet man and invited us all over to his house for lunch one day. As we were leaving he said to Elizabeth and me, 'I have a boat in Malta, would you and the boys like to come out on it one day? We can sail to Gozo – it's a beautiful island and the food is fantastic.'

The boys were actually leaving – Hugh was returning to film the movie he was working on and Dan was off on tour with Big Audio Dynamite – but Elizabeth and I took Maurice up on his lovely offer.

What he didn't tell us was that he didn't have a crew on his yacht and we had to help him navigate it out of the port, so Elizabeth had to take care of the ropes and I was in charge of a long pole to push us off the jetty and help us avoid crashing into the harbour wall. Fine, I thought, until the bloody pole started to retract just as we were heading off because I hadn't secured it properly.

'Maurice! Maurice! The pole's not working!' I shouted as his lovely boat headed towards the wall. At that point, he dived into the water to do God knows what and lost his swimming trunks in the process. Meanwhile, my pole was retracting more and more by the second.

'I'm very sorry, ladies, you don't need to see something like that,' he said, treading water butt naked. Elizabeth and I were standing on deck crying with laughter by now, and we started throwing everything and anything into the water so he could cover himself up – towels, blankets, you name it. Somehow he managed to save his boat from being damaged, thank goodness.

The hotel manager was another colourful personality – an ex-pat who kept holding excruciating drinks parties. His stock line was, 'Hello, I'm Mr Gat, but everyone calls me Pussy.' He looked a bit like Peter Ustinov as Hercule Poirot in the Agatha Christie movies.

The best character, though, was a dashing older guy who owned an Italian restaurant on the island, which was regarded as one of the top places to eat. He was Maltese and had obviously been pretty glamorous when he was in his prime – which was probably about twenty years earlier. His claim to fame was that he had dated Elizabeth Taylor for a week in Gstaad in the seventies, and he was still dining out on the story all these years later. The entire island knew – in fact, if you got into a cab and asked to be taken to his restaurant, the driver would invariably say, 'Ah, you know the owner? He was the boyfriend of Elizabeth Taylor.'

We first met him when we ate at his restaurant. He came over to greet us wearing the most terrible toupé and said, 'Hello, I've heard you're filming here. I know people in the film business. I was the boyfriend of Elizabeth Taylor for seven days in Gstaad.' Honestly, you couldn't make it up! He was very entertaining, though, and very nice, although he had a Swedish girlfriend who didn't seem to think so – every time he left the table, she'd say, 'I hate it here and I hate him. I want to leave.'

We found another restaurant in town run by an English girl. One night Dan, Steve, Elizabeth and I went there for dinner and Dan and Elizabeth ordered fish. When it arrived, though, they turned their noses up because it smelled really bad.

'I'm very sorry,' said Dan politely, 'but I think the fish is off.'

'There's nothing wrong with my fish, love. My fish is fine!' she snapped, enraged, and then asked us to leave. As far as I remember, Dan and Elizabeth got pretty bad food poisoning afterwards, so we never went back there again.

Although we were having fun off set, things still weren't going well on set. It was really hard work spending hours every day on a boat bobbing up and down in the ocean (Mel had been right!), and we often felt horribly seasick.

One day the director, Peter, came over to Elizabeth and me after he'd looked at some rushes and said, 'I know now this movie is not horror. It is not about love. It is not about Steven Spielberg sharks. It is a picowogical thriller.' I was glad we'd got that straight!

I'm ashamed to say that Elizabeth and I nicknamed the director the Smurf. We were always totally professional on set – I take every job seriously – but I had the feeling this could be a bit of a stinker – a Europudding, as we call it in the business. I even made the line 'Shave, pig' work, after failing to get Peter to change it to something more natural like, 'He should have shaved.'

'No, the line is "Shave, pig,"' he'd insisted.

We all had nicknames. I became known as 'Ratty' after a particularly terrible scene where Elizabeth suffocates me with a pillow and you see my legs frantically flapping around. Apparently they looked like little rat's legs. To be honest, if I'd been out there on my own, the job would have been horrific, but Elizabeth made it for me.

At the end of a day's filming, when we were heading back to shore, we'd find somewhere to sit down at the back of the boat, put a blanket over ourselves and share some headphones as we sang along to the Clash and Blondie, while the crew eyed us suspiciously. One evening, we were walking along the jetty on our way back to the hotel when we heard someone from the crew say in a thick German accent, 'Here come the English bitches.' Clearly our hotel upgrade still rankled.

The shoot really dragged on and we were always trying to relieve the boredom. We used to make up dance routines back at the hotel and scream with laughter, then Elizabeth told me about an acting coach she'd had who had told her she ought to call her autobiography *Shut Up*

Dream roles.
I was so excited to work with Christopher Plummer in *Hanover Street* (*above*) and he was lovely to me. On the right I'm playing the young Estella in the BBC's *Great Expectations* in 1981. I loved both parts and was beginning to really get the acting bug. I absorbed information like a sponge, listening, learning and always grateful for the opportunity.

The real me – not the
posh middle-class girl everyone
assumed I was. Rollerskating in
the street outside our house
in Avondale Gardens.

Is it just me or does Fella look
more like a donkey? God knows
where Dad found him.

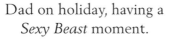

Dad on holiday, having a
Sexy Beast moment.

Mum in LA wrapped in lots of
clothes. That was when I realized
she was sick again.

I was gently making my transition from a child actress and was beginning to be cast in more mature roles. I'm very proud of the BBC's *Frost in May*, which was aired in 1982. I played Nanda Gray.

I was also so proud of *Diana*, which was shown in 1984. Here I'm with co-star Stephen J. Dean.

With Mickey Dolenz, who conceived and wrote the ITV show *Luna* – perhaps not a career highlight.

Outside our house with Gran, Jamie (looking very cool)
and Auntie Mary.

Love love love
Steve Dagger – like
a brother. We met
in 1984.

Playing Crepe Suzette in *Absolute Beginners* when I was seventeen. What a show off, shamelessly sucking my cheeks in. Oh to be young, daft and out of my depth.

In the same year as *Absolute Beginners*, I played Eppie in the BBC's *Silas Marner*, alongside Ben Kingsley.

Dad, Gran and Auntie Mary. Dad looked like an old man when he came out of prison.

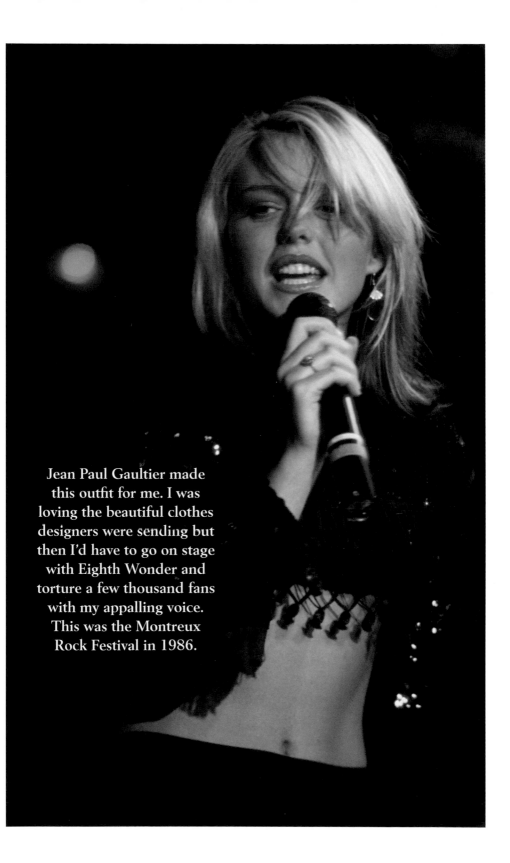

Jean Paul Gaultier made this outfit for me. I was loving the beautiful clothes designers were sending but then I'd have to go on stage with Eighth Wonder and torture a few thousand fans with my appalling voice. This was the Montreux Rock Festival in 1986.

I met Dan Donovan
in the autumn of 1987.
He was so handsome
I had to try hard
not to swoon.

Mel was the hottest star
in Hollywood when we
made *Lethal Weapon 2*.

and Drink the Champagne, so that became our catchphrase for the rest of the shoot.

Luckily, Mum was able to visit me, too, and we had a wonderful time showing her round the island. She was so nice to be around that her presence meant the Germans finally warmed to Elizabeth and me, which was no mean feat! Elizabeth's parents and her sister Kate also came out, and they treated me like family, which was lovely. In fact, for years afterwards I spent every Boxing Day with them.

Something that I still can't believe to this day is that we managed to talk the director into changing the ending of his movie. We were so behind schedule and everyone was desperate to get off the island and go home, so we persuaded him to end it with Elizabeth killing us all. His original ending was very complicated and involved us being rescued by a cruise liner, but I had visions of us never leaving Malta. The whole production was nuts from start to finish.

Although we didn't get any artistic satisfaction out of the job, Elizabeth and I formed an enduring friendship and had a brilliant laugh, and, for me, that's what life is all about. It's rare to spend so much time working closely with someone and yet never fall out. Elizabeth is an incredible woman – very funny and down to earth – and she has been a great friend to me over the years. I can tell her anything and it stops there. We might not see each other for six months at a time, but when we do meet up it's as if we saw each other only yesterday.

By the time filming finally wrapped on *Kill Cruise* I'd been married to Dan for a year and a half, but our schedules meant we'd barely spent any proper time together. Unsurprisingly, cracks were beginning to show in our relationship. He'd been touring in America with his band, so we were always in different time zones, and communication was patchy to say the least. We didn't have mobile phones or Skype back then, so it wasn't easy to keep in regular contact. When we both arrived back in London in November, it felt almost like we were strangers.

While I'd been away in Malta, Eighth Wonder had continued working without me, and a guy called Steve Brown, who'd worked on some of the early Wham! hits, had been brought in to produce some new material. By this point I was certain I didn't want to be involved any more, and I knew I was going to have to bite the bullet and tell Jamie and the rest of the band.

It was a shame because the band had been incredibly successful in other parts of the world – in Italy I felt like Madonna! But in the UK I was still getting attacked in the press and was constantly referred to as a bimbo, which I hated.

It finally felt like enough was enough when a couple of successful singers kept slating me in interviews. I had to send a legal letter to one of them. Funnily enough, I never heard a peep out of her again!

With the other singer, I decided to take things into my own hands one day after yet another vile comment appeared in print. I got hold of her phone number through a friend of a friend and called her.

'Hi, it's Patsy Kensit here,' I began politely. 'I just want to let you know that if you ever even utter the letter P again, I swear to God you'll regret it!' Then I put the phone down.

I'm not proud of it, but at the time I felt I had to stand up for myself. Years later, our paths crossed and she came over to me and said, 'Patsy, I just want to say I'm sorry.'

'That's fine, no problem. Thank you for the apology,' I replied.

Eventually, I plucked up the courage to tell Steve Dagger, Jamie and the rest of the boys that I didn't want to continue with the band. It was a blow to them but probably not a total surprise, and they could see I'd made up my mind. I'd already carried on with Eighth Wonder for a year more than I'd intended to because I didn't want to let Jamie down, but I'd had enough of slogging away at something I was never going to be great at, and I wanted to put my time and energy into acting.

I'm afraid to say my next film was also less than brilliant. Perhaps I should have realized when I found out it was about two air force pilots, one of whom gets captured by a UFO. Called *Blue Tornado*, it was an Italian action thriller also starring Dirk Benedict, who was famous for his role as Lt Templeton "Faceman" Peck in *The A-Team*. But, hey, it was filmed in beautiful Rome and my mum was able to come out with me. Luckily, though, something a lot better was on the horizon.

In March 1990 I met film director Don Boyd, who I admired a great deal, to talk about an Anglo-American project called *Twenty-One*. It was a great script, co-written by Boyd and Zoe Heller, about a twenty-one-year-old Londoner called Katie, who's trying to discover who she is and make sense of her life. The character talks directly to the camera about her dysfunctional family, dead-end job, complicated love life and heroin-addict boyfriend.

Parts like that for women only come along once in a blue moon, and it's incredibly rare to be offered a movie where you're in every single frame of the film. But because *Lethal Weapon* had raised my profile significantly in the US they were able to get the picture financed in my name, making it a really exciting prospect for me.

Shooting on *Twenty-One* wasn't due to start until July, and just before Easter I got a big offer from the US to star in a sci-fi action film called *Timebomb* alongside Michael Biehn, best known for his roles in the *Terminator* films, *Aliens* and *The Abyss*, and produced by Raffaella De Laurentiis, the daughter of legendary Italian film producer Dino De Laurentiis. I jumped at it because things weren't going great with Dan in London. He was about to head off on tour again, so he couldn't come to LA with me, but on the day I flew out, it was Mum who took me to the airport and Dan only turned up briefly to say goodbye because he had band commitments. My mum never got involved in our relationship, but she did say to him that day, 'This is poor form, Dan. You haven't seen Patsy for two days and now she's going to America for two months.' She felt he hadn't made the effort to see me before I left, but it was my fault as much as Dan's, as we both had jobs that constantly took us away from each other.

When I'd been shooting *Lethal Weapon* in LA I didn't make the most of it because I was always thinking about going home to Dan and my life in London, so this time I was determined to enjoy it, and I had a ball. I was a bit older – twenty-two – so it was easier for me to socialize and there was a big British community out there.

Sadly – and probably inevitably – things came to an end for Dan and me while I was making *Timebomb*. We'd simply been separated from each other too many times, and we eventually broke up over the phone. We talked about meeting up when I returned to London, but neither of us really meant it.

It was sad because Dan was my first true love, but realistically the chances of our marriage lasting were very slim, even without the long separations imposed by our schedules. We were just kids when we got together and neither of us had a clue what we wanted or needed from a relationship. Very few marriages that start that early survive, and we both made lots of mistakes.

I'd loved the romance of eloping to Scarborough to get married but I didn't stop to think about the future. When we first met I was at quite a vulnerable point in my life – I was still reeling from my dad's death and was being vilified in the music press, and Dan and his friends took me under their wing and gave me a sense of security and credibility.

But I must stress that although things didn't work out and neither of us were angels while things were breaking down, we had loved each other very much.

If I'm being totally honest, I wasn't thrilled about going home to London in July to film *Twenty-One*. I was having a good time in LA and I didn't have a husband to go back to any more, but I also knew that *Twenty-One* was the opportunity of a lifetime and that I shouldn't miss it.

However, I couldn't face staying at the flat I'd shared with Dan in Notting Hill – all I wanted was to get rid of it – so Steve found me a mews house to rent in Chelsea for the duration of the movie. We were shooting mainly on location around west London and the budget was tiny, so it had to be done in just twenty-nine days, and it had to be done brilliantly. There was no room for error.

The day after I got back from LA I had costume fittings and rehearsals. Somehow, the press had got hold of the story that I'd split with Dan, and when I opened the front door there was a swarm of paparazzi and reporters surrounding the house, so I had to run the gauntlet to get to my car. I'm not exaggerating when I say it was like that scene in *Notting Hill* where Rhys Ifans opens the door in his underpants only to be greeted by hundreds of photographers. Thankfully, though, I was fully dressed!

That was only the start of it – the press camped out in the street for days and the paparazzi even put matchsticks in the lock of my car door so the key wouldn't work and I'd be left standing in the street looking flustered as they snapped away (it was before central locking). Those guys are relentless. It was my first experience of that kind of thing and it's hard to deal with when you're only twenty-two. I remember crying in the make-up chair on a few occasions because I just wanted to hide under my duvet, but I tried really hard not to let it affect my work. My mum moved in with me, which made me feel a lot better because at least I had some company.

I remember coming downstairs one Saturday morning and opening the shutters in the living room to see about thirty journalists standing outside. That's when it hit me that it wasn't about me as an actress any more, it was about my failed marriage to Terence Donovan's son. That kind of press intrusion was exactly what my mum had been terrified of happening while I was growing up, and what she'd tried so hard to protect me from. But things only got worse, because very shortly after that the *News of the World* did a big exposé on my dad. Mum hadn't retired at this point – she was still working at the computer company – and she told me that she'd been very upset by the way she felt the firm's security guard had looked at her on the Monday morning after that story came out.

Of course, it must have affected Dan and his family, too, which I felt awful about. I spoke to Terence on the phone while all the press craziness was going on and he just said, 'Darlin', it's all rock 'n' roll. It's just rock 'n' roll, Patsy.' It was very cool the way he reacted. He was a lovely man and we always got on very well.

On the plus side, I loved Don Boyd to bits and there was a lot of positivity on the set of *Twenty-One*. In terms of style, the movie was similar to *Alfie* in that I had to do lots of monologues to the camera. Strangely enough, I drew on something Elizabeth Taylor had told me all those years before on the set of *The Blue Bird*. She'd said, 'Patsy, just before they clap the board, just for a minute, be still and you'll be ready to start the scene.'

Rufus Sewell played my drug-addict boyfriend. It was his first movie, and he was great in the part. I found it hilarious because Rufus and I had known each other as kids in Twickenham. I used to see him when I was getting off the bus to go to St Catherine's.

At the heart of the film there's a scene where my character, Katie, wakes up one morning to discover her boyfriend has overdosed on heroin and is lying next to her dead. I'm not a method actress at all, but I was definitely able to draw on how I felt on the day Dad passed away and my mum was cradling his head in her hands.

There was a good buzz about the movie and we started getting word back from the editing suite that it was going to be a good film, so in October I went to LA and met with various publicists to start preparing the PR campaign.

Later that month I also went to Paris to shoot a French TV movie for Canal Plus called *Does This Mean We're Married?* I'd agreed to it before *Twenty-One* happened and I got the part mostly because of the profile I'd had with Eighth Wonder. Filming lasted about a month and, bizarrely, I was playing an American stand-up comic. It was a diabolical film, but I got to stay in the most gorgeous hotel – Le Royal Monceau, which had a picture-postcard view of the Eiffel Tower from the balcony – and my mum got to come out and share my suite. While I was out there my agent at William Morris in London came to see me and we had dinner with Omar Sharif. He's a keen backgammon and card player, so I tried to chat to him about card games, but once I'd exhausted pontoon, patience and snap, I was out of my depth!

After a shaky start to the year with the breakdown of my marriage to Dan, 1990 ended on a high note. Just before Christmas I was offered a movie called *Beltenebros*, a much-anticipated film adaptation of a celebrated Spanish novel about political intrigue in Franco's Madrid, which was being filmed in Madrid with eminent Spanish director Pilar Miró at the helm. And to top it all *Twenty-One* was screened in LA in December with great reviews, and was accepted into the Sundance Film Festival. This takes place in Park City, Utah, which is basically a ski resort that just happens to have the hottest little film festival in the world for one week every January. Steve and I flew in, arriving quite late at night via a changeover in Chicago. When we got to our hotel it quickly became apparent that we had a hit film on our hands because Steve's inbox was stuffed with messages and business cards. There were notes from producers and directors suggesting meetings, and from agents who wanted to sign me, as well as media requests for interviews and lots of party invites.

The most urgent request was from Sheila Benson, who was one of the top writers on the *LA Times*. She'd seen *Twenty-One* and loved it, and wanted to interview me the next morning at breakfast for a cover story. It was the most massive break I could possibly get, and the story ended up on page one of the paper. Her review of the movie was literally a love letter about my performance, hailing me as the 'new Julie Christie'. Things couldn't have gone any better.

The film was screened throughout the week at Sundance, and in between meetings and interviews, Steve and I attempted to do a bit of skiing and drink some hot chocolate. I'm actually not a bad skier because I went on skiing trips with the school every year from the age of nine. However, Steve is less confident, so I headed off to a more challenging run, leaving him on one of the nursery slopes, where he managed to fall off a ski lift from a significant height. As he lay in a crumpled heap in the snow, trying to work out how to get up because his skis were at a crazy angle, he heard the swish, swish of someone skiing up behind him.

'Hey, man, are you Steve Dagger?' came an American voice.

'Er, yeah,' replied Steve, raising himself up onto his elbows to see a guy holding out a business card.

'I saw you with Patsy last night – here's my card. I just love *Twenty-One* and would love to be in business with you,' he gushed, handing Steve his business card before skiing off in a flurry of snow. He didn't even bother to help poor Steve up!

After a busy, exciting week at Sundance, we flew on to LA for more meetings with various studios to discuss upcoming projects. Because of its success at Sundance, *Twenty-One*, which had been independently produced, ended up getting a distribution deal with a company called Triton.

The positivity and buzz surrounding the movie in America was really good for me. Back home in England I was still the girl from *Absolute Beginners*, but in the States I was having my hot fifteen minutes – everyone wanted to meet me and sign me up. However, I don't thrive too well in those 'general meetings', as they're known in Hollywood, where there's nothing specific to discuss and it's all just small talk. I remember being at one meeting with some studio bosses when I noticed there was a pen stuck in the Styrofoam ceiling.

'God, what happened there?' I asked.

'Oh, Uma Thurman came in for a meeting and she put it here,' said one of the execs nonchalantly.

'So that's what you have to do to make your mark in this town,' I said, and everyone laughed.

10

Falling in Love Again

Rather than buy a new place once I'd sold the flat, I decided to live back at Mum's house in Hounslow, although I stayed over with friends in Notting Hill quite a bit, too. I was travelling a lot with work, so I didn't see any point in putting down roots. I was enjoying being single and going on a few dates, and I felt boosted by the excitement surrounding *Twenty-One*, so I was in a good place when I headed off to Spain in the spring of 1991 to start filming *Beltenebros*.

In the movie I play a stripper/cabaret artist, and the part required quite a bit of nudity and sex, so Steve had to negotiate what I would and wouldn't do beforehand. It's not unusual for your deal to specify exactly how much flesh you'll show – for example two inches of knee, a side shot of a breast and so on. I was supposed to be starring opposite Rutger Hauer, but he backed out, so the film was left without a leading man. I suggested Terence Stamp for the role of the assassin, and the director Pilar liked the idea, so he was cast. I'd met Terence socially in the past and admire him a great deal as an actor and as a person as well as loving his books.

Pilar was a very eminent filmmaker, but she wasn't the easiest person to get along with. She wasn't particularly kind or sympathetic, considering it was quite a difficult role. Steve ended up having huge rows with her over issues related to nudity that we'd already agreed on and that were specified in my contract. On the plus side, it was a dream to get the opportunity to work with Terence.

One day we were on location at the Palace Hotel in Madrid, filming in a corridor, when all of a sudden I heard a very irate Glaswegian voice. Terence and I were standing on either side of the corridor in our beautiful Sixties costumes and looked round to see a man I recognized as Jim Kerr of Simple Minds marching towards us.

'For fuck's sake! I need to get through. I've got a meeting downstairs,' he snapped. When he got to where I was standing he stopped abruptly and said, 'Oh, hello. What are you doing here?'

'Um, well clearly we're filming,' I replied cheekily. 'I'm really sorry, film crews always expect the world to revolve round them, don't they?'

We started having a chat and Jim asked which hotel I was staying at, then I saw Pilar glare over at us because we were holding up the filming, so we said our goodbyes and Jim went off to his meeting. I remember thinking how confident Jim was and I was intrigued.

Later that day one of the assistant directors brought over a note from Jim, which said how nice it had been to meet me earlier. He'd included his phone number and wrote that I should call if I was ever in Scotland and he'd show me the mountains. It was a beautiful message and very romantic – I still have it. I showed it to my mum, who'd accompanied me to Spain, and she thought it was very sweet, too, although she had no idea who Jim or Simple Minds were, so I had to explain!

That night when I was back in my room at the Holiday Inn I got a phone call from Jim and we had a long chat. Simple Minds had just released their album *Real Life* and Jim was about to head off back to the US on tour. Filming was winding up on *Beltenebros*, so I told him I was going back to London in a few days and he promised to call – which he did, almost every night. We could chat so easily to each other – we had a real connection. Then one night he rang and said, 'I'm getting on Concorde from New York to come and see you this weekend.'

Wow, impressive! I thought.

So Jim flew to London and we went for dinner at a Japanese restaurant called Hiroko, which was at the Shepherd's Bush Holiday Inn. He met me in the lobby of the Halcyon Hotel where he was staying and we walked to the restaurant together. We were having a lovely time, catching up on what we'd been up to, when Jim spotted fellow Scot Fish from prog-rock band Marillion. I heard Jim mutter under his breath, 'For fuck's sake,' not because he didn't like Fish, who was charming, but because he was on his first date with me.

'Jim! Oh my God, it's good to see you,' said Fish, walking up to our table. He then started talking intently to Jim about techy stuff like studios and sound desks, which being a writer and singer Jim wasn't really into. So much for romance!

After Fish left we drank some sake and Jim admitted he'd had a shot of whisky before coming out because he was nervous, which I found amusing once we'd got to know each other better because Jim's not a drinker at all.

After dinner we walked back to my car hand-in-hand and stopped to have our first kiss, which was very nice. Jim had to fly back to New York the next day, so he suggested going for a walk in Holland Park in the morning before he left for the airport. So, with plans made for the next day, I got into my car and drove back to Mum's in Hounslow. The next day I was running about an hour late to meet Jim, but he was very good-humoured about it considering he had a flight to catch, and we had a nice (albeit short) romantic stroll through the park.

I was also about to fly off shortly to work on my next movie project – a Disney picture called *Blame It on the*

Bellboy, which was being filmed on location in Venice. I was going through my moment of being hot in the States and had signed a two-picture deal with the studio (although the second film never happened) and I was able to command my biggest fee yet. The couture houses wanted to dress me for the movie, so I stopped off in Paris en route to Venice to look for costumes. It was a dream come true for me because I'd been passionate about fashion since I'd bought my first Chanel suit at the age of sixteen.

The movie is a good old-fashioned farce that revolves around mistaken identity among guests staying at the same Venetian hotel, and I play an estate agent called Caroline who's trying to sell a dodgy house. It was a wonderful cast – Dudley Moore, Richard Griffiths, Alison Steadman and Penelope Wilton – and there was great camaraderie on set. There was always a lovely dinner planned in the evening and we had a lot of fun making the movie.

Before he'd headed back to New York, Jim had promised to visit me in Venice, so he called me not long after shooting started and said he was coming over for the weekend. My first thought was, Great! Quickly followed by, Oh my God, what if he wants to stay in my hotel room? But he dispelled any awkwardness by quickly adding, 'Look, I've booked a hotel a couple of minutes' walk from your place, so I can have my own space.'

Thank God! I thought. Jim's from the Gorbals in

Glasgow and very down to earth, so he wasn't being starry or ostentatious, he was just trying to put me at ease.

Don't get me wrong, we liked each other a lot and there was definitely chemistry between us, but we didn't really know each other and I wasn't sure how things would pan out. It's stressful enough when you meet a new date for dinner and a movie, but this guy was flying thousands of miles from New York City to see me. That was a big deal, so I was relieved I didn't have the added pressure of worrying about hotel rooms!

The night Jim arrived in Venice he came to pick me up from my hotel, and the second I laid eyes on him I felt instantly happy. First we strolled to Harry's Bar, where we chatted over peach bellinis. I loved being in his company because he's such a funny, intelligent guy. I think there were a lot of surprises on both sides as we got to know each other better. He was definitely surprised to discover I had a sense of humour and that I was into music.

After dinner, we headed back to Jim's hotel for a nightcap and he showed me his room. Now my hotel was pretty fancy, but his suite took my breath away. It was palatial, with floor-to-ceiling windows overlooking the Grand Canal. Before he walked me back to my hotel, he gave me some beautiful roses that were in his room and we arranged to meet for lunch the next day.

The following morning I was walking through St Mark's Square with a couple of the costume girls to pick up something from the shops when I heard this Scottish voice shouting, 'Pat! Pat!' I turned round to see Jim standing with a group of guys, who turned out to be execs from his record company in Italy.

'Ah, Paddy Kenny!' they said in their thick Italian accents, grinning and reaching out to shake my hand while Jim sniggered. He was clearly someone else who found it highly amusing that Eighth Wonder were such a big deal in Italy! We chatted for a few minutes then I said, 'I'm with the girls and we have to find something for my costume, so I'll see you at lunch,' and we said our good-byes.

Later that day, when Jim and I were at lunch, he said, 'Why have you changed?' When I'd seen him in St Mark's Square I was dressed down in my puffa parka and jeans.

'Well, I was in my scruffy clothes,' I replied. I'd actually been embarrassed that he'd seen me looking so unglamorous.

'Oh, you looked so cool,' he said, sounding disappointed. Later on he told me that was the moment he fell in love with me: when he saw me striding across St Mark's in my puffa coat! So Venice was the beginning of our love affair and our relationship deepened from then on.

Filming wrapped on *Blame It on the Bellboy* in June and I headed back to London to finish shooting the interior scenes at Shepperton. While I was back I had a photo session with the photographer Andrew Macpherson for a piece in *The Face* called 'Patsy Goes to Hollywood'. And then I did exactly that and flew out to Los Angeles to do some advance publicity for the movie. It was an exciting summer on all levels.

Jim also asked me to spend a weekend up in Edinburgh with him and his daughters Yasmin and Natalie, who were about six and seven and a half at the time. Yasmin is Jim's daughter from his marriage to Chrissie Hynde of the Pretenders and Natalie is Chrissie's daughter from her relationship with Ray Davies of the Kinks.

I'll never forget coming through baggage reclaim at the airport and spotting the three of them waiting for me, because that was the moment I fell in love with Jim. It was amazing to see him with these lovely girls, just being a regular dad. He'd already confessed to me that he wanted another baby and I'd been broody since I was a teenager, so seeing him with the girls just blew me away.

I fell in love with Yasmin and Natalie, too – they were both adorable. Yasmin looked up at me and whispered, 'Are you a witch? Or are you a fairy?'

'Well, actually I'm a fairy, but I do know some witchy people,' I whispered back.

'I quite like witches, but I prefer fairies,' she said. Phew! I'd passed the test.

Jim's house was in South Queensferry, which is a

fifteen-minute drive from the airport, and we stopped on the way to pick up some chips for tea. It's such a pretty place and Jim's house was breathtakingly lovely – and huge! There was a beautiful beach and a little pier out front with a stunning Scottish castle in the background (where the girls thought the witches lived). It was idyllic and I couldn't help smiling as I thought of my little house back in Hounslow. When Jim did come round to Avondale Gardens he told me afterwards that he'd been shocked because he'd always assumed I was posh!

The whole weekend was fantastic – Jim and I discovered we had a mutual love of Scrabble, which became very competitive over the years and we used to play for hours on end. We went for walks on the beach and I even braved an indoor play centre with a ball pit where dozens of kids were jumping around and going crazy – any mum will tell you those places are hell on earth!

It was wonderful because I clicked with Yasmin and Natalie straight away and we did a lot of fun stuff together. After I'd got to know the girls better, I'd sometimes take them over to Ireland to visit Jim when he was recording there. One weekend we arranged to go over to celebrate Jim's birthday. Jim loved *This is Spinal Tap* as much as I did, particularly the scene where a troupe of dwarfs appear on stage dressed as gnomes and dance around a miniature Stonehenge set (if you haven't seen the movie, it's very funny!). In fact, at one point I even tried – and sadly failed

– to get twelve little people flown out to one of Jim's gigs in Germany to surprise him on stage. I'd love to have pulled off that stunt. So on Jim's birthday weekend, the girls and I got a gnome cake made for him from Jane Asher. They were squealing with delight when they saw it: 'Daddy's going to love it! He'll laugh his head off.'

We got on the plane to Dublin after a four-hour delay and ended up having an incredibly stressful flight, as I tried to protect the cake from getting bashed. And the girls, who were usually impeccably behaved, became bored and starting rolling balls up and down the aisle! 'Will you please sit down, girls!' I kept saying. When we arrived in Ireland we weren't talking to each other, and when we got to the meeting point and Jim saw our miserable faces, he said, 'What happened?' Of course, by the time we were halfway to the house, we were all laughing again. It was a crash course in parenthood!

Jim was recording in this big old manor house, complete with suits of armour, and it was a bit spooky for kids. Before the girls went to bed we put what was left of Jim's cake outside for the fairies and gnomes, then I got up in the middle of the night and said to Jim, 'I'm just going outside to do some bite marks in the cake so the girls think the fairies and gnomes have eaten it.'

'You're bloody nuts!' said Jim, turning over and going back to sleep.

I tiptoed through the house and went outside in my

nightdress in the freezing cold to where we'd left the cake at the top of some steps and started biting off chunks of it.

The next morning the girls came bounding into the room, 'Daddy! Daddy! Daddy! Come and see the cake!' They'd already been outside to check if the fairies and gnomes had eaten any of it. I loved doing that kind of stuff for them and it was right up their street. I just adored the girls and I still do. We're close to this day and I'm godmother to Yasmin's twin boys.

I thought it was very impressive that Jim and Chrissie had remained good mates after they split up. I remember feeling really nervous before meeting her for the first time because she'd been one of my idols. As a teenager I wanted to look like her – I wanted to dye my hair black and wear lots of kohl eyeliner and rock a white Yves Saint Laurent shirt with a skinny black trouser. She was just so cool.

I was worried that she wouldn't like me or would just dismiss me as some silly little girl, but I couldn't have misjudged things more. Chrissie loves other women and celebrates them, and it's wonderful when you meet someone like that. There was no weirdness and no rivalry, she was just lovely to me. As well as being a great person, an amazing musician, funny and uber-cool, she still looks bloody fantastic. She's someone I really look up to and we became good friends.

I also learned from Jim and Chrissie how to deal with the press a bit better. They're both very private people and have definite boundaries – they would never allow Yasmin and Natalie to be photographed, for example, because they believed that should be their decision when they were older. I realized that if I wanted to avoid disasters like my foray with the media around the time of *Absolute Beginners*, I had to keep a little bit of myself back.

My next acting role was the part of Hetty Sorrel in a BBC film adaptation of the George Eliot novel *Adam Bede*, which I accepted in July 1991. Giles Foster, who I'd worked with on *Silas Marner*, was directing so I was very keen on the project. I had a couple of weeks off before filming started in August, so Jim suggested I take my mum on holiday to his house in the Algarve, Portugal, then fly on to Germany to meet him as he was on a European tour with Simple Minds.

Jim absolutely adored my mum, and she loved him. In fact, not long after Jim and I got together he said, 'Tell Margie to leave her job. Let's get her on the payroll now.' He was incredibly generous in that way and he was wonderful to his own parents, too. So Mum was able to retire, and we looked after her financially.

When Mum and I arrived in Portugal, there was a car to meet us at the airport and take us to Jim's beautiful pristine white villa in the countryside. It had a sparkling blue swimming pool and stunning views, but it was pretty isolated, with just a couple of other properties nestled in the hillside, which made us feel quite nervous. Living among villains meant we were always prepared for a break-in! And we were used to having the security of concrete around us in London. Nevertheless, we managed to relax and have a lovely week together, and then Mum flew back to London and I flew on to Hamburg to catch up with Jim on tour.

I'd missed Jim and was so happy to see him when he collected me from the airport. He dropped me off at the hotel so I could shower and change, then he headed straight off to the venue for a sound check. I picked out a dusky pink Chanel suit to wear that night, which I dressed down with a vest and Converse sneakers.

When I got to the venue and the band came on stage I'd never seen anything like it in my life – the entire crowd in this huge stadium seemed to levitate! It was amazing to see Jim doing what he loved best and to see the reaction of the fans. I couldn't imagine what it must feel like to get that much love and adulation back from an audience.

After the gig, the band decided to 'do a runner', which is when you come off stage and get straight into a car and go, so you don't get stuck in traffic. I was still buzzing with excitement from the gig when we jumped into the back of our car. Jim and I hadn't said a word to each other when the driver put on the radio and we both started singing along to the exact same bit of a Dire Straits song called 'The Detectives' that was playing. 'You really *do* like music!' said Jim. I may not have been a great singer, but I've always loved music.

I definitely saw another side of the music industry when I was on tour with Simple Minds. It was in a different league to anything I'd ever experienced before. The catering was incredible and each band member had an assistant, so they literally didn't have to think about anything. Everything was organized, booked and transported for them. At the time I was having a pretty great ride with my own work – I'd been around the world, stayed in the penthouse of the Four Seasons and flown on the Warner Brothers private jet – but Jim showed me another level.

After Germany, we boarded a private plane to the south of France, and at the airport we got into helicopters, which flew us to our hotel near Avignon. It was a white chateau set in the most beautiful countryside and Robert De Niro had just stayed there. It was warm and sunny, so Jim and I had lunch on our balcony, then lay in the sun for a while. I was in love and life was just so beautiful. Everything felt perfect.

The concert that night was at Les Arènes de Nîmes, an open-air Roman amphitheatre that had been built as a bullring. The helicopters picked us up from the hotel and took us to the venue. Jim and I were in the last helicopter to leave, and as we flew over the amphitheatre the rest of the band were already on stage. I could see thousands of arms waving in the air. It's an image I'll never forget. When the chopper landed Jim literally ran straight on stage – it was that dramatic! Like something out of a movie.

After the show we flew back to the hotel and everyone gathered around a long white table in the garden, where we ate the most delicious meal. It was an amazing night.

It was on that same European tour that Jim proposed to me in Paris. It was a balmy summer's evening and we were standing on the tiny balcony of our beautiful suite at the Raphael hotel, looking at the twinkling lights of the city below, and he asked me to marry him. We'd had to climb out of the window to get to the balcony, so we felt like two teenagers breaking the rules. It was very romantic. I was crazy about Jim. I'd never met anyone like him – he's so strong and smart, and I learned so much from him. I remember thinking, God, life can't get any better. I half expected a bolt of lightning to come out of the sky and strike me down, because things were just too good to be true.

The next stop on tour was Madrid, which is where Jim bought my engagement ring – a large round sapphire with diamonds around it, just like Princess Diana's. When my mum saw it she said, 'Oh, darling, your ring is so lovely! But you know what? If you'd gone to so-and-so in Hatton Garden you could have got it a lot cheaper.' I guess she was right! I couldn't have asked for anything better, though, it all felt perfect.

After Madrid I had to leave the tour because I was due back in England to start work on *Adam Bede*, which was being shot in the Cotswolds. I don't think anyone involved with the production knew what to expect of me at that point, because I'd done *Lethal Weapon 2* and it was all over the newspapers that I was going out with Jim. Although I'd worked at the BBC consistently for years, I was starting to get the feeling that I wasn't quite their cup of tea any more. I definitely think I was viewed differently. It's amazing how people's perception of you can change just because of an incident in your life, then all of a sudden you're someone else. In reality, though, nothing about me had changed and I was totally committed to the role. I remember one of the make-up artists looking at my engagement ring and saying, 'I'm not looking after that bloody ring when you're filming!'

Jim came to visit me, bringing along one of the bosses of his American record company who'd never seen the English countryside, and I greeted them wearing my wig and corset. We were filming in the heart of chocolate-box England and I was staying at the Lords of the Manor hotel in the village of Upper Slaughter. It must have fulfilled every stereotype of England that American guy had!

Jim was playing a gig in Milton Keynes, and I desperately wanted to go and so did Iain Glen, the guy who played opposite me, and his wife Susannah Harker, so I kept asking the first assistant director and the scheduling guy, 'Will we be able to go?' Eventually we were allowed to, but I think the execs felt my head was somewhere else.

Iain was blown away by the gig and said to me afterwards, 'I've never seen anything so powerful and intoxicating. I can't imagine what it's like to see the person you're with command a crowd like that.'

At the end of shooting, Jim came with me to the Deauville Film Festival, where I was promoting *Twenty-One*, and it received more great reviews. From there we went on to the premiere in Paris, and at the end of September I was flown out to the US on Concorde to promote the film. Steve Dagger met me in New York, then we went on to Dallas, Seattle and finally to LA, where the movie was screened on 1 October at the Directors Guild. The excitement about the movie had gone into overdrive since Sundance and I was being touted as 'the new star from England'. The film opened on 4 October in the States and it did very well, particularly when you consider that it was a small independent production.

While I was in Los Angeles I also read for the part that Demi Moore ended up playing in *Indecent Proposal*. The casting process for the female lead went on for ages and I think they tested just about every actress in the world who was the right age! Adrian Lyne was the director and, of course, I'd worked with him many years before when he'd directed me in the Birds Eye commercials.

At the time I'd left William Morris in Los Angeles and signed with Gersh. I'd arranged to screen test for Adrian on 9 October, but when I got to the Paramount lot, the receptionist said, 'What are you doing here? Your agent called this morning and cancelled the meeting, saying you were sick.' She was talking about the agent I'd just left.

I was mortified – it was such an underhand thing to do. When I'd left William Morris, the agent I'd been working with said to me, 'I know everyone in Hollywood, and as hard as I've worked to help you, I'm going to work just as hard to ruin it for you.' I ran into that particular person years later and he apologized to me, but at the time it was pretty shocking.

Determined to remain professional, I apologized to the Paramount receptionist and explained that there must have been a mix-up because I'd recently changed agents.

'If Mr Lyne still wants to see me, then I can hang around,' I ventured hopefully. At that moment Adrian walked into reception.

'Oh, Patsy, I thought you'd gone back to the UK. I'm testing a couple of other girls, so come up,' he said, gesturing for me to follow him.

The screen test involved a lot of crying, which was pretty easy because I was so furious and upset over what my ex-agent had done.

I spent an hour and a half with Adrian and he was very sweet to me, saying, 'You've turned into a good little actress.' I didn't get the part, of course, but Demi Moore was sensational in the role.

In November, *Twenty-One* opened in the UK, and the year ended with *Beltenebros* being released in Spain. Despite all the issues we'd had on set, it was a huge hit, so 1991 finished well, both personally and professionally. I was in love with Jim and I felt that my acting career had been resurrected with *Twenty-One*. Things were looking up.

11

Becoming a Mum

Prior to our wedding, which was planned for 3 January 1992, Jim and I had been trying for a baby. We'd probably been trying for about eight months – since our first weekend together in South Queensferry – but nothing was happening and I'd started to get a bit worried. We had youth on our side – I was only twenty-three and Jim was thirty-one – so I'd expected it to happen quite quickly.

I made an appointment to see my gynaecologist, and the first thing he said to me was, 'Do you eat properly, Patsy?' At the time I was really tiny, but it had nothing to do with dieting, that's just how I was. Being young, I could pretty much eat what I wanted without gaining weight.

'Yes, I love food,' I replied.

'Well, I don't think it's going to happen for you unless you gain a few pounds,' he said.

I thought my diet was really healthy as it included lots of seafood and vegetables, but I made a mental note to pay more attention to what I was eating. But still every month my period would show up and my heart would sink. After a while I decided to be more proactive and bought an ovulation kit from the chemist. My fertile window of opportunity happened to clash with a weekend we'd planned in Ireland with Bono and his wife, Ali, both lovely, funny, kind people who were very good friends to Jim and me. We stayed with them and I remember saying to Ali when we were alone, 'I want a baby. I *really* want a baby!' and she was very excited for us.

Luckily, organizing the wedding proved a good distraction and I tried to put my worries about conceiving to the back of my mind.

Our wedding wasn't a showy affair at all – the ceremony was at Chelsea Town Hall and the reception afterwards for our families and close friends was at the Halcyon Hotel. I'd found a beautiful vintage Irish lace dress in a little shop just off the Portobello Road, and I wore a floral garland in my hair and carried a bouquet of cream roses.

When I pulled up outside the town hall for the service there were loads of paparazzi and a big crowd of people. I was amazed that anyone had turned up, but I had to fight my way through the scrum to get inside. The next day I read a story in the paper that said, 'At one point an old lady on her Zimmer frame was thrown to the ground by the heaving mob and all she was heard to say was

"Who the hell is Patsy Kensit anyway? I've never heard of her!"' It was hilarious.

I desperately wanted a piper at the reception, but Jim was having none of it. 'I don't want bloody bagpipes!' he kept saying. I thought it would be lovely, though – it wasn't a showbizzy wedding, it was just the people close to us and all his relatives were coming down from Scotland. So I pleaded with him until he gave in, and he told me afterwards that he was glad the piper came because it made the evening.

The food at the reception was amazing – lobster and caviar on ice with delicious champagne – and our wedding cake was iced using the same design as the Irish lace on my dress. Then in the evening we had little portions of fish and chips wrapped up in newspaper. It was so beautifully done.

The following day, Jim and I were going to Bali for three weeks on our honeymoon. Yasmin and Natalie, who'd been my bridesmaids, crept up to me at the reception and said, 'As you're going away tomorrow can we not just stay with you for the night so we can see you in the morning?'

'Of course you can!' I said.

So on our wedding night we had the two girls in camp beds in our room, which was fine as we were both exhausted anyway.

On the flight to Bali the next morning I started to feel horribly sick. I assumed I must have eaten something dodgy, although I couldn't work out what it could be. 'Urgh, I really don't feel very well,' I said to Jim.

'Just try to sleep,' he said. 'You're probably tired after yesterday.'

I slept for most of the flight, but when we got to our resort in Bali I still felt nauseous. The place was absolutely stunning, but I couldn't really take it in because I felt so queasy.

'Try not to worry,' said Jim. 'Relax tonight and we'll get the doctor tomorrow.'

The next morning we called the doctor – who also happened to be the local vet! – but he couldn't come until that evening, so I went outside and tried to have breakfast. The food was incredible, but I couldn't even look at it without wanting to vomit, so I hurried back to our room, put the air conditioning on full blast and threw up in the toilet.

'God, what do you think it is?' I asked Jim.

'I think you're pregnant,' he said.

It was an exciting thought, but I tried not to get my hopes up until I knew for sure. I slept for the rest of the day until the doctor knocked on our door that night. He was a lovely man and very reassuring. He took a urine sample and said the result would take a few days to come back – we were literally in the middle of nowhere, so nothing happened fast.

We had an agonizing wait to find out if I really was

pregnant, but thankfully the test came back positive and it was absolutely thrilling – we couldn't have been in a more beautiful, romantic place when we got the news.

I think a little bit of magic must have happened on the weekend we stayed with Bono and Ali in Ireland. It must have been the luck of the Irish!

Jim wrote me such a beautiful note, saying how happy he was that we were having a baby and that he'd always take care of us, and it's something I still cherish:

Nusa Dua Beach Hotel

Dearest darling baby! I cannot tell you how happy and excited I am about yesterday afternoon's news. After a whole week of apprehension, maybe and what ifs, I awoke today in a totally jubilant and optimistic mood and I feel that contrary to any silly little worries, this baby can only give you and I even more strength – after all nothing is stronger and more purposeful than the family unit. I do hope that you enjoy the pregnancy because, from what I have seen so far when you are around kids, I know that you will enjoy motherhood. Already this baby is a lucky baby to have a mum like you and I am the luckiest man to have you both. I swear to be a great husband and Daddy.

Confucius says: Try hard not to worry about silly little things or else baby will also get worried. Let Daddy worry and do the work, as it is his job.

We carried on with our honeymoon, but I didn't have morning sickness, I had all-day-long sickness, so Jim had to do a lot of stuff on his own. He used to love swimming in the ocean and paddling around on a board. One day, I was sitting on the beach watching him go further and further out to sea, when I started to panic. He was playing a trick on me because I hadn't been in the sea and didn't realize you could stand up with the water lapping around your knees and walk for miles.

I had visions of him perishing on our honeymoon, so I got up and started begging the lifeguards to go out and save him. I couldn't understand why they didn't seem bothered and kept telling me to calm down until I saw Jim stand up and start walking back to the beach, laughing!

After Bali we flew to Sydney, which I loved, but I was still feeling so ill. Every day I'd say, 'Right, let's go to a restaurant tonight. I'm feeling good. I can do dinner.' But as soon as the meal arrived I'd have to leave. I felt terrible for Jim because we were on our dream honeymoon and I was feeling constantly sick. And being intimate was the last thing I felt like.

While we were in Sydney we flew out to Ayers Rock on a tiny plane and I was just so ill. The stewardess was lovely, and when I told her I was in the early stages of pregnancy, she said, 'Try ginger. Make some ginger tea and keep some ginger biscuits with you.' I took her advice over the next few days and amazingly it helped.

Ayers Rock was stunning and felt very spiritual.

Strangely, I stopped feeling sick the moment we arrived. 'I'm starving, Jim. I have to eat now!' I said, suddenly feeling much better and overcome with hunger.

We were staying at a motel for a couple of nights, so we went to the cafeteria and said we'd like to order a meal.

'No, you have to wait fifteen minutes,' the waitress said abruptly.

'Is there any way I can order now because I'm pregnant and I haven't eaten for days,' I pleaded.

'Absolutely not,' she replied, refusing to budge. 'You have to wait fifteen minutes.'

I marched out towards reception with Jim in my wake, muttering that I was going to complain to the manager, when I looked up and saw a notice on the wall with 'Employee of the month' written on it and this woman's picture below.

'Really?!' I said. It was pretty funny.

We stayed for two nights and originally Jim was booked on an excursion to walk to the top of Ayers Rock. But he had a dream the night before that the Aborigines didn't want anyone walking on the rock, so he said he couldn't do it.

Instead, we asked the hotel if we could hire a car and we drove to the rock at five o'clock one morning. When we arrived the place was deserted and it began to rain, which is really unusual. I thought, Right, I've got to do this, and I took off all my clothes, put my belly against the rock and asked for its energy and power to go to my baby. I remember the warmth of the rock against my skin and the cool drops of rain on my face. Then all of a sudden the rain stopped and I looked up to see this beautiful rainbow in the sky.

The mood was broken by a giggling sound that seemed to be coming from inside the rock, then suddenly this little blond head popped out, and Aboriginal children started to emerge from the rock, dancing and playing. It was one of the most beautiful and spiritual moments of my life.

We left Australia and flew to Hawaii, then on to LA at the beginning of February, and that's where Jim and I parted ways. Jim flew back to the UK, while I stayed in Los Angeles for meetings about new film projects and to discuss the option for a second Disney picture – *Blame It on the Bellboy* had been released in the UK on 19 January, but had tanked at the box office, so the second movie didn't get made in the end, which was disappointing, but in my business you have to accept there will be highs and lows. Thankfully *Adam Bede* had been well received.

When I got back to the UK, I started looking for a house to buy in Holland Park for Jim and me. I found one place that I absolutely loved – a two-floor apartment on Landsdowne Road in a beautiful white stucco building with lovely communal gardens. I faxed over the details to

Jim, who was abroad at the time, and when he got back to London, he said, 'Let's go and see it.'

As we arrived at the apartment he turned to me and said, 'I've already put in an offer.' I couldn't believe it – he'd made an offer on the place without even seeing it because he knew I wanted it so much. I was blown away.

The place needed a lot of renovation before we could move in, so we got an architect called Colin Radcliffe involved, as he'd done a few jobs for Steve Dagger. Jim basically gave me a free hand to do whatever work was needed, which was very generous of him, and hiring Colin was fortunate because he introduced me to his wife, Angela, who is still my best friend to this day.

After meeting with Columbia in LA back in February I was offered the lead female role opposite Michael J. Fox in a movie called *The Concierge*. They thought we'd make a really cute couple, and at 5ft 3in there was no danger of me towering over him! But I was four months pregnant at this point and I felt I had to tell the studio. I was still tiny and my bump wasn't showing at all, but I didn't feel comfortable about lying. In the end, the studio couldn't get me insured, so they withdrew their offer and Gabrielle Anwar, the beautiful English actress who'd been in *Scent of a Woman* with Al Pacino, took the part.

Jim was away a lot writing new material with Simple Minds when I was pregnant so, rather than sit around at home by myself, I accepted a part in a film adaptation of the Henry James novella *Turn of the Screw*. It was a remake of the Deborah Kerr film *The Innocents*, which had also been based on the Henry James story, but while that movie had been really good, sadly ours wasn't. My bump seemed to be getting bigger by the day and I suffered from terrible heartburn, so I used to walk around the set swigging from a bottle of Gaviscon like it was going out of fashion! As the weeks went by, the heartburn disappeared and I could enjoy the pregnancy more, and I began to get very excited about meeting my baby.

At the beginning of September I was about two weeks over my due date when my obstetrician at the Portland Hospital in central London called me in to be induced. Within thirty minutes of being given some gel to kick-start labour I was on my hands and knees, groaning in agony. When I'd done my birth plan I'd decided I wanted a natural birth with no drugs at all, but when the nurse walked into my room that night like a cocktail waitress carrying a tray of pain-relieving drugs and said, 'What do we think, doctor?' I was in such pain I said, 'I want all of them! It bloody hurts!'

My obstetrician, who had just been to the opera, was still wearing his tuxedo and a pair of silver wellingtons, and I remember thinking he looked very dashing. He reminded me of Warren Beatty.

'We can give you an epidural,' he suggested.

'Yes, please!' I replied without a second's hesitation.

These days I think they can localize the pain relief better, but in 1992 you were completely numb from your chest down. Once I'd been given the epidural the doctor advised Jim to go home and get some rest because nothing was going to happen for a while.

'Honestly, go, go,' I said, waving him out of the room. When Jim came back first thing the next morning I was still in labour, and it dragged on and on throughout the day. I remember Jim was sitting in a chair across the room reading the *Guardian* when he suddenly looked up at me.

'What is it?' I asked.

'I just love you so much,' he said and then went back to reading his paper.

'Yeah, I'm sure you do! Thank you for that!' I laughed as I contemplated going into my eighteenth hour of labour – though joking aside, it was a really lovely moment.

Eventually, my doctor decided to give me an episiotomy and then he used forceps and a Ventouse cap to pull the baby out. It was a pretty difficult labour and I haemorrhaged afterwards and needed an injection to help my blood clot, but thankfully our gorgeous son James arrived safely into the world on 4 September 1992 and we couldn't have been happier. When he was placed in my arms, I had this overwhelming feeling of pure love. I'd never experienced such a profound emotion before.

It was about ten past five in the evening and my mum,

who'd been waiting outside the room while I gave birth, came in to see the baby. She picked James up, cradled him in her arms and started to cry. But they were tears of joy.

'Don't cry, Mum,' I said gently.

After I'd breastfed James a nurse came to take him away to a room with all the other babies.

'But I want him here with me,' I protested, passing James to the nurse reluctantly.

'Well, on the first night we like to have all the babies in a room where we can keep an eye on them,' she explained.

I couldn't sleep a wink that night because I was too excited, so I crept down the corridor to sneak a peek at James through the window. I'd never felt so happy in my life.

Even though James was a good baby, real life kicked in once I got home. We didn't have a nanny and on the sixth night of sleep deprivation with James next to me in his crib crying to be fed, I turned to Jim and said, 'What on earth have we done!'

'This is what it's like to have a baby, Pat,' he said, laughing.

I was only twenty-four and it was a complete shock to my system, and since none of my girlfriends had babies, I had no one to talk to about it either. In the end we decided to get a maternity nurse, who was totally brilliant. She helped me to get through the nights and settle James into a routine because up until then I'd been feeding him on demand. I only breastfed for three weeks because it didn't come naturally to me and the pain was unbelievable! I used to put frozen cabbage leaves in my bra to take the heat out and numb the pain. But then I got mastitis, so the paediatrician advised me to start giving James a bottle and reassured me that I'd done the important bit.

After six weeks with the maternity nurse, my gran, Auntie Mary and my mum started coming round to help out, but they'd forgotten everything about caring for babies! It was lovely to have them around, though.

One day I was changing James's nappy on the floor and my mum looked down at us and said, 'You're so young, Pat. It's like watching a child with a child.'

They all thought the world of James, and Mum especially adored him. Our joy during those first weeks of James's life was to be short-lived, though, because it wasn't long before Mum started to get sick again.

12

My World Collapses

I returned to Los Angeles in October for meetings about new projects. James wasn't even two months old yet, so I took him with me, along with a nanny. I guess I panicked about being out of the loop for too long when it came to work.

I had the opportunity to stay at home and enjoy being a mum and bake cupcakes – Jim never put any pressure on me to return to work – but I'd been working since the age of four and I didn't know any other life. In addition to that I felt nervous about the idea of not being able to earn my own living, and having enjoyed the success of *Lethal Weapon 2* and *Twenty-One*, it seemed madness not to capitalize on the opportunities that arose in the wake of those two films.

It turned out I was right about losing momentum, as nothing materialized from those meetings in LA. I found it interesting being back in Hollywood after having a child. Although I was only twenty-four and still young, even by

Hollywood standards, I sensed a shift in how I was perceived. Something had changed – perhaps the studio bosses didn't want the baggage of an actress with the responsibilities of a baby and a family. Whatever it was, six months earlier I'd been the hottest thing around, but now I was in no doubt that things move on quickly in Hollywood if you're off the scene, even if it's just for a few months. Already I felt like yesterday's news!

In the end I accepted a part in a movie called *Bitter Harvest* alongside Stephen Baldwin. It's probably best described as an 'erotic thriller', and I was offered a lot of money to do it, but I took the part mainly because I just wanted to get back to work.

Back home in the apartment on Landsdowne Road, things couldn't have been more perfect. I loved my baby so much, and as the end of the year approached, I felt physically back to normal and was sleeping properly thanks to James being in a routine.

But then Mum got sick again and ended up in hospital in Hammersmith. She'd had a cough for a while, and when she went to get it checked out she was told the cancer had returned and it was now in her lungs.

The first time I went to visit her I took James in his car seat and Mum was so annoyed with me. 'Please don't bring the baby in here, Pat. There are so many germs. Don't bring him in again!'

'OK, Mum,' I said gently.

I left James with Mum and had a quiet word with her doctor in the corridor.

'She's going to be OK, isn't she?' I ventured, unable to take in what he was saying. 'She'll bounce back, right?'

'No, I'm afraid she won't,' he said.

'Well, how long do you think she has?'

'It's hard to say – four, maybe six, months.'

'No, you're wrong,' I said. 'My mum has come back from the brink dozens of times over the years.'

'Look, there are two things we can do at this stage,' the doctor continued. 'She can go to Harefield Hospital and they can drain her lung and blow it back up again to relieve the symptoms she's experiencing. And we can also try chemotherapy.'

I spoke to Mum about the options afterwards, but she was adamant she didn't want to do either.

'No, I'll die on the table if I have that operation,' she said.

'OK, then what about chemo?'

'Absolutely not!'

My mum had refused chemo all her life. I've seen it work miracles, but my mum had been around cancer patients for twenty years and she always maintained that every person she had known who'd accepted chemo had died soon after, while she'd managed to keep going with radiotherapy, surgery and other drugs. I had no idea what was right or wrong, I just wanted her to get better.

Mum reacted differently to the news this time, though. There was an acceptance of how sick she was. In the past her cancer had been localized, so she'd had lumpectomies and mastectomies, but it was a whole different scenario now that the cancer had spread to her lung. She knew she wouldn't come back from it.

I left the hospital that day feeling utterly devastated. I had a knot in my stomach and I felt sick with fear. When I got home to Landsdowne Road I made a cup of tea and sat down with Jim. 'Mum's dying,' I said. Saying those words out loud for the first time made it seem real. I knew it would take nothing short of a miracle for her to beat the cancer this time.

Incredibly, though, she rallied, and whatever medication she was given helped to ease her symptoms, so she was discharged from hospital and was determined to soldier on and try to get back to normality.

I didn't want to leave Mum behind when I went to LA to shoot *Bitter Harvest* in early 1993, so she came with James, the nanny and me. I think the movie's really terrible and in hindsight I should never have done it. It's a film about bank robbers with a pointless topless scene. I've never had a problem with nudity if it's called for, but this was nudity for the sake of it, and it marked the start of me doing straight-to-video B movies that were well paid, but meant I went to work with a heavy heart. In retrospect, I was sabotaging my career. I shouldn't have panicked; I should have waited for the right thing to come along.

I know I didn't need to do those movies, but I've always been driven by a desire to earn my own money and support myself. If you want to succeed in acting, you have to be prepared to go without and turn roles down while you wait for the career-defining parts. I love the art of acting, but I come from a working-class family, I'd slept on a mattress on the floor and used an outside loo, I'd seen the empty cupboards when my parents barely had enough money for food, so I valued being able to earn. But, for my career, it was the wrong attitude to have. It's all about choices and I wasn't choosy enough.

I went to LA again in March of that year to shoot an episode of the cult US TV series *Tales from the Crypt*, which was directed by the American actor Kyle MacLachlan. He was dating the supermodel Linda Evangelista at the time and I remember her telling me on set one day when I was tucking into a big cake that I wouldn't be able to carry on eating the way I was once I hit thirty. They are words that came back to haunt me later!

I'd also accepted a part in a new Don Boyd movie called *Kleptomania*, alongside the US actress Amy Irving, which was filmed in New York and Atlanta. I think everyone hoped we could recreate the success we'd had with *Twenty-One*, but this picture was very low budget. I guess lightning doesn't strike in the same place twice and it wasn't a great sucess. I loved working with Don, though, and I respect him greatly.

I outdid myself with my next project. That summer I went back to LA with my mum and James to make an HBO fantasy horror movie with Mario Van Peebles called *Full Eclipse*. I probably should have been more concerned when a pair of werewolf fangs arrived in the post from LA so I could 'get used to wearing them'.

The story takes place in Los Angeles, where the police department has an elite squad of officers who turn into werewolves at night, and it was being directed by a guy I knew from LA called Tony Hickox, who was known at the time for shooting horror flicks and sequels. I was working eighteen-hour days because they were trying to do too much in the time they had, and I was completely shattered.

I think it has a cult audience, though, because my good friend Leigh Francis (aka Keith Lemon) told me it was his favourite movie of all time! In fact, when he had a fancy dress party for his fortieth birthday, he said, 'Come as that werewolf from *Full Eclipse*. Bring ya teeth!' He was dying to see the teeth, but sadly I couldn't find them.

While I was over in LA, I also screen tested for *The Mask*, which obviously went to Cameron Diaz, as well as reading for numerous other roles. Nothing came of any of them, though, and work-wise, 1993 was an incredibly frustrating year.

However, there was a glimmer of hope on the horizon when I met with the American director Allison Anders about a movie she was making called *Grace of My Heart*. It was about the music scene that emerged from New York's famous Brill Building in the Sixties and was loosely based on the life of singer-songwriter Carole King. That was one project I really hoped would come off.

When I returned from LA, Jim took me, James and my mum on holiday to Capri, a beautiful island off Italy's Amalfi coast. We stayed in a lovely hotel and the views from our bedroom balconies were breathtaking. It was idyllic and wonderful that we were all together again. I remember going into Mum's room soon after we arrived to find her gazing out of the window. 'It's so lovely here,' she said, smiling. She seemed distant, though, and I'd noticed she wasn't eating much, so I just knew she was starting to feel worse again. My heart sank, but I was determined to make the most of our holiday together.

We had a wonderful time – Mum and I spent the mornings wandering around the town and shopping in all the lovely boutiques and jewellery stores. One day I spotted a gorgeous emerald and diamond cross in a shop window and remarked how lovely it was. Then in the afternoons we'd swim in the hotel pool or lie on our balconies in the sun, popping to the mini bar every now and then for a cool drink or a slice of fresh coconut.

One afternoon, Jim and I were lying on the balcony reading when he said, 'Pat, go and get us a drink of water from the fridge, will you?'

'Er, you go and get it!' I replied, raising my eyebrows and going back to my book.

'Aw, please go and get it.'

'Oh, for goodness' sake, OK!'

So I went inside and opened the mini bar and there was the emerald and diamond cross I'd admired in the shop window. It was such a romantic thing to do and, as usual, Jim didn't make a fuss about his generosity.

After our holiday in Capri, Jim went off to America on business and I stayed in London with James. In November I started working on a TV movie called *Fall From Grace*, which is a World War Two spy thriller with a wonderful cast – the lovely Tara Fitzgerald, Michael York and James Fox, who I'd worked with on *Absolute Beginners*. During filming my mum became very sick – the cancer had spread pretty much everywhere and she finally agreed to a course of chemotherapy as a last-ditch attempt to buy more time. She knew there were no other options.

I admire Mum so much for dealing with her illness with such dignity, grace and strength. Most of us take it for granted that we can jump out of bed in the morning, brush our teeth and go to work or drop the kids off at school. But imagine what it must be like to get up every day for twenty years with the ever-present spectre of cancer. It must be incredibly hard. I've never been afraid of dying, but I'm afraid of being ill because I've seen up close what it's like to live with cancer. You can have all the money and success in the world, but if you don't have your health, you have nothing at all.

Mum was eventually admitted to the Middlesex Hospital on Mortimer Street, where I'd watched her being wheeled down to theatre twenty years earlier. Now here we were again. She was kept in for a few days, then they sent her home to Avondale Gardens with a bag full of meds and an oxygen tank, and I returned to the house with her.

For some reason, Mum was very distressed that we hadn't christened James yet. 'He's got to be baptized,' she kept saying. 'You've got to get that baby christened or he won't go to heaven.'

'OK, Mum, I promise,' I reassured her.

When I looked at all Mum's meds I was totally confused about what to give her and when, so I called our local GP, Dr Lewis, and he came over to the house Once he'd checked on Mum and we'd been through her meds, he took me outside the room.

'She's dying, you know?' he whispered.

'Yes, I know, but what should I do? Just stay here and hold her? I don't know what to do.' It felt totally overwhelming.

We tried to get her into a hospice, but there weren't any spaces. But if I'm being honest, I didn't want her to go into a hospice – although I'd told Dr Lewis I understood that Mum was dying, really I was still in denial. I wouldn't let myself actually believe it. I'd had twenty years of being told my mum was going to die, and I was so exhausted and stressed that I didn't know what to think. One minute I'd be begging God to take Mum and put an end to her suffering, and the next I'd be beating myself up for even having those thoughts. 'Please, God, just five more years, just five more months,' I'd pray.

In the end she was readmitted to the Middlesex, so every morning I'd get up at 4 a.m. and go to visit her on my way to the film set. She was usually sleeping and looking peaceful, so I'd sit with her for a little while and then go in to work.

Mum wasn't eating very much and the food at the Middlesex wasn't the best, so I hired a lovely chef from Leith's cookery school in Notting Hill and she cooked little meals for Mum, like tiny portions of fish pie. The nurses allowed her to use the little kitchenette nearby to prepare the food. I used to sit in that depressing ward, willing her to eat, but it was all in vain. She could never manage more than a mouthful.

One day I read an article in the *Guardian* about a new cancer wonder drug called Lenteron, so I took the paper into the hospital the next time I visited Mum and showed

it to the doctor, who looked about nineteen, but was probably my age.

'Can we try this?' I asked hopefully.

'I'm sorry, but your mum doesn't qualify for that drug,'
he said.

'What do you mean?'

'Well, you know the stage she's at. Your mum could
die any time.'

'Look!' I snapped. 'I've been told that a hundred times
over the years. This woman has paid National Insurance
her whole life. She's lived through a war. I will write you
a cheque now. Just give her the fucking drug!'

I was desperate and looking for anything that could
give us hope, but the doctor wouldn't consider it.

It was a very stressful time, and it didn't help that Jim
and I seemed to be spending more and more time apart
because of our work commitments. We'd planned to go
to the Seychelles over Christmas with a couple of friends,
so at least we had that to look forward to. One evening
our friends were coming over to talk about the trip and
fill in some forms, but before they arrived, Jim suddenly
said, 'I can't be here tonight, Pat. I need to go to the
hospital to see your mum.'

He was about to go off to LA again, before flying on
to India to shoot a music video. I was really cross with
him, not about the holiday plans, but because I was still
in denial about my mum's condition.

'It'll be fine. She's fine,' I said. 'You can see her when you get back.'

'No, Pat, I want to see Margie before I go.'

He knew that if he didn't go, he wouldn't see her again. He just knew. So he went and spent hours with her.

Around this time Mum wrote me a lovely letter, thanking me for taking care of her, and right at the end she said, 'Jim is a good man, Pat.' She adored him, but the truth was that our marriage was already in trouble – we just weren't together enough to nurture the relationship. I don't know if she guessed that things weren't going well, but one day when I went to visit, I must have been looking downcast because things weren't great at home and she said, 'What's wrong?'

'Nothing. Everything's fine, Mum,' I replied. I think that was the moment I became a woman. In the past I would have told her everything because we were so close, but I didn't want to upset or worry her when she was so sick, so I held back.

Mum hated it when I looked scruffy, and I used to turn up at the hospital on my way to work in jeans or workout gear and my puffa jacket. 'Why don't you make the most of yourself?' she'd say, shaking her head. She'd been the one to ignite my love of fashion, and it disappointed her when I didn't make an effort.

So one night after work, I put on a nice dress, a pair of heels and an Azzedine Alaïa leather coat I'd recently bought, and I went to visit Mum. Getting all dolled up after being on set for fourteen hours was the last thing I felt like doing, but it was so worth it when I saw Mum's face. It made her so happy.

'I want to introduce you to the new ward sister,' she said excitedly, lifting back the covers to get out of bed. When she stood up shakily I was shocked to see how emaciated she looked, even though she was still beautiful. It broke my heart. I took Mum's arm and we walked down the corridor to say hello to the sister, then I took her back to bed.

My mum had been so brave, fighting her illness for all those years, but one night she admitted to me that she was afraid of dying.

'Why, Mum?' I asked gently, taking her hand.

'Because I had to have an abortion,' she said, and she went on to explain that she'd got pregnant years ago, while she was in the middle of one of her rounds of cancer treatment, and that her doctor had advised a termination.

'Oh, Mum, I don't want to know that. Don't tell me that,' I said. 'You shouldn't be worrying or thinking about that.'

'I can hear the baby crying,' she continued, distraught. She was on morphine for the pain and I think she was hallucinating.

'Don't be silly, you're the most perfect person,' I said, trying to reassure her, but also to bring an end to the conversation. I just couldn't bear to see her so upset, but I should have let her talk. She needed to tell someone and talk it through, and I feel I failed her because I didn't listen. She'd listened to me and supported me for twenty-five years; she was the best friend I'd ever had. I still feel sad that I wasn't there for her at that moment.

On the evening of 17 December I went to see Mum after work to give her a kiss goodnight. She'd been deteriorating all week, but that night she was violently ill. She stared throwing up and she couldn't stop, and then she began vomiting blood and I couldn't look. I felt so ashamed of myself afterwards – what kind of person was I that I couldn't look at my own mum? Again, I felt I let her down at that time, but it was just too distressing to see someone you love so much in that condition.

When I got home later that night I called the hospital and spoke to one of the nurses on Mum's ward.

'Is she still vomiting?' I asked.

'No, she's peaceful now.'

'Thank God,' I said, relieved.

Before hanging up I made the nurse promise to phone if Mum's condition deteriorated. 'I just want to be with her when she passes because she was with me when I came into this world,' I said, sobbing. 'I don't care what time of day or night it is, please call me.'

The next morning I went in to see her at 4 a.m. and she was sleeping peacefully, so I sat with her for half an hour before kissing her goodbye and going on to work. At 6.15 a.m., I was sat in the make-up chair when I got a call from the hospital to say Mum had passed away. 'No, no, no,' was all I could say. I'd wanted to be with her to hold her hand when she died. I've never got over the guilt of not being with her.

All I wanted to do was go straight to the hospital, but we were about to shoot a scene, so I did it on autopilot and they made it as quick as possible, then James Fox sat with me until I was able to leave. We were on location at St Paul's in the City of London, and we sat together in silence, looking up at the sky. It was a bright crisp December day and the sky was so clear and blue. I'll never forget how wonderful James was to me that morning – he's a very spiritual man. It was the most peaceful and intimate gesture of kindness.

I got to the Middlesex after lunch and Auntie Mary was already there, with my cousin Daniel (Uncle John's son) and my brother Jamie. Jim was in India and my gran Bridget didn't make it either – by now I was convinced she'd developed agoraphobia, because she never left the house. It broke her heart when Mum died and she passed away herself exactly a year later.

We were never particularly close to our extended family. Mum was the glue that held everyone together, and after she passed away those relationships fractured, which is sad.

We were all standing around Mum's bed, talking about moving her to the funeral parlour, when I looked down at her and was struck by how beautiful her skin looked. She'd endured so many years of stress, yet there was hardly a line on her face. She looked so serene. Just then, Daniel said, 'Don't look, Pat. Turn away.' There was a little blood trickling from the corner of her mouth – it was awful.

When I returned home from seeing Mum I got through the rest of the day still on autopilot – I had to keep it together because James needed me. Then a couple of nights after Mum passed away, she appeared to me, as clear as day, when I was wide awake.

'I'm so relieved it's over, Pat,' she said. 'It was euthanasia. I felt so awful, but now it's over and it's such a relief.'

I felt as if she was at peace. It was probably my mind playing tricks on me because of the grief, and perhaps subconsciously it was my way of coping, but it provided a little comfort.

We all went to the funeral home to say goodbye to Mum. I was scared to touch her, but I knew I'd regret it if I didn't kiss her, so I bent down and gently kissed her forehead. The funeral took place on 21 December at the St Francis of Assisi Roman Catholic Church in Notting Hill and I was inconsolable. My doctor had given me sedatives to help me get through the day, but they made little difference. I felt as if I'd had a vital organ removed. Mum had been my best friend, my soulmate, my confidante and the one person who I could talk to honestly and really be myself with. Our relationship was probably quite co-dependent in some respects, but I make no apologies for that deep love that we shared. We relied on each other more than anyone else, and she'd been with me every step of the way throughout my career. I had no idea how I was going to manage without her.

· Jim was wonderful after Mum's death – he organized everything, with the help of his PA Sandra. He'd loved my mum and he understood our relationship because it was similar to his relationship with his dad.

After the funeral service and cremation, Jim and I invited friends and family to a little reception at the Halcyon Hotel to remember Mum and celebrate her life, and it felt good to talk to her friends.

I didn't have any bereavement counselling afterwards, which I might have benefited from – I guess it wasn't as commonplace as it is today – but I searched for comfort and reassurance everywhere and anywhere at the time. I remember bumping into a Turkish guy called Terry, who ran the sunbed shop in Notting Hill – I called him Terry the Turk – and afterwards I came back to the apartment on Landsdowne Road crying my eyes out. Jim was there and Chrissie had come round to see us.

'What's the matter, Patsy?' asked Chrissie.

'Well, I was talking to Terry the Turk at the sunbed shop, and he doesn't believe in the afterlife,' I sobbed.

'So your guru Terry the Turk from the sunbed shop doesn't believe in the afterlife?' said Jim, raising his eyebrows, and both he and Chrissie started laughing. It was a rare moment of light relief at a very dark time.

The Church was a real comfort to me then, as it had been for my mum during the difficult times in her life. Sometimes I'd just nip into church and light a candle and sit for half an hour, and it was very calming. These days I'm more of an à la carte Catholic – my beliefs have widened and I've got into meditation and Buddhism, too – but I love the familiarity and structure of the Catholic Church, as I've grown up with it.

But the biggest blessing of all was James – when Mum died I had to carry on and be strong for him. Without wishing to sound too dramatic, James saved me. I was so eaten up with grief that I don't know what I would have done if I hadn't had my baby – he was my reason to keep going. And we had him christened, as Mum had requested – it was just sad she couldn't be there with us to share the day.

Of course I had Jim, too, but our marriage was on rocky ground by this time. I often wonder if things might have been different for us if Mum had lived a little longer. She'd worked hard at her own marriage and knew it wasn't all bunny rabbits and rainbows, and I'm sure she would have helped me through the hard times. But with her gone I didn't have any strong family support when things got tough. You need your family at those times to give you a sense of perspective.

A few weeks after Mum passed away, I was looking through some of her things when I came across my parents' marriage certificate – from 1986. I couldn't believe it – when I was growing up I'd always assumed they were married. She must have had her reasons for keeping it a secret, but I felt really upset that she hadn't been able to confide in me. In the end I called Auntie Pat to ask her about it.

'Oh, darling, they did it when your dad was sick. Everyone knew,' she said.

'Well, why couldn't she tell me?' I asked.

Pat couldn't really answer that and it just felt like another family secret. It's in our DNA. I was really cross with Mum because we'd always been so close and I'd thought we'd told each other everything. I made a promise to myself that when I got to wherever I was going, we were going to have it out!

13

The End of a Marriage

Jim had bought us a lovely house in a beautiful place called Killiney in Dublin. We'd outgrown the apartment on Landsdowne Road, and the original idea had been that Mum would come to Ireland to live with us. But after she died I didn't want to commit to moving out of London. At the time I needed the familiarity of home. I felt too vulnerable to relocate to a place where I didn't know anyone and where I'd have to start from scratch, and I also had to be in London for work, so James and I ended up living at the Halcyon on and off. It was clear by now that Jim and I wanted different things and that we were rapidly heading in different directions.

I was so confused about everything after Mum passed away. I didn't know what I wanted any more. I'd spent my whole life anticipating her death, and yet when it happened I had no idea how to cope. Jim was incredibly supportive, but he couldn't replace my mum and I expected too much of him. It must have been tough for him, too, with a relatively new wife, a new baby and the death of his mother-in-law. It's a lot to deal with.

I can laugh about it now, but I remember lying in bed one night imagining in forensic detail how Jon Bon Jovi would look as a corpse! I was never a Bon Jovi fan, so I have no idea why I picked him to obsess over. I thought, I'm going mad. I'm literally going mad. But I wasn't, it was pure grief.

I also realized that I'd fallen into a pattern of choosing men who go away a lot, which is challenging when you're trying to sustain a marriage. Jim and I were always grabbing a moment together. I'm sure my dad's absences from home while I was growing up had an effect on the relationships I formed with men later on – I simply wasn't used to having a man in my life all the time.

My work took me away a lot, too. In January 1994, while I was still feeling very raw from losing Mum, I went to Australia with James to shoot a cop thriller called *Tunnel Vision*, directed by Clive Fleury. It was another project that paid well, but wasn't going to get me anywhere. When I came back to London I did a couple of photographic shoots – Uli Weber for the *Sunday Times* and Corrine Day for *Tatler.* I loved working with Corrine and I really admired her work – she took some great shots of James and me when he was just a few months old. Then in May I flew to Vancouver to shoot another thriller called *Dream Man*, opposite Andrew McCarthy, who'd been one of the eighties 'brat pack' actors who'd appeared in *St. Elmo's Fire*, *Pretty in Pink* and *Mannequin*. Once more, it wasn't a great script, but it was well paid. After a stream of mediocre movies, thankfully I landed a part in *Angels & Insects*, a Goldwyn picture based on the A. S. Byatt novella *Morpho Eugenia*. It was a role I really wanted and I campaigned hard to get it, going back time and again to read for the director, Philip Haas. It had a stellar cast of English actors, including Mark Rylance, Kristin Scott Thomas and Douglas Henshall, and I shared a dressing room with a lovely actress called Saskia Wickham. The story is set in the 1800s and is about a penniless naturalist called William Adamson (played by Mark) who befriends a keen amateur botanist, Sir Harald Alabaster (Jeremy Kemp). I play Eugenia, one of Sir Harald's older children, who marries William, while having an incestuous affair with her brother Edgar (played by Douglas).

I totally immersed myself in the role and it was a challenging shoot in some ways – dark themes are explored and the aristocratic Alabaster family are albinos, so every bit of my body hair was bleached from head to toe. During filming I went over to Dublin to visit Jim and I remember him saying to me, 'I can't wait until you finish this film and start looking normal again.' He wasn't being nasty – I did look odd. Pale and interesting isn't a good look for me. There was a lot of sex and nudity, too, and I did a full-frontal scene, which I felt fine about in the context of the script. Although it was hard work, it turned out to be a very good movie and it's still the project I'm proudest of to this day.

I remember Jim flying in from somewhere to visit me on set and things just didn't feel the same between us – there was a distance and I felt a bit numb about everything. I honestly think something died in me when my mum passed away and that I changed. When you experience the death of someone close to you, you can either retreat into yourself or go the other way and adopt a devil-may-care attitude, and I think I fell into the latter category. I'd been such a goody-goody all my life, and suddenly I started to rebel a little bit. I'd been so deeply loyal to Mum when she was alive; I would never have done anything to upset her. Losing her had a really profound effect on me.

Elizabeth knew I was having relationship problems and called one day. 'Come and meet me, Patsy,' she said. 'I've got to go to Harrods to get something, but we can have a good talk.'

So we met at the store and had a heart-to-heart, and at the end of the day Elizabeth tried on a Dior dress. She popped out of the changing room and said, 'What do you think?'

'Oh, just get it,' I replied.

'I remember your mum saying something similar to me years ago,' said Elizabeth. 'I loved this white Chanel coat, but I wasn't sure whether to buy it because it was really expensive and Margie said, "Darling, just treat your-self, you deserve it." She was such a lady.'

It might not seem much of a story, but I was touched by it. Elizabeth understood how much Mum meant to me.

I went away again in September, when I flew to Toronto to film *Love and Betrayal: The Mia Farrow Story*, a biopic for Fox TV produced by Tarquin Gotch, who'd worked with John Hughes in the eighties. It was a decent script and I enjoyed the role, which focused on Mia's relation-ships with Frank Sinatra and Woody Allen. I'd actually read for Woody when he was casting *Husbands and Wives* a couple of years previously, which was an honour because he doesn't see many people.

Normally when I'm filming on location I go to work, get back to the hotel, have dinner and go to bed, but in Toronto I really made the most of the social life and had an amazing time. James was with me, but I had a nanny to help. I'd been working non-stop since my mum died and I think I needed to let go and enjoy myself. Billy Connolly, who's a really good friend of Jim's, came to town for a gig, so I went along to that. I'd already seen him many times and he's always fantastic. The Pretenders were in town, too, so I saw Chrissie and went to their gig.

I also read in one of the local listings mags that Oasis were coming to Toronto to play at some tiny club, so I asked the guy who was doing my hair if he fancied going to the gig with me. It was sold out, but we managed to blag our way in – by total fluke I got talking to a guy outside the venue who turned out to be Noel Gallagher's guitar roadie, Jason. When I explained that we were having trouble getting tickets, he managed to get us in, and we stood by the side of the stage for the whole gig. By this point I already knew the words to every song from their debut album *Definitely Maybe* and I loved the show.

Afterwards, there were two ways to leave the venue, on either side of the stage, so as the universe would have it, singer Liam Gallagher went one way and I went the other. I ended up in the car park where the Oasis tour bus was parked, and the band – minus Liam – were already boarding it.

'Come on the bus and have a chat with us all,' shouted Noel. I spent a few minutes talking to them about why I was in Toronto and then I said, 'So, do you all support Man United then?'

'No, I'm a fucking Man City fan!' said Noel, clearly outraged.

Despite my football faux pas, they were all lovely to me, and as I was getting off the bus, Noel said, 'Take a number for Mags, our tour manager, and call if you want to come to any more gigs.'

Love and Betrayal turned out fine – I got no complaints from Mia! And when filming came to an end I flew from

Toronto to New York to shoot with Rankin for hip new style magazine *Dazed & Confused*. I was already at the studio when Rankin and the stylist Katie Grand walked in carrying two bin bags full of clothes and talking excitedly about the Stone Roses and the Oasis album, which they whacked on the stereo for the shoot.

I had a great time that day and we all got drunk. I'd been in Toronto for nearly fifteen weeks, working really hard, and with people who were a lot older than me, so it was a relief to let go and have fun. I thought Rankin and Katie were great and we became fast friends. They've both obviously gone on to be super-successful, but they've never changed, even though Katie's bin bags have been replaced by Louis Vuitton luggage!

Rankin took a photo of me lying on the floor holding a nearly-empty bottle of tequila – my hair's in a quiff, I'm wearing a man's suit and I look like Elvis, Keith Richards and KD Lang all rolled into one! But despite what a lot of people think, that whole rock-chick image isn't the real me – I had moments like that, but at the end of the day I was a working mum with responsibilities.

By the time filming wrapped on *Love and Betrayal*, I hadn't seen Jim for four months. He'd been recording in LA and then on tour in the US with Simple Minds while I'd been in Toronto. Our marriage was fast unravelling and rumours were starting to surface that we were having problems. After the *Dazed & Confused* shoot I flew to a private island called Petit St Vincent in the West Indies with James and his nanny for a holiday, then we headed back to London, where Jim and I planned to spend a family Christmas at the new home he'd bought us in St John's Wood. The house needed to be totally renovated, so I paid for all the building work. I've always been very proud and never wanted to be financially dependent on a man. It was another reason I took so many dodgy film roles. And I'd never forgotten my mum worrying about paying off the loan she and my dad had taken out to buy their council house in Avondale Gardens. As a consequence I hate owing money or being in debt to anyone.

But Jim was trying everything to make me happy and make things right between us. Once when we were up in Scotland, he said, 'Let's go for a drive.' So he drove me to this little castle and stopped the car in front of it.

'Wow, this is beautiful!' I said and Jim threw me a set of keys and said, 'It's yours.' It was an incredible gesture – the property came with a title, a loch and acres of stunning countryside – but I'd been just as moved when he'd bought me a little bottle of Penhaligon's rose perfume when we were first dating.

Back in London, though, we continued to lead separate lives. Jim had to go away again before Christmas, so when I found out Oasis were playing at the Cambridge Corn Exchange, I rang two writers I knew from *The Face* to ask them if they wanted to go to the gig with me, then I called Chrissie and invited her along, too. 'Yeah, I'm in,' she said. So I booked a car and a driver to take us up there. We all loved the band, but *The Face* guys were uber-fans and wanted to listen to demos and B-sides in the car on the way there, while I wanted to hear 'Columbia'. The show was amazing and afterwards Oasis's tour manager, Mags, invited us backstage, so I said to the boys, 'Are you coming with us?'

'Um no,' they mumbled, shuffling their feet. 'We'll just wait here.'

'Why don't you want to come and meet the band?' I asked, confused.

'Because we just don't want to ruin it for ourselves. We don't want to know any more than we've seen.' It was very sweet.

The backstage area was jam-packed and the band was surrounded by fans. Liam was standing in the corner, so Chrissie made a beeline for him, leaving me trailing in her wake. 'Do you want guitar lessons?' she asked him after she'd introduced herself. She was messing with him. She's obviously a brilliant guitarist and a legend in her own lifetime, and they were all in awe of her. Finally, I said to Liam, 'All right? I missed you in Toronto.'

'Yeah, I fucking hate all that shite,' he said, and that was pretty much all we said to each other!

What I loved about Oasis was their openness – they

were totally authentic and they hid nothing. It was very liberating. And they never apologized for anything they did or said – you had to admire their front. Their attitude was, 'If you don't like it, fuck off', which was very punk rock, if I may be bold enough to say that, having been about ten years old when the Sex Pistols changed the world.

About two weeks later I crossed paths with Oasis again. I was getting on a plane to Glasgow to pick up James from his gran's, and the band happened to be getting on the same flight. I was wearing little round John Lennon-style glasses, and as I walked past Liam's seat he said, 'Oh, I like them specs.'

'Thanks, I got them in New York,' I said. I was on the verge of saying he could have them, but then I thought, Actually, I quite like these glasses. I'm keeping them. I'm so glad I did because he was always admiring people's glasses – 'top bins' he'd call them – and he built up quite a collection because they'd just give them to him!

I was sitting at the back of the plane and Liam didn't turn round once. I remember thinking he was cute, but nothing more. Noel went to the loo and said hello, and invited me to the gig in Glasgow, but I couldn't make it because I had to be back in London for work. Noel was always a gentleman and their elder brother Paul (aka Bod) is such a lovely guy.

By now, Jim and I were living separate lives. We did spend Christmas together at the house in St John's Wood, but neither of us had a good time – we were two people on different paths. I think we'd both changed, though I'd probably changed the most. I was still really young when I'd married him and we'd had James quite quickly, plus we'd had the extra pressure of long separations. We both realized that things couldn't carry on the way they were, and sadly we agreed to separate. We decided not to draw attention to it by making an announcement, and Jim went off somewhere with Simple Minds while I stayed in London.

There's no doubt it affects the whole family when a marriage breaks down. My mum was really upset when my marriage to Dan ended, and she would have been devastated to think I'd split up with Jim, who she loved and respected very much.

I believe in marriage with all my heart and I've never made light of it – I just seem to be terribly bad at it! I think there's a perception that I get married for all the wrong reasons, but I was so in love with Jim when we got together. It was the real thing and, possibly, if I'd known then what I know now about relationships and life in general, I might have worked harder at my marriage and things might have turned out differently for us. Although, Jim might disagree of course! I feel very lucky to have met him. We may have fallen out of love, but we still loved each other as friends and he has always been there for me.

Although I was struggling emotionally in the wake of my marriage breakdown and still coming to terms with my mum's death, work was a good distraction and 1995 started well in that respect. I'd got the part in the Allison Anders movie *Grace of My Heart*, about the Sixties pop music scene, and shooting began in March. There was fierce competition for the role and in the audition there was a scene where I had to cry and with everything I'd been going through in my personal life, the tears came very easily. Allison had always wanted me for the part – she'd become a friend and we shared an interest in music (she's a huge Beatles fan). I found out afterwards that one of the female producers had said, 'I don't trust an actress who can cry on cue like that.' But that's Hollywood.

The cast was great – Illeana Douglas, who played the lead; Matt Dillon; John Turturro; Bridget Fonda and Eric Stoltz. It also had a great soundtrack, with some original music written by Burt Bacharach.

It was a lot of fun to make and it's a good film. Martin Scorsese was the executive producer – he was going out with Illeana at the time and the picture was his gift to her. I thought I'd probably never see him on set because he's such a legend, but he was there every day. He loves actors and he's just so captivating and funny – and, of course, he was a big fan of *Absolute Beginners*. Once we had a conversation about Catholicism and he kept saying to me, 'Why would you do that to your children? Why? Why?' He wanted to talk and he engaged with everyone. We had to do some pickup shots later on in Central Park and he had to have tents around him or he would have been mobbed.

It was the first movie I'd worked on where I didn't want to get straight into my car at the end of the day and head back to my hotel. I wanted to hang out and watch everyone work. It was a great experience and the film was loved.

That spring there was a great buzz about *Angels & Insects*, which got into competition at the Cannes Film Festival in May. I started to feel that I was back doing good work again and it was an exciting time. Steve Dagger accompanied me to Cannes and he spent the whole time worrying about how my fantasy football team was doing on the Frank Skinner and David Baddiel show *Fantasy Football League*! Steve picked my team and I ended up finishing runner-up to novelist Nick Hornby, which was annoying as he's an Arsenal fan and we're Spurs fans. If my dad had been alive he would have loved helping us with it!

The next few months were really busy and I was starting to feel stronger. In the summer, Steve and I went to Milan to sign a deal with Dolce & Gabbana to model and endorse their clothes, then in September, *Angels & Insects* was screened at the Toronto Film Festival, where it was a big hit. After the screening I went with the cast to a bar to celebrate and we were downing shots with Brian De Palma, Uma Thurman, Timothy Hutton and Sean Penn. Sean loved the film, which was a huge compliment as he's a genius actor. I knew him because he was a good friend of Jim's and had hung out with Jim and Chrissie when he was married to Madonna. The following month I filmed a guest spot on *French & Saunders*, which was a spoof of the *Batman* movie and a lot of fun to make, then I flew to Europe to promote *Angels & Insects*.

The next thing in my diary was presenting an award with INXS singer Michael Hutchence at the MTV Europe Music Awards in Berlin in November. If I'd known what was going to happen, though, I never would have gone. The next morning a photo appeared in the papers of Michael and me standing together, and it looks like I've got my hand down his trousers. I'd actually had my hand on his arm, but the image was doctored to remove my hand. It was really awful because I loved Michael to bits and had felt bad for him that night because INXS had been so successful, but now there was a new music scene emerging that he wasn't part of. Both of us had to get lawyers involved over the photograph, but the damage was already done. It was pretty shocking and I'm sure

Su and Lou, aka me and the gorgeous Elizabeth Hurley in character on *Kill Cruise*.

Playing Kiefer Sutherland's girlfriend in *Chicago Joe and the Showgirl*. He is one of the funniest men alive.

With Rufus Sewell in *Twenty-One*. It was his first film but
we'd known each other since we were kids.

With Jim Kerr at the Deauville Film Festival, 1991.
I was crazy about him – he's so strong and smart.

Playing Hetty Sorrel in *Adam Bede*, in 1991.

Mum with James, in Los Angeles in 1993. I was there to film *Bitter Harvest* and didn't want to leave her behind.

I loved the role of Eugenia in *Angels & Insects* and am very proud of the movie as a whole. Below with Mark Rylance, my onscreen husband. The costumes were wonderful too.

Hanging with pretty cool folk – Eric Stoltz (*far left*), Illeana Douglas and John Turturro on *Grace of My Heart*. I didn't want to leave the set, I was so happy.

This is one of my favourite photos of Liam, taken on his birthday
– we look like two teenagers at a school disco.

On our honeymoon, sailing around the Amalfi coast.

With Ardal O'Hanlon in *See U Next Tuesday* on the West End stage. Getting up on stage night after night rebuilt my confidence.

Returning to television in the wonderful role of Sadie King on *Emmerdale*. I'm a bitchy blonde man-eater.

After *Emmerdale* I played
Faye Morton on *Holby* for
four years. A gentler character
but with her own secrets.
Here I'm with Luke Roberts,
my screen husband.
We became good friends.

I was so touched that
viewers voted to keep me
in *Strictly Come Dancing*
until week nine. My partner
Robin Windsor was brilliant
and so supportive.

In the past few years I've felt the happiest I've ever been
and I'm excited about all the future holds.

there are still lots of people who think the photo was real.

On the night of the awards I was walking back to my table when I felt someone tap me on the back, and when I turned round it was Liam Gallagher.

'Oh God, how are you?' I said.

'I'm all right. How are you?' he replied.

'I'm good, I'm good,' I said before taking my seat. A bit later I went to the hospitality bar with a couple of the people from my table and Liam was there.

'You're too beautiful to be married,' he said.

'What?' I shouted because I couldn't quite hear him above the music.

'You're too beautiful to be married,' he repeated.

'Well, you need glasses so—' And before I could say any more, he'd disappeared with a woman!

14

Cool Britannia

I next crossed paths with Liam at the end of December 1995, while I was up in Manchester appearing on a Saturday night TV show called *Pyjama Party* to promote *Angels & Insects*. It was a slightly bizarre chat show hosted by Katie Puckrik, where members of the audience dressed in pyjamas. Steve Dagger and my close friend and make-up artist Jackie Hamilton-Smith were with me. Jackie had some friends in the city, so she suggested we hook up with them at a bar after the show.

Most of the time I'm really boring after a job and just go home to bed. 'Oh, come on, Patsy!' said Jackie. 'Come out, it'll be fun.'

To be honest, I probably needed to have a bit of fun. And now that things were over with Jim, I wanted to pick up my social life again. 'OK, I'm in!' I said.

We arranged to meet Jackie's friends at a hotel, and when we walked into the bar there was a group of about fifteen people sitting around a table, and one them was

Liam. We decided to go on to another bar in the city, but I wanted to pop to the ladies' first, so I asked where it was and Liam got up from his chair. 'If you walk through there you'll see a sign like that,' he said, standing with his arms out to the side like the sign on a loo door. 'That's what you want to look out for.'

It was really funny.

When I got back, we left to go on to the next bar, and on the way there one of Liam's friends said to me quietly, 'You know the kid likes you.'

'Um, well a) I think I'm like five years older than Liam, and b) Don't be ridiculous!' I replied, laughing. Liam had just turned twenty-three and I was about to be twenty-eight in March.

But all night Liam kept moving seats so he could sit next to me, although he didn't say very much.

I think Steve Dagger, who had his manager's hat on, must have had his heart in his mouth watching the whole thing unfold. Eventually, it was time to go home, but when we were walking back the group got split up and Liam went one way and I went the other. Again!

On the walk back to the hotel I said to Jackie, 'That was a fun night, wasn't it? Liam's a lovely guy.'

Then when we got to our hotel there was a message for us at reception, inviting us to Liam's hotel. But as we were making our way over to their hotel, Liam and his friends were on their way to ours, so we missed each other again.

'Look, come on, this is ridiculous,' Steve eventually said, losing patience. 'I think the best thing to do is call it a night and head back to the hotel.'

I'm pretty sure he wanted to get me out of Manchester as quickly as possible, because every move Liam made at that time ended up in the tabloids, and Jim and I hadn't officially announced that we'd separated. 'Yeah, you're right,' I agreed. But as we were walking into our hotel, Liam and his friends were walking out.

'There you are!' Liam said. 'I've been looking for you.' So everyone trooped back in to have a drink at the bar.

Liam and I ended up going for a walk along the canals, and he stopped to give me a kiss. It reminded me of the kind of thing I'd done as a teenager, and the excitement you feel after that first kiss.

I thought Liam was a good-looking guy, but I was quite surprised I was on his radar. After I'd done the *Dazed & Confused* shoot with Rankin and Katie Grand in New York, I did an interview for the magazine with Jefferson Hack, and when he'd asked me what music I was into, I'd said I liked the Oasis album *Definitely Maybe*. And I'd added that if I were a teenage girl, I would definitely have Liam Gallagher's poster on my wall. I'd forgotten I'd even said it, but apparently Liam had read it.

Like Jim, there was something familiar about Liam when I met him – maybe it's got something to do with his Celtic looks. Both Jim and Liam reminded me of the Irish boys I'd grown up seeing at mass on Sunday and the boys I grew up with on the estate, who threw rocks at my hat! I understood where they came from and felt an affinity with their backgrounds. I've always been attracted to self-made people.

But Liam was very young and I could also see the temptations surrounding him. Having been married to someone who was very successful in the music world, I wasn't naive about how intoxicating it can be – and it was all new to Liam.

After our first kiss that night, I said goodbye to him, and the next day I travelled back home to London. I didn't really expect to hear from him again, in fact I was doing a shoot for Italian *Marie Claire* that week, and Steve turned up and said, 'Have you heard anything from Manchester?'

'No, I haven't,' I replied. 'Look, it was a really fun night. We pulled each other and had a kiss, but it's probably got trouble written all over it, so I'm happy just being a fan of the band.'

Two hours later my phone rang and it was Liam. 'I'm coming to London,' he said.

'Right, when's your train getting in?' I replied.

And that was how our relationship started. At the risk

of sounding clichéd, it was a rollercoaster ride from that moment on.

I remember being at the Groucho Club with Liam on our first date and Gary Kemp came over to say hello.

'How are you, Patsy? I didn't realize you'd split up with Jim,' he said.

'Yeah, but we're still good friends and we've got an amazing kid,' I said. 'But you know what? I'm never getting married again,' I added, laughing.

I'd thought Liam was engrossed in a conversation with someone else at the time, but he turned round and said, 'What? You're never getting married again?'

'No, darling, I'm not. Look, it's been twice!' I said, laughing again.

Then on our second date at the Steeles pub in Primrose Hill, he suddenly said, 'I want to have a kid; if I have a girl I want to call her Melody, and if it's a boy, Lennon.'

It was very romantic, but there was a part of me that couldn't believe he wanted to be with me because he was so young and he had the world at his feet. I went round to see Chrissie not long after Liam and I started seeing each other and although she adored Liam she said, 'Patsy, you do realize he's gorgeous and his band's about to be the biggest thing in rock 'n' roll. There will be so much temptation coming his way, how could he not screw everybody!'

Jim and I had made a promise to each other that if either of us met someone else we'd tell each other straight away and that we'd make our separation public, so on 17 January 1996, we released a joint statement announcing that our marriage was over. It was all very grown-up.

Career-wise things were great for me at the time. Later in January I attended a screening of *Angels & Insects* at BAFTA in Los Angeles, then I spent a few days in the US doing promotion for the movie, including an interview on CNN. At the start of February I went to Dublin for more promotional work at the Irish Film Festival, and to appear on *The Late Late Show*, and on 9 January the movie opened in LA, Toronto and San Francisco to very good reviews. And I was also nominated for the *Evening Standard* Best Actress award for the movie, but I was pipped to the post by Kristin Scott Thomas. The awards were televised and one of my friends said it was hilarious seeing me so demure and 'thespianed up' because the following week I attended the Brits with Liam, rocking a completely different look in a suede mini-dress and some boots given to me by Tom Ford for Gucci.

The Brits on 19 February was the first time Liam and I were seen together at an event. The press had a field day over us being an item, but that was just the start of the tabloid storm that became a feature of our lives over the next few years. It was a crazy night and Oasis, who were all blitzed, won everything – best album, best group and best video.

That night, Liam lent across the table and said, 'Do you want to come back to mine and help me pack?' He was about to go to America with the band, so he needed to go back to his mum's in Manchester to collect some of his things. James was with Jim, so I said, 'Yeah, of course.'

There was a big MTV party after the awards, but Liam didn't want to go, so we just went back to his hotel. Over the years we disappeared on our own a lot after gigs and events. I remember there being a big party after the Earl's Court gigs in 1997 and someone asked the photographer Jill Furmanovsky, who used to follow the band around a lot, 'Oh, are Patsy and Liam not here?' and she said, 'No, they wouldn't be caught dead in this environment.'

The truth was, we'd often go straight home and have spaghetti hoops on toast! Don't get me wrong, we had our rock 'n' roll moments, but more often than not we lived a very pedestrian, suburban sort of existence. And we had a genuine bond – we just clicked on every level.

The day after the Brits, Liam took me to Manchester to meet his mum, Peggy, for the first time. She is an amazing woman, and she became like a mother to me over the years, as well as being wonderful with James, too.

When I first saw the Gallagher house in Burnage, it felt so similar to where I'd grown up in Hounslow. As

Liam opened the front door, Peggy was coming down the stairs, and I immediately noticed how young she looked and how sparkly her eyes were. We started chatting away to each other and then Liam put his arm around me and gave me a kiss in front of Peggy and his brother Paul. It felt like the most natural thing in the world, and it was lovely to be with him away from the circus surrounding the band. Up until that point things had blown a bit hot and cold because there was always so much going on in Liam's life – Oasis were at the height of their fame and success at the time.

That night we got fish and chips, got into bed and watched the Brits on telly. I couldn't get my head round gravy and chips, though. It's such a northern thing. It has to be salt and vinegar for me!

We went back to London the next day and Liam flew to the States, while I stayed at the house in St John's Wood with James. It was difficult being separated from Liam at such an early stage in our relationship and I really missed him. He had a beard at the time, which I liked because I thought girls might not be so attracted to him! I'd say, 'Yeah, keep the beard, it's a good look.' But it was impossible. He was gorgeous, with or without the facial hair.

When Liam was away, Jim came over to see James and the three of us went for a walk in a little park near the house. While we were walking, Jim put his arm around me – we were still good friends and it was just an instinctive gesture. Of course, someone photographed us and the pictures appeared in the tabloids the next day, along with stories saying that Jim and I had got back together. I called Peggy straight away and told her it was all nonsense and that Jim and I were just mates.

I appeared on Chris Evans's show *TFI Friday* soon after that and when I walked on to the set I jumped up and kissed a poster of Liam that was on the wall, and it was the first time I talked publicly about him. Then a couple of days later I did a shoot with Corrine Day for the cover of *Tatler* before flying to New York to appear on *The David Letterman Show* to promote *Angels & Insects*, which was the number-one independent film in the States at the time.

After New York, James and I went to Barbados and my friend Jackie Hamilton-Smith and the lovely Robbie Williams, who she was dating at the time (she's now married to the actor Sean Pertwee), decided to come out and meet us. Andy Coulson, who was a journalist working for the *Sun* at the time, was there too. Oasis was a big thing for *Sun* readers, so he always seemed to be around, and was forever calling Steve trying to find things out.

In March, I flew back to New York to appear on Conan O'Brien's show, largely to promote *Angels & Insects*, but we also talked about *Love and Betrayal: The Mia Farrow*

Story, and Steve came over from London to meet me. By coincidence, Oasis were playing a gig in New York the next day, and Steve said to me, 'Where's the after-party?' Being with Spandau in the eighties, he was used to music industry parties at fashionable nightclubs with super-models and lots of champagne.

'Oh, they're going to the pub,' I said, smiling. 'An Irish pub to drink Guinness!'

After Easter I started shooting a German movie called *Human Bomb* – a hostage drama set in Berlin – opposite Jürgen Prochnow, who I'd worked with on *Kill Cruise*. It was a lovely cast and an enjoyable job. And when filming wrapped in May I was due to head to Manchester with Liam, as Oasis were playing a gig at Maine Road, and then afterwards Liam was moving into my house in St John's Wood, which I was really looking forward to.

Before we went to Manchester he bought a Bristol car from a showroom near Olympia. We both used to admire this car every time we drove past the showroom and I'd always say to Liam, 'I love that car. I've always wanted one of those.' So one day we went in and bought it.

It was a beautiful silver classic car from the sixties that looked similar to an Aston Martin, and it had vintage leather seats that smelled just like the ones in the chauf-feur-driven cars that took me to Pinewood Studios when I was five.

The man who owned the showroom looked about two

hundred years old and his name was Anthony Crook. I said to him, 'The car is going to be checked over, right? It's not going to break down on us or anything, is it?'

The guy started laughing and said, 'How could you trust anyone with the name A. Crook, eh?! Ha, ha, ha.' He'd clearly told that joke a few times over the years.

'My God, is he for real?' I whispered to Liam.

Anyway, we bought the car and offered to give Oasis bassist Guigsy and his lovely girlfriend Ruth a lift up to Manchester. They'd just bought kittens, and they brought them along, too, so there was constant miaowing coming from the back seat. Liam didn't drive, which meant I was at the wheel, and we'd barely got onto the M1 when the rear-view mirror fell off and then the indicators stopped working. By the time we finally got to our hotel, I think Guigsy and Ruth were traumatized!

'We're not coming back to London with you in that car. Thanks, but no thanks!' they said.

The day after the show at Maine Road, which was amazing, we went to Peggy's to pack Liam's stuff and take it to the house in St John's Wood. As we were leaving, Peggy, who was standing outside the front door, started to cry. Liam had been travelling a lot with the band, staying in hotels and using his mum's as a base, but now he was flying the nest properly with his girlfriend. Being a mum myself, it broke my heart. In fact, I said to her not so long ago that I wished we'd turned the car round and gone back to get her, so she could have stayed with us in London for a few days or a week or for ever.

In lots of ways Peggy has been a role model for me. She's an inspirational person because she brought up three boys on her own, and they all love and adore her. When a couple gets together I always think it's easier for the girl's mum because she's normally part of the package; it's different for the boy's side of the family. Peggy ended up coming down to London a lot to stay with us, but at that moment it was really sad.

I went out to Los Angeles at the start of June for a whole week of meetings with film studios, but I ended up coming back after a day because I wanted to be at home with Liam. I found it hard at the beginning of our relationship, because when we were together it was as if no one else existed, then he'd walk out the door and, although I knew he'd meant every single word of what he'd just said to me, the minute he left I was in constant turmoil about where he was and what he was up to. I was probably living every sixteen- to twenty-one-year-old girl's fantasy, but in reality it was really tough.

Although there were difficult moments during our first year together, the good far outweighed the bad. One of the best evenings we had was seeing Burt Bacharach sing at the Royal Festival Hall in June. Noel went on stage to perform 'This Guy's In Love With You' with Burt, which was so lovely I wanted to cry. I remember looking over at Liam and it was the most perfect moment. I was wearing a white Bianca Jagger-style trouser suit that Savile Row tailor Richard James had made for me, and Liam had never looked so beautiful in a tweed jacket he'd bought from Harrods on one of our first shopping trips together.

After the show we went backstage and met Burt, which was a dream come true for us because we are huge fans, and Liam and I had our picture taken with him. It was a perfect evening, and then the next day we flew to Capri and spent a week sailing around the Amalfi Coast.

We also had an idyllic holiday on Anguilla, in the Caribbean. I'd never heard of it before we went, but the resort was paradise – secluded villas and white beaches that stretched for miles. It was just heaven. One day Liam and I decided to go into town, which consisted of about three shops and a sleepy bar, where a local reggae musician called Bankie Banx was singing and playing guitar. Bankie recognized Liam and shouted, 'Oasis! Oasis!' Liam decided he wanted to jam with Bankie, so I said I'd drive back to the hotel and come back for him in an hour.

Within five minutes of being back at our villa, though, I thought, I'm going back to get him now, so I jumped into the jeep and started driving back towards town along a deserted dusty road. All of a sudden a figure appeared on the horizon, like Lawrence of Arabia against a backdrop of shimmering heat waves, and as I got closer, I could make out a Mancunian haircut and a very distinctive walk. 'Bloody hell is that . . .? It's Liam!' So I put my foot down and pulled up alongside him.

'I came early because I missed you,' I said.

'I missed you, too, and I wanted to come back,' he replied, jumping into the jeep.

It was very sweet, because although it was a short drive back from town, it was a pretty long walk. Liam did lots of lovely things like that. It's strange looking back at that time. It wasn't without its low points, but I remember it vividly, as if it's in Technicolor. It makes me laugh, it makes me cry, but it's almost as if it happened to someone else.

That summer Jim and I instructed lawyers to start divorce proceedings and Liam proposed to me. We were up north for a boxing match, staying at a lovely hotel in Cheshire, and we were in our room getting ready when Liam turned round and said, 'Will you marry me?' I couldn't believe it. It really was the last thing I expected.

'Of course!' I said without hesitation. I was so madly in love with him. 'Let's not tell anyone, though,' I added. I just wanted to enjoy it without lots of fuss. Guigsy and his missus Ruth were with us on the trip, so of course Liam told them straight away! It was lovely because they were both so happy for us and it was a really special night.

Liam and I went back to our hotel afterwards in a kind of love bubble. The fight had been televised on Sky

Sports and a girlfriend of mine had watched it with her husband. She called me afterwards and said, 'Will you bloody stop kissing that guy! We kept seeing the two of you with your tongues down each other's throats. For God's sake, woman!'

When we got back to London we went to Hatton Garden to pick rings – my mother would have been pleased! Liam got an Irish Claddagh ring in gold with a ruby stone in the shape of the heart. And I got a simple emerald-cut diamond.

We didn't do an announcement, the story just leaked out that we'd got engaged. One afternoon soon afterwards, Liam and I walked round to Gascogne restaurant in St John's Wood hand-in-hand. It's not there any more, but one of my best friends, Grainne, and her husband Andy Fletcher, the keyboard player with Depeche Mode, used to own it, and we'd often go there for Sunday lunch. We wanted to tell them about our engagement and show them our rings.

After lunch we strolled back to the house and there was a photographer outside waiting for us. It was a really warm summer day and I had no make-up on and my hair was in a ponytail, and Liam just looked like a regular guy. The photographer took our picture and it's still one of my favourite photos of Liam and me together – no styling, no hairdressers, no posing. We just look like a young couple in love.

There's another picture I love that was taken on one of Liam's birthdays. I'd had a yellow submarine cake made for him and someone took a photo of us just after he'd cut the cake. We literally look like two teenagers at a school disco; we're both smiling and we look really happy. And we were happy. Those moments were authentic. It's very easy to get a one-dimensional view of a relationship from what you read in the papers.

I remember being at shoots or business meetings with Liam and people would be genuinely surprised by how we were around each other. There was one producer Liam worked with who said, 'Oh my God, you guys really are in love, aren't you?' The trouble was, at that point we'd had a few public spats, and those moments came to define our relationship in the eyes of the press.

One night, shortly after Liam moved in with me, he didn't come home. Peggy was down from Manchester staying with us at the time. One of the staff at the Halcyon called me to say he was in a room there with a group of friends and a well-known model. So I drove over there and booted the door of the hotel room. It was like an IRA drop-off – Liam was pushed out of the room and the door was slammed behind him.

'Fucking hell, Pat, what's going on?' he asked, looking all confused and disorientated.

'You arsehole, Liam. What are you doing? Your mum's staying with us!'

We got into my BMW to go home, but I was so angry I wanted to hit something and I didn't want it to be Liam! So I got out of the car and karate kicked the door. Liam got out wearing one of those Bill and Ben hats.

'Aww, not the car, Patsy,' he said. It was *my* bloody car!

Typically, a photographer had captured the whole thing and, although I wasn't a fan of the tabloids at the time, the headlines the next morning were very funny. My favourite was 'Patsy Cantona-sit!'

But after that it wouldn't have mattered if we'd never rowed again. As far as the media was concerned the die was cast.

Probably the most historic Oasis gigs were the two dates they played in the grounds of Knebworth House in Hertfordshire in August 1996, each one to a massive 150,000 people. The hype and press attention around the shows were extraordinary. It was a huge deal and it was wonderful to be there and see the band in all their glory, playing to all those people.

On the first night I remember Liam and Noel walking up the ramp to the stage and it was almost as if I was watching them in slow motion. There were other guys from the support bands standing at the side of the stage and they all looked awestruck. It was as if Liam and Noel were two kings – we were all fans.

Liam and I ended up getting no sleep at all that night.

We spotted some buggies that were used for transporting people around backstage, so we decided to nick one and take a little trip round the site. Liam drove us out of the backstage area and we were confronted by this sea of litter that went on for miles. It was 3 a.m., so everyone had gone home and it was completely silent. It was actually one of the happiest nights of my life. Liam turned to me and said, 'I want you by my side all the time. I don't want you taking your clothes off in any more shite movies. I want to take care of you and your son.'

We managed to drive off site and the next thing we knew there was a blue flashing light coming towards us.

'Quick, do a U-turn,' I said to Liam.

'I can't do a quick U-turn, Pat, it's a fucking buggy!'

A police officer got out of the patrol car and walked over to us.

'Evening, Mr Gallagher,' he said, at which point I transformed into 'Panto Patsy', which was Liam's name for me when I was being ridiculously polite and overly apologetic.

'Oh, my goodness! We were just so over the moon about the gig we didn't realize we'd gone off site, officer,' I tried to explain. It turned out we'd gone so far off site we were about to join the motorway in our buggy!

'It's not safe for you guys out here,' he said. 'I'll escort you back.' We meekly followed him back to the site.

By the time the first support act started we'd had no sleep at all, so the management found us a motel room close by and we fell into a deep sleep. When we woke up we'd forgotten Liam had to do a gig! It was a mad panic to get there in time and Liam left all his clothes behind. I had this big cashmere sweater, so he said, 'Give us that' and he put it on, and then I blow-dried his hair for him. He looked very cool that night – very Mick Jagger – and he sang like a bird. But I don't think I got any brownie points from the management for keeping him up late with our buggy adventure. I sat at the side of the stage wearing a Seventies-style wide-brimmed hat and Liam dedicated a song to 'The cat in the hat', which was very sweet.

That night, Chrissie came with Yasmin and Natalie, and Liam dedicated 'Live Forever' to Yasmin. I think the reporters were all going crazy trying to work out who Yasmin was and if she was Liam's new girlfriend! There's a great picture that Jill Furmanovsky took of Liam and me in silhouette watching these amazing fireworks at the end of the gig. It was an incredible weekend.

After Knebworth, Oasis embarked on a US tour and I hooked up with Liam again at the MTV awards in New York in September. The next day I had to fly to Los Angeles to attend a screening of *Grace of My Heart* at the Writers Guild and then I had a whole week of studio meetings and promotion. But by the time I'd touched down in LA, it was all over the papers that Oasis had split up and that I was responsible for it, which simply wasn't true.

I did what I had to do in LA and got straight back on a plane to London. Steve Dagger tried to persuade me to stay on for the studio meetings, but I was too worried about all the stuff that was being written about Liam and me and if it would upset him. The band were already back in London hiding out somewhere and I was picked up from Heathrow by two burly security guards who bundled me into a car and did a 360-degree turn before screeching off, trailed by dozens of paparazzi. We even drove straight over the middle of a mini-roundabout!

The media interest in Liam and me went off the scale after that, but in all honesty, I cared way too much about what other people thought of our relationship.

In October, Liam and I were invited to Milan for a Versace menswear show and Liam jumped up on the catwalk and started walking with the models. It was actually very funny, but at the time I was annoyed with him because he left me sitting there like a lemon. Looking back, it didn't matter – I should have laughed it off and let him get on with it – but I was too worried about other people's perceptions. It was partly because the whole world seemed to be examining everything we did under the microscope, but I'd also been in a marriage that was very different to my relationship with Liam. Jim was a good few years older than me, but Liam was still so young – only a couple of years older than my son James is now, which just seems crazy – so I regret worrying about stupid stuff like that.

Donatella was wonderful and clearly didn't give a monkey's about catwalk-gate! We were in Milan for a few days and the next night she invited Liam and me over to her apartment and we had the most phenomenal dinner. We went up in a gilded elevator and her place was just stunning – opulent but not ostentatious – with rose-scented candles burning in every room.

Gianni was there and so was Elton John. I was struggling at the time with all the stuff that was being written about us in the papers – most of which was a load of rubbish – and I remember Elton saying, 'Why are you reading it, Patsy? It doesn't matter if you're the strongest person on the planet, you shouldn't start your day like that. I don't read anything, nothing.'

'It's because I've had to sue over stories in the past,' I explained.

'Yeah, but you have a manager and lawyers who will let you know if something is libellous. Don't read it.'

So from that day onwards I stopped. I pick up a broadsheet now and again and I read the fashion mags, but that's it. I'm not interested in reading about someone's fat bum!

The next morning Donatella – who is without doubt one of the most generous people I've ever met – insisted on sending me off with some beautiful couture dresses.

A dream come true for a fashion addict like me and Versace have continued to be very generous with their clothes to this day.

The following night we went to Gianni's home for a glass of champagne – he was just lovely and so gracious – and then we attended a Mario Testino exhibition and had dinner afterwards. Cars picked us up from Gianni's place to take us to the event, and we were dropped off at a beautiful square in Milan that was lit by candles. Gianni took Donatella's arm and led the way, and Liam and I followed, holding hands. It was just otherworldly – a truly magical night.

At dinner Liam was sitting next to the editor of Italian *Vogue* and Mario, who was on my right, kept saying things like, 'I want to photograph you both naked!'

Liam was like, 'Awright, mate. I'm sat here with a knife and fork in front of me and you're saying you want to photograph my missus nude?' Everyone at the table broke into laughter. They thought he was adorable.

'Can you just ease him in gently, please?' I laughed.

A dish of quail's eggs came round and Liam took one look at it and said, 'I'm not fucking eating that,' and Donatella said, 'Me neither, darling. I don't like this,' just to make him feel at ease. It was a class move.

Liam charmed the socks off everyone that evening, and Donatella absolutely loved him. We all came from very ordinary backgrounds and I think that was one of the things that bonded us.

That autumn I did a few magazine photo shoots – Mario Testino for *The Face*, the cover of British *Vogue* and then, on 12 November, Liam and I shot the 'London Swings Again!' cover of *Vanity Fair* at the Hempel Hotel in Bayswater with a great photographer called Lorenzo Agius.

I guess it's now regarded as something of an iconic image – with the two of us lying on Union Jack bed sheets – because it became synonymous with the whole Britpop thing, but it was a pretty unremarkable shoot. Sorry to disappoint! It's a great picture, but there was no Sixties magic dust in the air.

The magazine held a party afterwards as a kind of celebration of London and all things British. We met Mick Jagger there and he invited us to his Christmas party at his house in Richmond. When we arrived I was desperate for the loo, so Mick pointed me in the right direction and Liam – putting on his best Mick Jagger voice – said, 'Awright, Mick. Don't try it on with the missus.'

We had a lovely time, but as the party was winding down, Liam said to Mick, 'I'm here because of "Jumping Jack Flash" and you're a fucking dinosaur.' He was being funny and Mick was very good-humoured about it, but I was dying inside and went into full Pantomime Patsy mode, steering the conversation on to Marianne Faithfull and what she was like.

I think doing shoots together like the *Vanity Fair* cover stoked the fire a little bit when it came to generating interest from the tabloids. You've got to expect it if you agree to do that kind of thing, but it's hard to get the balance right. Liam also invited it in many ways, as he didn't have rigid boundaries with the media like Jim and Chrissie had. But he had very strong views about the fans that camped outside the house. 'These kids are buying our music and coming to our concerts,' he said. 'They shouldn't ring the bell but if they want a fucking auto-graph, they can have one.'

I remember one of the first times Liam and I had to face the press as a couple. We were flying back into Heathrow and there was a group of paparazzi waiting for us before we hit customs, and my first boyfriend Darren Stone's dad was one of them.

'Hello, Patsy,' he said.

'Hello, Mr Stone, how are you?' I replied, stopping in front of him so he could get a picture of us.

'How's Darren?' I asked as he clicked away.

'He's really good, thanks.'

'Great, will you send him my love?'

'Always do, Patsy, thanks.'

'Thank you, Mr Stone, you have a nice day – and see you soon!'

The look on Liam's face was priceless. 'Mr Stone?' he said, clearly wondering how I'd got to be on such good terms with a paparazzo.

'Yeah, Darren's dad,' I replied, grinning.

15

A Wedding, a House and a New Baby

Liam and I had planned our wedding for February 1997, but one morning, about a week before the big day, we looked out of the window of our rented house in St John's Wood to see an entire film crew outside. We couldn't believe it. *The Big Breakfast* TV show was being broadcast from the street in front of our house and there were girls wearing wedding dresses getting out of a limousine – it was a circus!

We turned on the TV and it was surreal, watching it all going on while we were inside getting James ready to go to school. 'So this is the dress that Patsy could be wearing,' said one of the presenters. It was completely nuts, and Liam and I just looked at each other and said, 'We can't do this.'

We had about ten boxes of Cristal champagne in the hallway, ready to go to the venue in Knightsbridge, but now the press had discovered the date of the wedding, we felt we had no option but to call it off.

It was literally days before, so it was a nightmare having to cancel everything, and it was embarrassing, too. Predictably, the tabloid headlines all screamed, 'Liam's got cold feet!' Great.

After that we went on a crusade to get married privately. In those days you couldn't marry in a hotel like you can now, so we ended up begging the people at Westminster Register Office at Marylebone Town Hall to marry us at 7 a.m. on 7 April.

It was a lovely spring morning and I wore a Lolita Lempicka dress and a Dolce & Gabbana summer coat, both in Man City blue! We didn't invite anyone to the wedding – just our witnesses Colin Radcliffe and a guy called Kevin who cut my hair at Michael John (I was on a break from Daniel Galvin, who'd been cutting my hair since I was fourteen).

After the ceremony we went to Blake's hotel in Kensington, where we were staying for a couple of days, for a fry-up and champagne. But we only managed to keep the story under wraps for a few hours and it was on the six o'clock news that night. It was great, though – we felt like two renegades. The big wedding we had planned would have been wrong, and I was glad that in the end it was just the two of us, so thank you *Big Breakfast*!

When we told our friends and family we'd got married,

a few people were concerned for us because they knew we'd just come off a big row (it must be the fiery Irish genes).

The trouble was that Liam would still occasionally go AWOL, leaving me at home to pace the floor. When he would eventually walk through the door he'd always be sporting a new pair of sunglasses that someone had given him. And I'd always pull them straight off.

'Not the bins, Pat, not the bins!' he'd plead.

I would take some satisfaction in snapping the glasses in half!

The house we were renting at the time belonged to Simon Cowell's brother and Liam and I broke the bed, which Simon always reminds me about when I see him. And we weren't jumping on it – it was broken the good old-fashioned way! The *Sun* actually bought the bed because Simon's brother was selling up and they ran a competition to win it.

That house had been costing us a fortune, so when the lease was up we moved into a tiny terraced house nearby, which Noel and his wife, Meg, had been renting, as they were about to move into their beautiful big place in Primrose Hill.

I honestly think we spent our happiest times in that little house. It was just Liam, James and me, and the only other person who visited regularly was our cleaning lady, who came in twice a week for a couple of hours. Life was simple.

Then we bought a big house on Elsworthy Road in Primrose Hill that needed renovating. I was fearless back in those days. I remember Liam went on tour while we were having the loft converted and there was tarpaulin and scaffolding for about six weeks while I was there alone with James, and everyone knew where we lived.

It was a fantastic place – my friend Angela Radcliffe's husband Colin did it for us, and we had everything we could possibly want. But all of a sudden we needed a lot more help and more people around us to run the place. It was a shame because our lives started to get overtaken by that kind of thing, but a posh house and lots of money won't make you happy if you lose sight of what's really important.

We employed a housekeeper and other staff, but I found it hard to hand over my home to strangers. I'm not that comfortable with people doing everything for me – I'm almost apologetic! I have friends who were born into money, and for them it's entirely normal, but that wasn't the case for Liam and me with our backgrounds. The dynamic in our home changed, and it was an adjustment for all of us after the lovely cocoon of our tiny terraced house.

Then there was the press onslaught every time we walked out the front door to go to the supermarket or do the school run with James. A photographer got a picture of us with me carrying the shopping bags and Liam walking behind with James. And I was made to look like I was spineless and downtrodden. After that Liam made sure he carried the shopping! I remember a friend saying to me, 'Well, why do you do the weekly food shop? You shouldn't be doing that. Get someone else to do it.'

'Why shouldn't I do it?' I replied indignantly. But in the end I did stop – it just wasn't worth it. Even though I didn't buy the papers and gossip mags, I would walk past them in the supermarket, and I couldn't help taking a peek at the headlines – according to the press I was always crying or I was too thin or I looked depressed. Stupidly, I let it get to me.

From the outside it probably looked as if we were out every night and part of some big scene, but as a couple, Liam and I were actually really ordinary. One night, not long after we moved in together, we went to the local swing park and sat on the swings chatting. On another occasion we sat on the kerb outside Abbey Road Studios talking about the Beatles until 3 a.m. We kept ourselves to ourselves. Yes, there were social occasions when we'd party like everyone else, but most of the time we were at home with James.

We didn't socialize with the band much either – when you're working that closely with your brother, as Liam was with Noel, you don't want to spend all of your downtime with each other. Everyone did their own thing, really.

I remember we bumped into Pete Townshend in an airport once and got chatting to him – we are both massive Who fans – and he said to us, 'So where's everyone else? Is it just the two of you?' I think he expected us to have a big entourage.

'Yeah, it's just me and Patsy,' replied Liam.

'Wow, that's good. That's really good,' he said, clearly surprised.

Liam and I did go on some amazing holidays together, but other than that we lived really normally. The only thing that wasn't normal was the massive intrusion into our privacy. I accept that it's hard to complain if you've shot a cover for *Vanity Fair* together, but it doesn't make it any easier to deal with.

I couldn't get used to having Oasis fans camped outside the house 24/7 either. They were always writing on the wall outside the house, so I had to get it sand-blasted every week! Looking back it was hilarious – they'd write things like, 'Patsy is a fat ugly cow', and, 'Liam, remember our night in Brazil? Call me!'

When it came to work, I'd lost a bit of momentum over the previous few months. I went to Los Angeles for ten days that summer for meetings about new projects, but to be honest, I just wanted to be back at home in London. My heart wasn't really in it. Then, in the autumn, I was offered a part in US sitcom *Friends*, which was one of the biggest and most successful shows on the planet at that point. My American agency at the time was Gersh, which is known for its power in the TV world, and *Friends* was an offer you didn't pass up. The idea was that I'd come into the show as a guest for three months, playing Ross's new girlfriend Emily, then, if all went well, there was the possibility of it becoming a regular part. I think the show's bosses were fans of *Absolute Beginners* and *Lethal Weapon*, which is how the offer came about.

That type of show is shot over the course of a week – you start the table reads on a Monday morning, then more jokes and dialogue changes might get written into the script, then there are rehearsals, which build up to a full rehearsal, and then you shoot as live on a Friday. Everyone who worked on the show was absolutely lovely, and the actors were so good – so polished and sleek – but my mind was elsewhere.

Steve Dagger was due to come out and see the show being recorded on the Friday, but before he had the chance, I rang him to say I didn't want to do it any more and that I was coming back to London.

When you join an American TV show, regardless of whether you're doing two episodes or twenty, they have an option to sign you up for five years, so they can tie you in if things are going well. And when you guest on a show like that where people have been working together for years, you have to be a very strong person to go in and do your job. But at that point I felt quite fragile and afraid of everything.

I just couldn't commit to it. I knew I needed to be at home if my relationship with Liam was going to survive. It was already a struggle keeping things together with his touring schedule, and if James and I had moved to LA – even for three months – it would have fractured everything. I'd learned from my time with Dan and Jim that absence does not make the heart grow fonder, it simply makes you grow apart.

No one forced me into pulling out of *Friends* – it was my decision. I was madly in love with Liam and I chose my marriage over the job. The show's bosses were fantastic and understood my reasons for leaving and, luckily, English actress Helen Baxendale was in town and could replace me in the role straight away. But my agents at Gersh weren't very happy about it, and I guess I can't blame them, so in the end I felt I had to leave. Whatever they did, they were never going to get me anything as good as a role on *Friends* – that was the Holy Grail in the TV world at the time.

I was offered a part in a TV mini-series in January 1998 about the Mafia called *The Last Don II*, for CBS. The first series had been very successful and it didn't require a big time commitment from me, so I decided to take the role. It was also being filmed in Toronto while Liam was on the

North American leg of the *Be Here Now* world tour with Oasis. We hooked up in Toronto, but I was doing night shoots so had to sleep all day and Liam, being a brilliant stepdad, took James to see *Titanic*. During the movie Liam told me he was desperate for a pee, but couldn't leave James because it was at a crucial moment in the film. They were like two girls! When they came home I was getting up for work and they were both like, 'Ah, it was so sad. It was the most amazing movie.' Liam was so great with James – he still calls him Jimbo or Jimmy to this day.

But Liam couldn't stick around because he was off to tour the US before heading on to Japan, Australia, New Zealand and South America. It was relentless and it felt like he was always on the road, and with James at school, there was no way I could follow him all over the globe. After weeks of being inseparable he'd walk out the door and be gone for weeks and it was as if we weren't married. I knew full well the temptation that was thrown his way and inevitably it caused huge problems between us and we broke up for a month. I went to stay with my friend Grainne Fletcher, then I moved into a flat I owned in Palace Court, which I'd bought off Jim.

My way of dealing with the split was to throw myself back into my work. My relationship with Liam had probably started to affect my career. In the acting world, the perception of me changed after we became a couple. I was suddenly seen as this tabloid creature, and it diluted who I was. Years before, joining Eighth Wonder and being seen as a wannabe pop star wiped out years of worthy acting roles, and I think my marriage had a similar effect. Plus Oasis and Liam were such a force of nature that I was always going be in their shadow.

So in the autumn of 1998, while Liam toured the world, I made three movies. The first was a British comedy called *Janice Beard* with Rhys Ifans, in which I played the glamorous bitchy boss of a typing pool. I also played Angie Best in a George Best biopic, and I made a movie with Richard Chamberlain called *The Pavilion*, which was filmed in North Carolina. It wasn't a wonderful movie – I think it was shocking actually – but something wonderful happened while I was filming it. Liam and I had got back together, so he came out to visit me in the States, and while he was there I became pregnant. Even though things had been difficult between us over the previous few months, we were both beyond thrilled with the news. Having a baby together was always something we had really wanted.

Because of my pregnancy, work took a back seat as 1999 got underway. I felt ill pretty much all the time. At least with James the terrible morning sickness disappeared after twelve weeks, but I was sick all the way through my second pregnancy and had constant heartburn. My baby bump also got big very quickly, and I looked about five months pregnant from really early on.

When I was about halfway through my pregnancy, I went to Cannes with Liam, who was recording an album there with Oasis, and attended a *Janice Beard* screening and party and I wore a silver Versace dress that Donatella had made for me. On the work front, though, that was pretty much it.

Liam and I found out we were having a boy during one of my last scans. They hadn't been able to tell us at our previous appointment because of the position the baby was lying in. I'll never forget Liam punching the air and dancing around the obstetrician's office, shouting, 'Yes! It's a boy!' He was overjoyed, and of course we'd already picked a name – Lennon.

I went into labour about six weeks early, when I was on my own one day at the house on Elsworthy Road – Liam was recording and James was at school. I asked James's nanny to pick him up from school, then I called Liam to tell him to meet me at the Portland Hospital as soon as he could, and he was there at lightning speed. This time, my obstetrician recommended a Caesarean, because the baby was early and he wanted to get him out quickly. And when Lennon was placed in my arms on 13 September 1999, he was just gorgeous – absolutely tiny at six and a half pounds, but perfect in every way. Liam and I were delighted. The next day one of the nurses showed me the newspapers and there was a picture of him standing outside the hospital with a huge grin on his face and the headline, 'It's a boy!' I already knew Liam was going to be a great father because of how he'd been with James, so I never had any doubts on that score.

When James came to the hospital with his nanny later that day he was furious that I hadn't waited for him to get back from school, because he was so desperate to see his little brother.

Because he was born early, Lennon had to stay in an incubator at the Portland's special care baby unit for about three weeks. He looked like he was in this little fish tank, and we'd put a Man City strip with 'Lennon' on the back in there with him. James had had a Celtic one with 'James Kerr' on it.

My plan was to stay with Lennon and breastfeed him as Liam was due to go back on tour. He didn't want to leave us, but I insisted – he'd made a commitment and he had to work.

Lennon is such a blessing and has brought me such joy. He was an incredibly good baby from the start and rarely cried. I had a maternity nurse booked prior to having him, but after three weeks she said, 'You don't need me any more.' I was more experienced and confident second time around – I'd been so young when I'd had James and I didn't have a clue what I was doing!

Whenever I think of Lennon, I just picture his smile – it lights up the room. He was always giggling when he was a baby and he's still such a happy person, as well as being a very polite, good boy. He reminds me of my mum in lots of ways. Both my sons look exactly like their dads. When James was born, Yasmin and Natalie came to the hospital with Chrissie to see him, and they brought a photo of Yasmin when she was a newborn to show me how much she looked like James. I really am very lucky to have James and Lennon – they're both adorable. Liam obviously chose the name Lennon after John Lennon, and Yoko sent us a beautiful card that read, 'To Lennon, welcome to the world, love love, love, Yoko', along with blankets and clothes from their babywear line – I had no idea there was a range of baby merchandise! Yoko is such a strong and interesting woman, and I was very touched that she'd thought of us. It was incredibly generous.

16

Dark Days and New Beginnings

By the summer of 2000, my marriage had hit the rocks again, and this time it was beyond repair. So I took the boys, moved out of Elsworthy Road and into the small flat I owned in Palace Court, Bayswater, until I could find a bigger place for the three of us. It was overwhelmingly sad, particularly as Lennon wasn't even a year old, and I couldn't help feeling that I'd failed.

I regretted walking out on Liam almost immediately and made a brief attempt at a reconciliation. We'd split up before I'd become pregnant with Lennon and had got back together, but this time we were both in very different places. I think he had moved on while I still had feelings for him, and my heart was broken into a million pieces when we split up for good.

It really saddens me to have failed so miserably with my boys' dads. Jim swept me off my feet. I thought I was worldly and well-travelled when I met him but really I was out of my depth. He taught me so much, and he's a wonderful father and a great friend. He is and always has been strong for so many people. With Liam, in many ways it was the perfect relationship I'd dreamed about when I was sixteen. On our first dates we just stayed up all night talking and sharing secrets. We even dressed the same – in Gucci duffel coats and desert boots – a bit like teenagers. One of the first things he bought me was a T-shirt from Dublin airport – he didn't have much cash at the time. I kept it and still treasure it, just as I treasure the bottle of Penhaligon's rose perfume from Jim.

At the time I remember listening to the No Doubt song 'Don't Speak', which is about a break-up, and that opening line about always being together just struck a chord with me because that was how Liam and I had been. When he wasn't on tour we were joined at the hip and he always wanted to be with me – even if I was going to the supermarket for a pint of milk! He was very protective and loving. When we were together there were fireworks, and a chemistry that lasted to the end, but I guess it just wasn't meant to be.

I'm not naive – I'd heard all the rumours about his womanizing and I knew exactly what was going on behind my back, but I want to focus on the good times because there were plenty of them. And I want Lennon to pick up this book and know how much we wanted him and that he was born out of love, and to see that there's another side to the tabloid stories.

It would be all too easy to blame Liam for everything, but the truth is, I made mistakes, too. In fact, I'm happy to admit that I made mistakes in all my marriages. When a couple breaks up, there's usually fault on both sides. I had to take a long, hard look at myself. I changed a lot after my mum died – her death broke me and I desperately wanted Jim and then Liam to love me the way she had. But no one could replace that unconditional love – and it would be insulting to Mum's memory to think they could. I see that clearly now but at the time I was looking for someone to put me back together. That must have been hard for Liam, and in hindsight, I put way too much pressure on him.

His intentions were always good, and to his credit, he wanted to marry me and have a family, and he took on James when he was just twenty-three. A lot of guys wouldn't have been interested in taking on the responsibility of being stepfather at that age, but Liam was and is incredible with James – in fact, he gave him his first proper job with his clothing company Pretty Green.

Looking back, it was just an impossible situation because of what was on offer to Liam when Oasis took off – he had everything handed to him on a plate. I was five years older with two marriages behind me, so we approached our relationship very differently. I also think the people around us both were concerned about us being together, and at times it felt like we didn't have a lot of support in either camp, except from Peggy.

And it's bloody hard being married to a rock star! I watched the Martin Scorsese documentary about the life of George Harrison, and was struck by his second wife Olivia saying that when she was asked about the secret to a successful marriage in the music industry, her reply was always, 'Don't get divorced.' I thought, Wow, she's wise, it really is that simple – if you want to stay married, don't get divorced!

It's very hard for these guys to come off stage after so much adulation and go back to their wife and a normal life. If they leave a wet towel on the floor, you're like, 'Why can't you pick up the bloody towel?' Well, it's because they've never had to – they've always had someone to do it for them. The comedown must be immense.

I honestly think the fans get the best out of really gifted musicians – on stage is when they're at their most glorious. When I was fifteen, I was the girl in the audience at Haircut 100 gigs thinking, I wish I was his girlfriend, but now I'm older, and hopefully a bit wiser.

I had a bit of an epiphany when I went to a Paul McCartney concert after Liam and I split up. I was much happier just being a fan, and I felt so relieved that I wasn't going home with someone from the band! I had a great time, I sang along, and then I went home at the end of the night without having to do a runner. It was wonderful!

The months following the break-up with Liam were hard, though. I was on my own again with two children so I had to keep it together for them, and I had to rebuild my life. We'd put the house on Elsworthy Road up for sale, and I found an apartment to rent which was close to a good school for James.

I also had to try to pick up my career again, and I knew it was going to be harder now that James was settled in school and Lennon was only a baby. I took a really small part in an Allison Anders movie called *Things Behind the Sun*, then I made an indie flick in Ireland called *Bad Karma* – that pretty much sums it up – opposite Patrick Muldoon, in which I play a mental patient who believes she's the reincarnated lover of Jack the Ripper! Then the year ended with *Aladdin* at New Wimbledon Theatre alongside Martin Clunes, Griff Rhys Jones and Julian Clary, which was a one-off performance recorded for ITV.

As 2001 kicked off, so did divorce proceedings. Liam and I appointed lawyers and we had to deal with all the usual difficult stuff associated with divorce. At least I knew that Lennon was always happy to spend time with his dad, and his happiness at the end of the day was what was most important. Liam was with Nicole Appleton who was a terrific stepmother. Lennon adores her, and we've become good friends over the years. She and Liam had a baby boy, Gene, giving Lennon another half-brother he loves.

In February I appeared on the cover of *Arena* magazine. I'd done a very glam and pretty provocative shoot with Uli Weber after splitting up with Liam. I appear topless inside the magazine and I had breast implants at the time, which I subsequently had removed. Uli is a great photographer and *Arena* was a respected title, but I didn't know who I was at that point and I hate the photos. Everything I did in the last eighteen months of marriage – including having implants – was about trying to get Liam's attention and I made poor choices. Part of me thinks I did that shoot to try to make Liam regret our break-up. But looking back, I don't recognize that person – it feels like it was another girl. Even though lots of actresses were doing quite sexy magazine shoots at the time, I feel bad for my kids that I did those pictures.

It ended up being a very busy year in terms of work. In April I accepted a small part in a US comedy called *Who's Your Daddy?*, which was hyped a lot at the time, but sadly didn't amount to much. On the positive side, I was still being offered roles in the States, and I was glad that I'd been able to establish myself over there, because it's not an easy thing for a British actress to do.

Towards the end of May I went to Vancouver to shoot a TV show called *Strange Frequency*, which is a bit like *Tales of the Unexpected*. It was around this time that I noticed I'd started to put on weight. One day I was going to meet Angela Radcliffe for an early dinner at Gascogne, but I called her at the last minute to say I couldn't come.

'Why?' she asked.

'Well, because none of my clothes fit me,' I explained.

'That's ridiculous, Patsy, I only saw you last week.'

'I'm telling you, nothing fits me.'

And that was the start of four of the most awful years of my life. I was so confused about this body I'd suddenly acquired. It wasn't vanity, I just didn't understand why I'd suddenly ballooned. I was thirty-three and I didn't recognize myself any more. It honestly felt like I'd been taken out of one body and put in another.

I'd always hovered around the eight stone mark, give or take a couple of pounds, but when I stepped on the scales, the needle crept up to nearly twelve stone. It was completely shocking and I hadn't been aware of it at all – it felt like it happened overnight and I didn't understand how.

Up until that point I could eat whatever I wanted without gaining weight – it was just something I never had to think about. And if I did put on a few extra pounds, like I did on holiday with Selena before *Absolute Beginners*, I lost the weight without any effort.

Suddenly, Linda Evangelista's words of warning about my metabolism changing after thirty began ringing in my ears!

'You know you're not going to be able to eat like that after you're thirty?' she'd warned, watching me tucking into cake.

'I'm just lucky,' I'd replied dismissively, going for another mouthful.

'Honey, overnight God flips a switch and it all changes,' she'd cautioned, wagging her finger. How right she was!

So I started training like an athlete, but no matter what I did I couldn't seem to shift the weight. I think my body was in recovery from all those years of running on adrenaline. I'd been in a state of high anxiety my entire life. Since I was five years old I'd worried myself sick about everyone and everything – if my mum was going to die, Dad's trip to 'South Africa', whether or not I'd accidentally blurt out something about his criminal background, and more recently the stress of trying to keep my relationship going. When all those worries were gone, I honestly believe my body just shifted down the gears and stuck in neutral, and I gained a whole load of weight – 'emotional weight' from years of trying to keep it all together. I'm an emotional eater – I eat when I'm happy and I eat when I'm sad. In the past my metabolism had been able to deal with it, but not any more.

That summer I took on a couple of Brit roles – a guest slot in an episode of BBC1 hospital drama *Casualty*, and I was also cast in a movie set in the north-east called *The One and Only*, in which I had a very glam role, though

I battled with the costumes I was meant to wear because I'd put on so much weight. There was a lovemaking scene, which I wasn't comfortable with because of how I felt about my body. I remember during one scene the producer came over to me and said, 'Just hold your stomach in a bit in this shot, Patsy.' I guess she was trying to be helpful, and she was nice about it, but it was awful.

They did a group shot of the cast and I remember Steve Dagger saying afterwards that his heart was in his mouth because he knew what was coming. When the photo was released the tabloids had a field day, and that's when the whole 'Fatsy Patsy' and 'Patsy Scoffs-it' thing started. I knew better than anyone what had happened to my body, but I didn't need to be told in such a cruel way.

One day I was in my flat when a particularly tenacious tabloid journalist rang the buzzer and asked to speak to me.

'OK, I'm coming down,' I said. I knew talking to him was the quickest way to get rid of him but there was no way I was going to let him into the flat.

'Do you want to come and sit in the car with the driver?' he asked when I opened the front door. My first thought was, I bet this is being taped!

He produced some photographs of me out running. 'Can you tell me who the father is?' he asked.

'Um, what are you talking about?'

'Well, look at the pictures,' he said.

'Look, I've just gained some weight,' I said truthfully.

'Patsy, honestly, who's the father?'

'There is no father. I'm not pregnant, I've got a sweat belt on!'

The conversation ended there and I went back upstairs. I never got used to the press ringing my doorbell in search of a story. Even if it's your job to find things out, I believe everyone has a moral obligation to treat people the way they'd want to be treated themselves.

After that, all the same publications that had criticized me for being too thin a few years before started having a go at me for being fat. It's bullying and it's disgusting. I would never, ever make someone's size an issue. And although I wasn't buying the newspapers and gossip mags, it was hard to avoid seeing some of the stuff because it stared out at me from every corner shop and supermarket. There was one picture of me on the front of a magazine with my cellulite circled, looking like a seventy-year-old man. It was horrific! Sometimes I'd be putting an apple pie on the conveyor belt at the checkout and the woman behind the till would look at it, clearly thinking, Shouldn't you get some more salad, love? I couldn't get away from it.

I was terrified of leaving the house because there were always photographers hanging around outside. I'm sure I would have ended up agoraphobic like my gran if I hadn't had James and Lennon to look after. Nowadays, no one gives a damn, which is heaven. I can go out looking like a bag of laundry and no one bothers to snap me. Bliss! But back then I became so self-conscious that I avoided mirrors completely, and there are about two years when I'm not in one single photograph with my sons.

Looking back, I'm not bitter about any of it, though. I think you just have to draw a line under it and move on.

I was around eleven and a half stone in August when I went to Toronto to shoot a low-budget US feature called *Darkness Falling*, with Jason Priestly and Janet Kidder. I didn't think the script was great, but I needed to work and the money was good.

I'll never forget the looks on the faces of the producer and director when they met me off the flight to take me to a costume fitting. They didn't recognize me as the person they'd hired. They were clearly shocked by my weight gain and it was just awful.

Back in London, Steve received an email from the producer accusing him of misleading them about me. It was quite a sexy role that required skimpy costumes, which I would have slipped into easily only a few months earlier. The office had innocently sent out my card with my vital statistics on it, which was standard practice when I got any role, but they weren't accurate any more.

Thankfully my next role was less reliant on how thin I was. The following month I was back in Toronto for the lead in a TV movie called *Loves Music, Loves to Dance*, which was adapted from the Mary Higgins Clark novel and was a good project.

After that was an episode of the BBC thriller series *Murder in Mind* with Nigel Havers, and at the end of the year I went to Milan to take part in an Eros Ramazzotti concert to reprise the duet we'd done when I was in Eighth Wonder.

It had been a challenging year, with the divorce and trying to battle my weight gain, but at least it had been productive in terms of work. However, in 2002 I made only one movie – an indie thriller called *Shelter Island* with Chris Penn and Ally Sheedy, which unfortunately didn't quite come off as a movie. My weight was a problem once again, so it was awkward.

For the rest of that year, I just enjoyed being mum to James and Lennon and started looking for a house to buy for us. Although I did go to LA in January 2003 to do pilot season, where actors audition for the major US networks, my heart wasn't in it. I just didn't feel confident because I was still overweight. Even if I'd been offered a TV project, I'm not sure I would have had the confidence to do it. Hollywood is a pretty challenging town if you're not thin and looking your absolute best.

The boys and I moved out of our rented place and into a house I'd bought in Notting Hill, which was lovely and it helped us feel more settled. Then in mid-August I began rehearsals for the role of Marlene in West End comedy *See U Next Tuesday* with Nigel Havers and Ardal O'Hanlon. It's an adaptation of a French play called *Le Dîner de Cons* by Francis Veber and there had been a very successful movie version of it. The story involves a wealthy publisher who entertains his friends with a weekly dinner party every Tuesday, to which they all have to invite an 'idiot' to ridicule. The play was only meant to run for three months, but ended up running for six and it got good reviews.

I don't think the rest of the cast expected me to stay on after the first week of rehearsals because I had a terrible stomach bug, but I went in every single day and I never missed one performance during the run.

Geoffrey Hutchings, who was a brilliant stage actor, was also in the play. Sadly he's passed away now. I know he didn't think much of me initially, though we ended up becoming great mates. The one thing I had on my side was that I'd been acting my whole life, and I knew that if you have a pulse, you go to work. If they send you home, that's fine, but you turn up. I was always totally professional. I think people had forgotten I'd grown up in the business, because of the band and my high-profile relationships.

Getting up on that stage night after night felt like a real achievement after everything that had happened in the previous couple of years, and through doing it I rebuilt some of my confidence. I knew I had two matinees a week and a show each night, and I thrive on that kind of structure and routine. It also fitted in really well with the kids. Theatre work gives you a lot of freedom once you're up and running, so it meant I could still do the school run with the boys.

One night, as I was parking up at the Albery Theatre (now the Noël Coward Theatre) on St Martin's Lane before work my mobile rang and it was one of my acting agents.

'Listen, Yorkshire Television have called. Hear me out before you say anything, but the executive producer on *Emmerdale*, Steve November, would like to meet you. The casting director has seen the play. Would you be interested?'

'OK, I'll take the meeting,' I said, thinking I had nothing to lose.

So Steve came down to London and met me to talk about playing the part of super-bitch Sadie King. The meeting went really well, and he was totally upfront about what I'd be expected to do.

'You know you'll have to talk to the red tops,' he said.

'Yep, I know.'

'And you know it'll be six-day weeks at the beginning, and you'll be up in Yorkshire even on Saturdays.'

'Yeah, I understand.'

It was good timing for me – I needed to shake things up a bit; I felt ready to take on a new challenge and I'd never worked on a soap before.

At the end of 2003 I did an interview with Leigh Francis (aka Keith Lemon) for his TV comedy show *Bo' Selecta!* The two of us gelled straight away and became firm friends. In fact, if my boys are away, I sometimes have sleepovers at Leigh's house and force him and his lovely wife, Gill, and their two girls to watch episodes of *The Only Way Is Essex*! I love working on Leigh's projects and I owe him a lot.

The period after splitting from Liam hadn't been easy, but the boys and I were doing really well and I was slowly rebuilding my career.

A couple of years after we separated, Liam and I decided to get Lennon baptized. We asked Liam's elder brother Paul, along with Steve Dagger, Elizabeth Hurley and my friend Grainne Fletcher, to be Lennon's godparents. It was a small christening at a little Catholic church near my home in Notting Hill, with just Liam, me, the godparents, James and Peggy.

Lennon was about three years old and we got him a little white Ralph Lauren suit to be christened in. I walked into the church holding his hand and he spotted his dad standing at the back of the church and led me over to him. He looked up at both of us and took our hands, and the three of us walked down the aisle together. It was so moving, and he looked like a little angel in his white suit.

Children have an amazing way of reminding you what's important. That day we were both so proud to be his mum and dad.

17

Patsy Reinvented

On a freezing February morning in 2004 I found myself standing in a village in West Yorkshire being lashed by sleet and a force-10 gale. It was my first day on the set of ITV soap *Emmerdale* and I'd never experienced a location shoot where there was a 360-degree wind before! Every time I got into position and the camera started rolling, my hair would suddenly flip around and we'd have to do the take again.

At least the cast and crew couldn't have been nicer and more welcoming. I shared a dressing room with the lovely Australian actress Emily Symons, who'd also been in long-running Aussie soap *Home And Away*. Everyone got along really well, which was a blessing as soaps move fast; when you join one you have to hit the ground running and, boy, did I get chucked in at the deep end. The schedule was relentless and I knew it was going to be hard on the family, too.

I didn't want to uproot the boys from their schools

and their lives, so I had to do a lot of commuting every week between London and Leeds. Fortunately, I had the support of our wonderful nanny, who'd been with us for years, and we managed to juggle things so it worked. Nevertheless, I got to know the M1 a little better than I wanted to! I made a rule that I wouldn't be away from the boys more than three nights in a week and sometimes I'd drive home just so I could read James a bedtime story, then I'd sleep for a few hours and get up again at 4 a.m. to head back to Yorkshire. The rest of the cast kept telling me I was nuts and that I was going to end up driving into a ditch and killing myself.

I think a lot of people in the acting profession used to look down their noses at soaps, which is totally absurd. I learned a phenomenal amount from everyone on that show. Working on a soap like *Emmerdale* involves unbelievably long hours and very hard work, and those actors nail it day after day. The amount of dialogue they have to learn is incredible and there's very little time to prepare. I know movie actors who would fall apart under that pressure. It's a different culture and a very different way of working, but I loved it. I can honestly say that I healed up north.

My character Sadie King was wonderful to play – a bitchy blonde man-eater! Still, the first few months on the show were bumpy. No one asked me to lose weight for the role and I was probably at my heaviest at the time

– almost twelve stone. I'm only 5ft 3in, so every extra pound is magnified on me. I couldn't bear watching playbacks of my scenes on set, so I tried to avoid it whenever I could. It was like watching someone I didn't know. A review of my first episode was pinned up in the green room – all the reviews used to get posted there – and I couldn't bring myself to ignore it. It said something along the lines of, 'She waddled up the cobbles to the Woolpack with a fat arse.' I mean, really! It was scathing. So after that I ignored the reviews, which enabled me to just get on with the work.

The show's ratings started going up not long after I joined – obviously nothing to do with me – and we began doing hour-long episodes that went up against *EastEnders*, and *Emmerdale* was winning the ratings war. It was great for me that I'd joined at a time when there was so much positivity around the show.

Over the weeks and months the reviewers warmed to me, and my character, Sadie, was popular with the audience, too. Then I started getting nominated for awards, which was wonderful and unexpected. I hadn't gone into the show for plaudits, I just thought that if I could get myself on TV again regularly then people might remember I'd been an actress my whole life. And I think that's what happened. It was the beginning of my reinvention. I was nominated for Most Popular Newcomer at the National Television Awards the year I joined, and then I picked up the title of 'Best Bitch' two years in a row in 2005 and 2006 at the *Inside Soap* Awards.

Emmerdale also helped me to lose weight. A few of the girls on the cast were doing Weight Watchers and going to the meetings, so I decided to give it a go too. I'd tried every faddy diet under the sun by that point, but I'd fallen into the classic trap of eating practically nothing or nothing that I actually liked, then feeling so hungry I'd overdo it. As a result, I wasn't losing any weight at all. To be honest I'd almost resigned myself to being overweight for the rest of my life. But once I started following Weight Watchers I noticed the weight gradually coming off. It wasn't sudden, it was slow and steady. And I wasn't hungry or craving 'naughty' things because no foods were banned, so I was still able to eat food that I enjoyed. I'd finally found a diet I could maintain. It took about eight months, but I managed to get down to nine stone by sticking to the plan, and I began to feel like my old self again.

The bosses at *Emmerdale* were also very generous in allowing me to take a bit of time out to do other projects. I appeared in a series of *A Bear's Tail*, a *Bo' Selecta!* spin-off, in which I play the adopted mum of Leigh Francis's very rude and flirtatious teddy bear!

Then at the end of the year I appeared in *Aladdin* again, this time at the Richmond Theatre, alongside Simon Callow and Christopher Biggins, and I loved it.

I also played a part in an indie crime thriller called

Played, which was written and produced by Mick Rossi. Steve Dagger and I had met Mick, who used to be in an English punk band called Slaughter & The Dogs, on a trip to LA when he'd interviewed me for a magazine. We'd hit it off so he asked me to take part in his movie, which was micro low budget – he was calling in all sorts of favours to get it off the ground. He managed to persuade lots of big stars to take on roles or cameo appearances, including Val Kilmer, Gabriel Byrne, Joanne Whalley, Vinnie Jones and Anthony LaPaglia, for little more than expenses.

The project had been rumbling on for two or three years and Mick would call Steve regularly with updates on how the finance was coming along. In the end, the money was put up by John Daly, whose company Hemdale had made some very successful films, including *Platoon* and *The Terminator*. *Played* wasn't a commercial success, but you had to admire Mick's energy and commitment, and it was screened at a number of film festivals.

Although I felt settled at *Emmerdale* and loved the routine and structure it gave me, after two-and-a-half years the commute to Yorkshire every week was just becoming too much. I decided it was time for the wonderful Sadie King to make her final exit and I left *Emmerdale* in September 2006. I owed the show a lot – it was the rebirth of my television career and it undoubtedly helped to rebuild my self-esteem. I would have stayed on if it had been filmed nearer London – and if the bosses had wanted me to, of course – but my kids were growing up so fast and I was missing them. I wanted to be at home with them and to be around more often to do the school run and cook dinner and kiss them goodnight. It was all about my family.

But working up in Yorkshire had been such a positive experience for me and I'm very glad I did it. During my first year on the show one of the things I remember most was being cold all the time, but by the second year when one of the girls from the costume department asked, 'Do you want to wear your coat, Patsy?' I'd say, 'Oh no, I'm fine.'

'Your blood's thickened, lass!' they'd say, laughing. 'We've toughened you up!'

When I was leaving, my lovely wardrobe lady came over and gave me a big hug and admitted that after my first day on set, the crew were all saying, 'Patsy won't be back tomorrow.' I think they all had me down as some kind of southern softie!

'But, God, didn't you prove us wrong?' she added. 'We've been so impressed with you, Patsy.'

It was very sweet – it meant more to me than anything. Without a doubt, joining the cast of *Emmerdale* turned out to be one of the best things I've ever done.

After leaving I had a six-week break, then I started work on the BBC1 hospital drama series *Holby City*, playing troubled ward sister Faye Morton. It was wonderful to be offered a part in another very successful long-running drama series – and it also felt good to be back at the BBC. It felt like coming home. Like *Emmerdale* the schedule was tough and the hours were long, but it was filmed at Elstree Studios in Borehamwood, which is on the outskirts of London, so at least I could be home every night for James and Lennon. On *Holby* I always made sure that any guest actor felt at ease – after rehearsing with *Friends* for a week, I realized how hard it is to come into a show where the cast have all been working together for years.

I also became good friends with Luke Roberts, who played my husband, Joseph Byrne, on the show and I can honestly say that in four years of working very closely together we never rowed once and I could tell him anything.

In 2008 while I was working on *Holby* I was approached to take part in *Who Do You Think You Are?*, the BBC1 show that takes a forensic look at a celebrity's family tree. I'd always been a fan of the show, so I agreed and they said they'd go away and research the backgrounds of both my parents to see if there was a show in it. I was pretty sure that they'd come back with my dad and they did.

One of the first things they told me was that Dad was already married to another woman when he met my mum.

I'd had no idea – it was yet another family secret – but I guess it might explain why my parents took so long to tie the knot.

I found the show really hard to do at first. Delving back into my dad's past revealed some hard facts about the poverty he grew up in around Bethnal Green and the criminal activity that both he and my grandfather were involved in. After a couple of days on the show, I didn't want to do it any more because I honestly thought I was going to end up finding out that I was related to Jack the Ripper! That's the way it seemed to be heading and I felt very nervous about what they'd uncover. And it felt horrible raking up all the stuff about my dad again.

The people working on the programme were all very cool and patient, and things ended up taking an unexpected and pretty amazing turn. I found out my father's ancestors were goldsmiths and walking stick makers (respectable and skilled trades) before the family fell on hard times. I also discovered that my great-great-great-great grandfather was a much loved and respected clergyman called James Mayne. He was the curate of St Matthew's Church in Bethnal Green in the 1830s and President of the Bethnal Green Association for the Relief of the Destitute Poor, which had illustrious patrons such as Prince Albert.

James Mayne was awarded a Master of Arts degree from Lambeth Palace by the Archbishop of Canterbury for his charitable work with the poor in Bethnal Green, which was a very rare and special honour. His last posting was to the small country parish of Hanslope in Buckinghamshire where he's buried underneath the church altar.

I feel so proud and privileged to have such a remarkable man as an ancestor. I'd always assumed that I'd inherited the spiritual side of my character from my mum, but it seems there's a thread of it in my dad's family after all and a very significant one, too. I was pleased the show ended on something so uplifting, and not with the world of sixties organized crime.

That year I also turned forty, which I guess is a milestone. I've never been one to make a big deal of my birthday, so I just went out for dinner with a couple of friends. My reluctance to organize parties of any kind must be a throwback to my childhood and Mum not allowing Jamie and me to have friends over to the house. Even now I'd worry that people wouldn't show up! But I can honestly say that I've never worried about getting older and I've never lied about my age. After what I went through with my mum, the only thing that's important to me as the years go by is keeping in good health because I want to be around for my sons for a very long time.

I'd also started dating Jeremy Healy, who I'd known since I was sixteen because we used to hang out in some of the same circles. He'd been in eighties pop act Haysi Fantayzee and is now a DJ. We married in April 2009, but split up a year later. To be honest, I think there are some things that are best left and this is one of them. There's really nothing to say about the marriage other than it didn't work and I regret it. It was over very quickly, which I felt very embarrassed about, but I had to get up, dust myself down and face people. I never spoke about it at work and none of my colleagues on *Holby* ever made anything of it, so I never felt uncomfortable, which was really nice of them.

I also felt it was important to show my kids that if you get knocked down, you can bounce back and move on to something better. What kind of role model or mother would I have been if I'd just stayed in bed and felt sorry for myself? Plus, I had to get up and go to work.

But after playing Faye Morton for four years, I decided it was time to move on from *Holby City*, too. I desperately wanted to take some time out to concentrate on my family. I seemed to spend my whole life either rushing home to see the kids or trying to get to one of their schools in time for something. James was about to turn eighteen and I suddenly panicked and thought, My God, in the blink of an eye he's going to be a man! I really didn't want to miss out on those precious years I had with the boys before they flew the nest. Any mum who goes out to work will know how that feels – you constantly struggle with the guilt of being away from your kids.

At this point the three of us were rattling around in

a big house in Highgate in north London so I decided to sell up and downsize to an apartment in west London, which meant I could be mortgage-free and could afford to be more choosy about what work I took on. And I can honestly say that since we've shrunk down a little bit the boys and I have been happier than ever.

After it was announced that I was leaving *Holby*, I was asked to take part in *Strictly Come Dancing*. I wasn't due to finish at *Holby* until the end of December 2010 and with *Strictly* starting in September I knew it was going to be bloody hard work trying to juggle the two. But I believed that *Strictly* would be a good thing for me to do because, in the wake of another failed relationship, my confidence was at rock bottom and my self-esteem was in tatters. I'd piled the weight back on, too. I got a bit cocky after joining *Holby* and stopped following the Weight Watchers programme properly, so my weight hovered between ten and a half and eleven stone. I figured all the dance training would help me shape up again.

I was pretty naive about what would be required of me on *Strictly*, though. I thought I would learn a bit of dancing and it would be lovely, but it was physically and mentally exhausting, and very competitive, too. My professional dance partner Robin Windsor was brilliant with me and so supportive and kind, but every time I heard that theme music strike up to open the show I was gripped by terror, my mind would go blank and I'd instantly need to go to the loo! It was utterly nerve-wracking. To walk on to that dance floor stone cold sober in front of a live audience and try not to fuck it up is simply terrifying!

I fully expected to get kicked out in the first week, but the public vote kept me on the show until week nine. I couldn't believe it and was genuinely touched that people watching at home bothered to pick up the phone to keep me in.

Strictly was a great distraction at the end of an incredibly tough year and it did help me to slim down, too. Training for six hours a day (plus all the terror-induced adrenaline that was racing around my body) meant that I lost about a stone and a half, so I was back down to around nine stone again, and I felt really fit. I also took part in the *Strictly* live tour at the start of 2011, but when that wrapped in February and I stopped training, the weight started to creep back on and, before long, I'd put on a stone. I was annoyed with myself for undoing all my hard work. Although I wasn't as big as I'd been when I joined *Emmerdale*, ten stone is still too heavy for my small frame. I guess I'd just relaxed a bit too much after the tour and I wasn't paying attention to my diet. Just a few months later, though, something happened that made my weight issues pale into insignificance.

Because my mum had developed cancer very young I've always been fastidious about well woman check-ups

– I have an annual smear test and an ultrasound, and I've been having yearly mammograms since I was in my twenties. So one Thursday in September I went to have a smear and ultrasound scan. My regular gynaecologist had retired, so this was my first appointment with a new doctor. I was in his office having the scan when he said, 'Oh, you have quite a big ovarian cyst there and it looks irregular.'

I panicked immediately and blurted out, 'Do you think it's cancer?'

'Why on earth would you jump to that conclusion?' he replied, appearing irritated. I was thinking the worst but with my family history it was hard not to.

'You need to go right now to the lab on Wimpole Street to get some blood taken and then I'll call you next week with the results,' he added.

'Look, you have to be straight with me,' I pleaded. 'You've just told me it looks irregular – does that mean it could be cancer?'

'We need to do more tests before we know for sure what's going on,' he said.

I was about to play the wicked queen in *Snow White and the Seven Dwarves* in panto at the Churchill Theatre in Bromley and rehearsals were starting soon. (Lennon was with his dad that Christmas so I was able to take this on.)

'Well, I start work in a fortnight—' I started to say, my mind racing with fear and panic, but before I could get another word out, the doctor chimed in.

'You people in your industry. Honestly, you're being taught a lesson here about what's important,' he said, shaking his head.

Of course the panto wasn't important next to my health, but I was in the middle of a major anxiety attack and I was just saying the first thing that came into my head. I told him I wanted a second opinion that afternoon, so he arranged an appointment for me with a consultant on Harley Street.

I was a sobbing mess when I left the office, clutching my referral letter. I was still shaking when I had the blood tests later that day on Wimpole Street, but the nurses were lovely to me. I'm a big baby when it comes to needles at the best of times. After that I walked round to the consultant's office on Harley Street. He was nice and very calm, and booked me in for a CT scan straight away, which would provide a more detailed image of the tumour.

I went home that night feeling wrung out with worry, but at least I'd had the blood work done and the consultant had said he'd call me as soon as the scan came back.

I knew I was in trouble when my mobile rang at 11 p.m. that night. It was my consultant telling me he'd organized for me to have an ultrasound at 7 a.m. the next morning with a top guy in his field. Fuelled by nervous energy, I got showered and dressed the next day. James would drop Lennon off at school later, so I could drive straight to Harley Street.

When I walked into reception there were already five or six women waiting to see the doctor. They were clearly all cancer patients – they had no hair because of chemotherapy. Sadly, it was a look I was all too familiar with, having seen it many times before when I'd visited my mother in hospital as a child. I was struck by how beautiful the women looked, and how serene – just as my mum had done. And in that moment I could picture myself sitting next to those women, in the same position. I felt there was an inevitability about it after what had happened to Mum.

As I waited for my name to be called, I closed my eyes and said silent prayers to Jesus, Buddha, my mum – whoever was up there! 'Please, God, I'll never take my life for granted again. I'll change to be a better person,' I kept repeating.

All the staff were lovely, including the doctor who confirmed that I had a large tumour. As he looked through some papers I studied his face for clues to how serious my condition was.

'You have a very big complex tumour – 18cm,' he said, raising his eyebrows. 'Any idea how long you might have had it?'

'Well, I have a smear test and ultrasound scan annually, so it couldn't have been there a year ago,' I stammered, suddenly feeling weak with fear. It had obviously grown very rapidly.

We discussed my options – a hysterectomy or removal of the tumour only – and he recommended the latter. He told me there was an area of the tumour that he was concerned about, so he said he'd biopsy it once it was removed. After talking through the details I was booked into the London Clinic for surgery on the Monday morning.

I was glad it was all being dealt with very quickly, but after the appointment I walked back to my car with tears streaming down my face. I thought about my boys and what would happen to them if I wasn't around. Of course they had their dads, but I kept thinking about them being separated from each other and it broke my heart.

I got through the weekend busying myself with normal mum stuff and kept everything low key so as not to worry the kids. On the Monday the op went well and the area of the tumour the consultant had been worried about turned out to be benign, thank God. I was hugely relieved.

I was shown pictures of my cyst afterwards. It looked like a big white football and there were lots of little pockets with teeth and hair in them.

I was back on my feet very quickly after the surgery and started rehearsals for *Snow White* as planned. And I was glad that when the panto was over I'd be able to spend lots of quality time at home with James and Lennon. I felt even more sure that giving up my regular gig on *Holby* to prioritize my family had been the right thing to do.

After my health scare I decided I had to tackle my weight again – not just because I wanted to be slimmer, but also for the good of my long-term well-being. I'd planned a holiday to Turkey with some girlfriends in the summer of 2012 and one day, while I was pondering what I could pack that wouldn't display too much flesh, I vowed that as soon as I got back from the trip I was going back to Weight Watchers.

None of my friends are the sort to parade around the pool showing off in a string bikini and we'd all been trying to lose a few pounds before the trip, but my efforts hadn't been very successful. Weight Watchers was the only diet plan that had ever worked for me.

A couple of days before I left for Turkey I got a call from one of my agents, who said, 'Look, I'm not saying you're fat or anything, but Weight Watchers have just been on the phone and they want to talk to you about being an ambassador for them. Would you be interested in talking to them about going on the programme when you get back from your holiday?'

'Oh my God! It's divine intervention! Can we take the meeting before I go? I can be there in ten minutes!'

'I'll see if they can do it tomorrow.'

Although I was desperate to go back to Weight Watchers, they'd introduced a new Pro Points plan and I'd been used to the old points system. But when they explained it to me at the meeting the next day, it was really easy to understand and you actually get more food for your point allowance. A lovely girl called Katie Inglis was nominated as my leader, so she weighed me and I was nearly eleven stone. Again! I'd been avoiding scales, so it was a bit of a wake-up call.

I had a lovely time in Turkey, but every day I'd get up two hours before everyone else to go for a swim because I didn't want anyone to see me in my swimming costume. Of course none of my friends would have ever made me feel bad about my body, but I just didn't feel comfortable in my own skin.

When I got back to London in August Katie weighed me and I'd lost three pounds, so subconsciously I'd already started to make better food choices. And then by mid-December, after doing Weight Watchers for four months, my weight was down to 8st 13lb, which was the slimmest I'd been in years. I felt great and I was really proud of myself. And I'm happy to say that my weight has been pretty steady ever since – I fluctuate between 9st and 9st 5lb – and I feel like myself again, which is the best bit.

I'm someone who loves food and I've never felt it's the enemy, so I couldn't survive on a restrictive diet where you can only have purple food or algae shakes or whatever the current fad happens to be. If I want a slice of pizza or spaghetti I can have it with Weight Watchers – that's why it works for me. And I can cook family meals for James and Lennon, and adapt them for myself.

Once I'd lost the weight, I went on a regional tour with Weight Watchers to speak to other members. It hadn't occurred to me to wonder what kind of reception I'd get, whether I'd get punched or hugged. I'm sure a lot of the people in the crowd assumed I wasn't really doing the programme and probably had my own sushi chef on hand, and I definitely had to win them over. But I'm like every other woman out there who's struggled with her weight. And, when I stood up and admitted to weighing my clothes before stepping on the scales at a meeting, I felt the room thaw instantly. There was a real connection. We all take off our watches and anything else that might add a few ounces – if I could take off my bra and knickers I would.

I feel very protective over the members now because if you confessed that sort of thing to someone outside the meeting room they'd probably think you were a bit unusual!

In June 2013 I became really ill with pneumonia. I'd had it before when I was working on *Holby* and apparently once you've had it you're susceptible to getting it again. James was just about to go off to Sicily to start working in his dad's hotel, but he told me he wasn't getting on the plane until I saw a doctor.

'I'm calling Dad and telling him I'm not going unless you get checked out. I can't leave you like this,' he said.

So I called my GP who came over to the apartment and confirmed that my right lung was full of fluid, and I was admitted to the London Clinic straight away.

When the chest consultant was examining me he said, 'You've got something in your stomach. Your belly is really distended. Can't you feel this?'

He guided my hand to the left side of my abdomen, but I couldn't feel anything.

'A year ago I had a benign ovarian tumour removed, so it might be scar tissue,' I suggested.

What I had noticed in recent weeks was that I'd wake up in the morning with a (relatively) flat stomach, but by the end of the day I looked as if I was seven months pregnant. It was exactly how my mum looked in the last few years of her life.

'Well, I think you need an MRI,' said the consultant and with that I was wheeled upstairs to have the scan immediately.

The MRI showed that I had two cysts – one on the left ovary and one that was resting on my pancreas. They were big – about 6cm. However, the consultant explained they wouldn't be able to operate until I'd got over the pneumonia.

When I was back in my room I put my head in my hands and started sobbing. 'God, why is this happening again?' I said out loud. I just wanted some reassurance –

as with last time, everyone was being vague, but there was also this horrible sense of urgency. I wanted to see my cancer specialist Tim Davidson, who'd been doing my mammograms for years. At that point one of the nurses came in and asked if I was OK.

'No one's giving me any answers,' I explained through my tears. 'I just wish I could see Tim Davidson.'

'Give me a minute,' she said, leaving the room. When she returned, Tim was with her – I couldn't believe it. It must have been divine intervention because he happened to be doing his rounds at the time. I gave him a big hug because I was so glad to see him – he knew me and my family history.

'Patsy, try to stop worrying. I'll need to look at the results of the MRI scan but do you want any more children?'

'No,' I said.

'Right, then one option is to have a hysterectomy.'

'Fine,' I replied. 'I'll have a double mastectomy, too. I don't care, I just want to live for my boys.'

'Look, you're very sick and if you do have a hysterectomy, that is a major operation. That's more than enough to be getting on with.'

He was very reassuring and calm, which helped me to be calm, and he said he'd bring in one of his colleagues to look at the cysts. In the end we agreed I should have a hysterectomy once I was fit enough to undergo surgery.

I had to stay at the London Clinic for a week to be treated for the pneumonia with intravenous antibiotics. James had finished at Liam's company Pretty Green to take up his new job in Sicily, so he came to visit me every day and we went over his driving test theory together – and he passed. James was absolutely amazing that week – a tower of strength – but I played everything down because I knew he wouldn't get on the plane if I told him I was going to have surgery.

After a week I was sent home from hospital with antibiotics and nebulizers, and was told I'd get a call with a date for the op. In the meantime, I had to wave off James, who was starting his new job in Sicily. Lennon and I took him to the Gatwick Express and it broke my heart watching him get on that train. He looked so young in his baseball cap, but he was all organized with his suitcase. After he boarded the train he popped his head out of the door and mouthed to Lennon, 'Look after Mum,' and Lennon put his arm around me.

It was a new and exciting chapter in James's life and I was happy for him, but I couldn't believe my baby had grown up and was leaving home. Needless to say I was a wreck and I burst into tears as soon as his train pulled off!

Three days later I was back at the London Clinic to have my hysterectomy and I was very scared. I was shocked that the cysts had grown so large and so quickly. I honestly thought, This is it. I must have cancer this time.

I was convinced my luck had run out, so I tried to prepare myself for the worst.

I was in theatre for five hours, then in intensive care for twenty-four hours because of my blood-clotting problem. Lennon had been at camp with the school, but when he returned he came to the hospital to visit me and insisted on sleeping in a chair next to my bed for two nights. I kept telling him to go home, but he wouldn't. He was looking after me just like he'd promised his brother.

I was on a morphine drip for a week, then I was sent home with lots of painkillers and HRT medication to await the results of the biopsies on the cysts. My consultant didn't seem too worried about the one that was attached to my ovary, but he was concerned about the other one. I know how quick and cruel cancer can be – one day Mum would be fine and the next she'd be in hospital and gravely ill, so I was worried. But I couldn't let on to James and Lennon how scared I was. As a single mum I'm very conscious that I have to be a mother to my boys and not a friend – I don't want to use them as a crutch. I saw way too much of sickness when I was a child, which was no one's fault, but I never want to expose my kids to anything like that.

When I got home I put the biopsy results to the back of my mind, which is very unlike me as I'm an obsessional thinker. My OCD kicked in and I started rearranging cupboards and making to-do lists, even though I'd been told to rest. But it took my mind off things. As the days went by I started to feel more hopeful that the tumours were benign – I assumed if they'd found cancer they would have called me pretty quickly.

Then one morning a letter arrived from my consultant's office. I took a deep breath, braced myself and ripped it open. I scanned the text quickly, then sat on my hall stairs and cried with relief – the tumours weren't cancerous and I'd been given the all-clear.

Over the next few weeks my emotions were all over the place because of the HRT, and I felt disorientated and very forgetful, which was frightening. For about three days I genuinely thought I was losing my mind. Thankfully I saw a specialist who is monitoring me and helping to get my hormone balance right. I wasn't able to exercise or drive my car either, but that stuff didn't matter in the grand scheme of things. I was just so relieved and so grateful that I didn't have cancer.

I decided that when I was feeling well again I would get tested to find out if I'd inherited one of the high-risk cancer genes from my mum. And if I have, I won't think twice about having a double mastectomy. My goal is to live to a grand old age so my sons won't be without me. I never want them to go through what I had to go through with my mum.

I haven't once regretted having a hysterectomy, but I did have a little period of mourning for that part of myself. It was almost like saying goodbye to my youth and it was a very definite marker that I was moving into a new and very different phase of my life. The factory was most definitely closed! But it had given me two wonderful sons, which I'm eternally grateful for.

I did miss having my mum to talk to – someone older and wiser to tell me it was all going to be fine and that I would feel like my old self again. When I felt up to venturing out, I went to Daniel Galvin to get my hair cut and the lady who runs the cloakroom, Norma, took me aside and said, 'It's going to be fine, Patsy. It'll take six or seven months, but you will feel better.' I was so grateful to her for that moment of kindness.

At the start of July, Lennon and I went to Sicily for two weeks to visit James. We managed to miss our flight from Gatwick after getting stuck in traffic and ended up staying at the airport hotel so we could catch another flight early the next morning. 'Typical!' was James's response.

But when we eventually arrived in Sicily, I immediately felt a hundred times better and it was so good to see James. In fact, I was so excited that I broke the 'no swimming for six weeks' ban imposed by my consultant and I started to bleed. I called a doctor out and after examining me he said I was fine, but ordered me to rest for the rest of the trip. James was very cross when he found out my operation was a lot more than 'zapping a little cyst', which is what I'd told him.

I had a blissful two weeks reading on my terrace and eating pasta for breakfast, lunch and dinner. There were no cupboards to tidy, no lists to make and nothing to organize – it was exactly what I needed. And I couldn't think of any other people on the planet that I'd rather be there with than the most important men in my life – my beautiful boys, James and Lennon.

Epilogue

I was walking into town through Regent's Park with Lennon recently when he turned to me and said, 'You love doing this, Mum, don't you?'

Until that moment I hadn't quite realized just how much I value being able to put on my trainers and walk through London. Fifteen years ago it wouldn't have been possible – there would have been twenty paparazzi following me.

I don't miss that kind of attention at all. I love having the freedom to leave my house and go wherever I want, do whatever I want and look however I want without it ending up in the papers.

The past three years have been some of the happiest of my life. I stepped off the treadmill, cleared the decks and put all my energy into being a mum. And I'm so glad I did because I would have regretted missing out on that time with my sons in years to come. What matters to me is not material things but my kids. They are my greatest blessing.

But now James is off travelling the world and working for his dad, and Lennon is older, I'm looking forward to going back to work. Their dads look after them beautifully and brilliantly, but I've always worked to support myself, which is something I'm really proud of.

I believe you can survive in this business past a certain age as long as you're not trying to cling on to the past and if you have the courage to reinvent yourself, which I believe I have done. Now I feel that I'm at the absolute beginning of a completely new chapter in my life and I'm excited about what the future holds.

This girl from a west London council estate is very grateful to have been given the opportunities to realize her dreams. I wanted to act, I wanted to make movies, I wanted to fall in love and have children, and all of that's happened.

There have been some terrible highs and lows in my life and I sometimes feel in interviews that I'm expected to wrap my life up neatly in a box and say, 'Yes, I'm here, I've done it, I'm happy, I won't make those mistakes ever again.' But that's daft. When you're talking about your life the paint is never dry on the canvas. I endeavour to remain engaged, to grow, to accept the internet is here to stay and I'd better learn how to use google! Above all, despite these bumps in the road, I still believe in love and remain to this day a hopeless romantic. I'm sure Elizabeth Taylor would approve.

Acknowledgements

I want to thank my family. My boys, James and Lennon, and brother Jamie Kensit, I love you very much. And Selina – so happy that you and Jamie are together. Also thanks to Auntie Mary and my cousin Dan.

Natalie, Yasmin and the gorgeous twins Vinnie and Jackson – your fairy godmother loves you very much.

Sean Mitchell and Adam Bolton, I love you both like family. Thank you for all your support.

For always being there and taking care of me since I was fourteen, thank you, Steve Dagger.

Jackie Vickers (JV!) and Sofsi Talbot-Rice, I don't know where I would be without you, thank you also for taking care of me since I was fourteen!

Thanks to all at my management, Urban Associates, especially the unstoppable Neil Howarth, thank you for believing when I didn't, I'm so grateful. And Amanda and Danielle, thank you for making things calm and positive.

Ian Johnson, thank you and I totally adore you.

Acknowledgements

Thanks to Joyce Deen (JD!), my PA and Jewish mumma, and Luciana – couldn't do without you both, you are never leaving me!

Also my best friend for twenty-two years, Angela Radcliffe – thank you for keeping all my secrets. Maximus and Colin Radcliffe. Thanks to the Glam Squad: Sally O'Neil, Moya Saint and Lorraine McCulloch. You have the technology to rebuild me!

Thanks to Ingrid Connell for your patience and making this a joy to do as opposed to the nightmare I envisaged . . . and all at Pan Macmillan. A huge thank you to Clare Higney who helped put my story into words, and Saffron (it's not bedtime material yet but maybe one day Saffron will have a peek at what her mum was doing just before she arrived . . .).

Index

Index

339

Index